THE GREAT RIGHT HOPE

Book One of The Si ̄
[
M. J. J

C000060172

ISBN: 978-0-
Paperback Version – 2nd edition

Published by LL-Publications 2009, 2014
www.ll-publications.com

Edited by Zetta Brown
Proofreading by Janet S.
Book layout and typesetting by jimandzetta.com
Cover art and design ©2013 by Patrick JP Currier
(www.patrickjpcdesign.com)

Printed in the UK, USA

Other Books by M. J. Jackman

The Sid Tillsley Chronicles
The Great Right Hope
A Fistful of Rubbers
Acracknophobia

All are available from Amazon, BN.com,
and other online retailers!

A Few More Reviews for

A FISTFUL OF RUBBERS

Book Two of The Sid Tillsley Chronicles

"When blood thirsty vampires are a threat and are not your main concern, you know you have problems...Intriguing and offbeat, *A Fistful of Rubbers* is a strong recommendation."

—John Taylor
Taylor's Bookshelf/Midwest Book Review

"The action of Sid's right fist, supported by his Middlesbrough pals, and fuelled by Bolton Bitter beer, drives the story on its drunken, bruising and hilarious journey."

—Geoff Nelder
www.compulsivereader.com

"What I really liked about *A Fistful of Rubbers* is the interaction between Sid and the boys and the well-crafted dialogue. I really have not read anything quite like it. It is so refreshing to read a quirky and original vampire story that does not regurgitate the same old plotlines and characters that are so common in this genre. What we get instead is a fresh perspective and characters who are seared into your brain, whether you want them there or not."

—Bitten by Books
www.bittenbybooks.com

And finally, it ends with

ACRACKNOPHOBIA

"It's a mystery, a wonderment, how Jackman kept track of the twists and body count. Not even the most teeth-sharpened vampire aficionado will be able to guess how this one ends. I commend this book to all readers of both humour and vampire genres. Enjoy."

—*Geoff Nelder*
Cafe Doom

Acknowledgements

This is TGRH v2.0. If you own version 1.0, congratulations! You're gonna be stinking rich some day. If you don't own version 1.0, congratulations! You're gonna read the ULTIMATE EDITION, with DVD commentary and stuff.

Version 1.0 didn't have any acknowledgements, and most of the usual suspects are named in books 2 and 3. However, I just want to add a couple of my big inspirations. Dr. Belfield, thanks for your help on this one and my last few WIPs. Also, Jez, cheers for all the chats in Loughborough Leisure Centre car park (not dogging). Your work is incredible, a unique and wonderful legacy to leave behind. Keep going, buddy.

For you, Peelo.

Again.

1

BRIAN WIPED BEER FROM HIS FACE WITH HIS SLEEVE. He sighed a heavy sigh, for being a scholar was hard work sometimes. "You all right, our Sid?" he asked.

Sid Tillsley, the perpetrator of the drenching, gave his chin a well-needed dabbing. "Aye, you caught me by surprise, that's all."

"Look, it's quite simple, really, mate," said Brian. "If you flash your headlights twice, it means you want to go over and take a look at the action."

Brian dodged left, fast, as Sid spat out another torrent of beer, splattering the pub's nicotine-stained wallpaper. There was no chance of the mess being cleaned up and there'd be no complaints either, for this was The Miner's Arms, and this was the Smithson Estate, the roughest council estate in Middlesbrough, and therefore, the North of England, and therefore, the universe.

"You sure you're all right?" asked Brian.

Sid stared at the table in front of him, his mouth gaping. "I don't get it, Brian. I just don't get it."

Brian was in a position to explain, because he was a man of the world. He'd made it out of Middlesbrough at least half a dozen times, once as far south as Sheffield, not that he liked it, mind. "Sid, me old pal, we're all different. It's a funny old world out there these days. This dogging lark is just the tip of the iceberg."

"Shaggin' was such a private matter when I was a lad." Sid looked away into the distance. "It was so private, I did it on me own till I was twenty-five."

"Aye, things have certainly changed. There are loads of crazy fetishes around now; swinging and dogging are pretty standard." Brian laughed. "Just think what some of them Germans get up to!"

Sid took a moment to consider this, scratching his great bald dome and rubbing his unshaven double chin. Suddenly, his face darkened, and it was already heartattack red to start with.

"I am NOT being invaded, Brian," he growled.

"Eh?" said Brian, screwing his face up.

"Them Germans. They ain't invading me."

"Invading? What you on about?"

Sid rose up in his seat, his clenched buttocks giving him the extra height. "I ain't havin' it!"

Brian sighed. "No, mate, you've got it wrong *again*. What I meant—"

Sid's fist banged down on the table. "My uncle was a Dambuster, Brian."

Brian's brow furrowed. "No, he wasn't."

"That ain't the point!" Sid was becoming angry, and Sid wasn't a man to anger. Sixfoot five with shoulders still out of proportion to his height, he was built like a silverback gorilla, albeit a morbidly-obese silverback gorilla whose days of tree-swinging were well and truly behind him. On top of the shoulders sat his big, bald head where not a single hair had survived the storm of male-pattern baldness. A five o'clock shadow covered Sid's face and ran down his neck to join the thick, black, curly hair that carpeted his chest. A nose broken at least a dozen times split two dark, beady eyes. His thin lips covered a set of yellow teeth earned for years of hard, hard smoking. Thick rolls of fat sat on the tops of his shoulders and rose to just under his ears. Technically, he owned a neck, but you'd have to take an X-ray to prove it.

Sid's attire for the evening consisted of a black leather jacket that was made from a whole cow, accompanied with a pair of skintight blue denim jeans. Under the jacket, Sid wore a faded Esso Tiger Token T-shirt. In his younger days, he wore the combination to try to look like the Fonz, but that hadn't lasted long, for alas, Father Time had not been kind, and Mother Nature had been a bitch in the first place.

Brian decided honesty was the best policy. "I haven't got a fooking clue what you're going on about."

"I ain't having one of *them lot* watching me."

"Them lot?" asked a confused Brian.

Sid's anger waned only to be replaced by awkwardness. He tore up three beer mats in the matter of seconds. "You know, *them...lot... them lot* that dance on the ice, on the telly."

"Torville and Dean?"

"No!" Sid contemplated it. "Well, he probably is, like. But I mean *them lot*, the ones who like to wear...clothes. Nice clothes. *Them lot* are always wearing those nice clothes, them ironed clothes...from shops. You know them shops, Brian...them shops." Sid nodded at Brian, as if his rambling was significant.

"I think a lot of people wear clothes from shops, Sid."

"No! You know...they look after themselves. They use all them products, like, what's it called?" Sid clicked his fingers in thought.

Brian was impressed with his multi-tasking.

"That deodorant thing!"

Brian grimaced. "You really should start wearing deodorant. We've had this chat before."

"Howay, Brian! What I mean, is that they groom, Brian. They *groom.*"

Brian rubbed his goatee beard. "So do I. Northern women love an oiled goatee. Half of the lasses from Newcastle think I'm Zorro."

"No! They groom, they groom… their part. Their *part!*"

Brian shrugged. "So do I, Sid. It maximises aerodynamics."

"Yeah, but you're Middlesbrough's Finest Swordsman."

And that he was.

Brian Garforth was one of Middlesbrough's most successful ladies' men. Born without a virginity, he'd conquered all of the 'boro in his forty-five years, even though he was no oil painting. Even his impeccably kept thin moustache and little pointy beard couldn't rescue his looks. He was short and skinny-fat, an unappealing combination of skinny limbs and a pot-belly. He wasn't well-endowed either, and his penis was like a war veteran: grizzled.

Brian dyed his hair jet black on a weekly basis so that the world would never know about the grey lurking beneath. His hair was slicked back over his skull, but a slightly balding patch could be seen under the brightest of spotlights, although mentioning it always resulted in the spilling of blood. Brian was always suited and booted. Tonight, he sported a red woollen suit with a matching thin red woollen tie. A black Italian shirt matched his shoes.

So no, the reason for his unrivalled sword skills had nothing to do with his looks but came down entirely to his intellect, his perspicacity, and his Machiavellian silver tongue.

"Aye," he said, "I'm great with me cock."

"Anyroad, Brian, *them* lot! You must know what I'm on about. They drive them cars, them women cars with flowers in the front and parkin' assistance. Do I have to spell it out? I thought you were smart! They like the company of other men, in the family way." Sid waggled his bushy eyebrows.

"Sid, are you talking about gays?"

"Sssshhhhhhhh! Don't say the name!" Sid turned quickly in his seat to check the entrance to the pub.

Sid's display of stupidity amazed Brian. "Sid, they won't appear when you say the word, ya daft git. They ain't the opposite of Rumplestiltskin."

Sid screwed his face up. "Rumple—eh?"

"Rumplestiltskin. If you say his name, he disappears. You must have heard of Rumplestiltskin. It's an old fairy tale."

Sid's eyes widened at the phrase "fairy tale." Suspicion soon replaced the shock. "You seem to know a lot about these *fairy tales*. Have you been up them dogging sites, Brian? Have you been up there, being watched by German *them lot?*"

Brian sat back. Suddenly, he was on dangerous ground. Sid was the most homophobic man in Middlesbrough, and therefore the North of England, and therefore the universe. Like most idiots, his phobia didn't extend any further than the male half of the species. Lesbians were OK with Sid, mainly because he didn't know what they did. He assumed they watched a lot of soaps together and had double the cleaning power of most households.

Luckily, Brian Garforth, being the most educated man on the Smithson Estate, was more than capable of dealing with the situation "No, Sid," said Brian with caution. "No, Sid, I haven't." Brian paused to allow the words to sink into his friend's large but slow brain. "You know that Janice who works in chippy up on Charleston Street?"

Sid nodded, still sporting a suspicious glint in his eye.

"Well her hubby Charlie has been getting into it apparently."

Sid's Gay Defence System roared into action. His massive face flushed, and then the colour drained, and then the cycle repeated. He was like a pink strobe light. This was his infamous *Pink Alert*.

"Charlie? He's a...a German now?" *Pink Alert* forced other bodily functions to shut down, especially thinking, which was never high on the priority list. It was similar to when Captain Kirk diverted all of the Starship Enterprise's power to the front shields and weakened other parts of the ship.

Sid always kept his rear shields at maximum power.

"No, Sid," reassured Brian, holding his hands up, but in a very masculine manner. "I heard that he goes up there on Wednesdays and Fridays to meet LADIES," shouting the word added to the heterosexuality of it all, "which I confirmed at a later date."

"How?" demanded Sid.

"Well, after hearing Charlie was out Wednesdays and Fridays, I started going round and servicing Janice, his WIFE!"

Suspicion drained from Sid's face, and Brian gave a satisfied smile. Sometimes Brian surprised even himself with his complete mastery of the spoken word.

Sid dug out his fags, a packet of "El Sphinxo" Egyptian cigarettes. He'd earned four hundred of them for helping local Egyptian entrepreneur, Anhur Jahari, steal three tonnes of sharp sand from local playgrounds and take it to the construction site of what would be Middlesbrough's first Egyptian Experience Centre. Even Brian, a bona fide culture vulture (he watched a film with subtitles once; he didn't like it mind), was sceptical of its success.

Sid loved smoking. He both metaphorically and literally died for it. He was the definition of a chain-smoker. His brand: anything cheap. In the last decade, he'd paid zero tax to the government for cigarette duty. Every cigarette that had passed through his lungs had been ripped off or smuggled in from abroad.

"So," started Sid, all fear of Brian's homosexuality having subsided, "are you thinking of giving this dogging lark a go then?"

Brian shook his head. "Nah, I'm seeing Janice two nights a week, and then, there's Maureen from deli at Morrisons. Oh yeah, I've just started seeing that Karen who works in The Duke's Head, as well."

"Karen?"

"You know, the funny-looking one with the limp who works behind bar. Works with her tits out on weekends," said Brian matter-of-factly. "Anyway, I can't be doing with any more lasses at the moment. Too many names to remember."

"Bloody hell, mon! Three on the go!" said Sid flabbergasted. "So this doggin' lark, then, you just go out, pick a lass and start a shaggin'?"

"Well it ain't quite that simple, like. Dogging's been all over the news lately, but you still have to make sure you're in the right place, at the right time. You can't just whip out the old man in Tesco's car park. It normally takes place in nature reserves and lay-bys. Oh, and the coppers are trying to knock it on the head. You can get banged up for it, like."

"Sound complicated. So, why're you telling me about it?"

Brian hesitated. It'd come to the crunch and it was time to tell his good friend the reason he'd brought it up. He didn't want to upset the big fella, and not just because of his fearsome reputation of handing out swift, right-handed justice; Sid was his best friend. "You haven't been doing too well with the ladies of late, have you?"

"What do you mean? I split up from that lass not too long ago," he said defensively.

"That was over a year ago now, fella, and Gladys, well, she wasn't exactly Middlesbrough's finest now, was she?"

The big man reminisced over Gladys and her feminine wiles...and it didn't bear thinking about. Brian couldn't comprehend how a man could become physically or emotionally attached to a sixty-two-year-old retired prison guard whose party trick was extinguishing cigarettes on her nipples.

Sid grinned. "Any port in a storm, you know that." Although everybody knew he'd never risk docking in Greece.

"Well anyway, I thought that maybe a good-looking, young go-getter like yourself may not have time in his busy schedule for dating. Maybe a bit of no-strings fun would do the trick. What do you say?"

"Me? Go dogging? I'll think about it, Brian," said Sid unconvincingly. He banged his pint glass down. "Now then, mate, I do believe it's your round."

"Sid, I've already bought you two beers and you haven't put your hand in your pocket yet." Brian knew what was coming next.

Sid coughed for dramatic effect. "Brian, me ol' mate, I don't pick me sickness benefits up for another couple of days." It was a well-rehearsed yet poor performance. "Don't suppose you could lend a good man a ten pound note, or possibly buy him an ale to soothe his dodgy heart?"

Unfortunately, this particular performance had been seen before. Historically, the only performances that had been witnessed more were those involving Mick Hucknall's penis.

"I've already bought you two beers, and there's as much chance of me seeing that tenner again as you not taking the lift."

Sid's second mortal fear was stairs. The bald head dropped.

Brian sighed. "Tell you what, mate."

Sid's head rose.

"You can earn that tenner."

Sid's head dropped again.

"If you pick me up some stuff from shops next week. How 'bout it?"

Sid stroked his chin. He knew something was afoot. "What stuff? Why can't you get it yourself?"

"It's just...erm, I'm busy next week and I need to pick up a few things from Abdul," said Brian looking sheepish.

"Abdul? Ain't he the guy who owns that mucky shop?"

"Err...yeah," admitted Brian.

"What are you buying from a mucky store?"

This was a delicate situation for he was Brian Garforth, Middlesbrough's Finest Swordsman. He was proud of his swordsman reputation, and entering such an establishment could ruin it all. Unfortunately, the most intelligent man on the Smithson Estate couldn't think of a single good excuse why he'd need to. Being a swordsman, he had no need for mucky magazines or videos as he literally never had to take matters into his own hands. A swordsman had no need of those plastic abomination dildo things. And all that fetish stuff was for blokes who didn't know how to pump hard enough.

However, Abdul Zafar, purveyor of gentlemen's interest magazines, did have something Brian wanted to try. Brian's art of seduction had developed with age, like the swordsmanship of a Samurai master. However, this Samurai master's sword was not as sharp as it had been in recent years. The old Samurai master had the goods to deal with any particular adversary on any particular day. Nevertheless, to face an opponent more than once was now proving difficult, or in all honesty, nigh on bloody impossible. Brian needed a little help from a little blue pill, having recently come to terms with maybe possibly needing Viagra for occasional use...just in case—probably won't need it at all—definitely wouldn't...just as a safety net.

Abdul had the cheapest stock in town, but Brian had to find a way to obtain the goods without anyone knowing. He'd decided to ask Sid, his most trusted friend.

"Sid, I want you to buy me some Viagra from Abdul. I'm asking you to perform this task in utmost confidence. You have to keep this under the radar, on the down low. This sort of thing being leaked is life or death to a swordsman."

"What's up with your pecker, Brian?" asked Sid, innocently.

"You bastard!" The Middlesbrough Casanova's face turned crimson. This was like Maradonna losing his football; Leonardo Da Vinci losing his paintbrush; or Rod Hull losing Emu, the world's most elaborate wanking sock.

"Calm down, Brian. You're too sensitive!" reassured Sid. "Of course I'll pick up your stuff, and I won't mention it t'anyone," said the modern-day saint.

"Thanks, Sid." said Brian relieved. "You truly are a good—"

"Sixty quid for me troubles."

"You bastard!"

"Brian, I'm putting my reputation on the line entering this seedy back-street shop," said Sid, like he was the pillar of the community.

"Very well," conceded Brian through gritted teeth. "But if word gets out to anyone about me experimenting with sexual enhancers, then I'll let a few secrets out about you!"

"No problems, Brian. May I have the cash in advance, please?"

"Half now and half on delivery. I'll give you the money you need for the stuff later in the week." Brian reached into the top pocket of his jacket and pulled out his imitation crocodile skin wallet. He took out thirty pounds and handed it to Sid, who took the money graciously, got up, and moved his massive frame to the bar.

SID EYED THE BEER HUNGRILY AS HE APPROACHED.

"Same again, Sid?" enquired The Miner's Arms' landlord.

"Yes please, Kev."

Kevin Ackroyd pulled two pints of Bolton Bitter; two exact pints down to the millilitre. Sid, Brian, and a select few were the only patrons to get served the legal limit. It wasn't because Kev liked them, it was because they'd give him a shoeing if he didn't.

If Sid was a Russian doll, and you took the top off Sid, then the top off mini Sid, then the top off the mini-mini Sid, and then added a ginger 'tache, you'd have Kevin Ackroyd. He was about five and a half feet in both directions, and where Sid's shoulders were out of proportion to his body, Kevin's belly was out of proportion to his. The nose was not broken as was Sid's, but was incredibly red with the years of alcohol abuse.

Sid lit his eightieth Egyptian of the day. "How's the extension going round back?"

The landlord's face dropped. "Don't get me started, Sid. The bleedin' missus nags all day long about building a new bedroom. She wants to move her bleedin' mother in, doesn't she? As if my shit life couldn't get any shitter?"

"Sorry for askin', Kev, didn't realise. How much do I owe yer?"

"£3.92 please."

Sid passed over a ten-pound note and waited for his change.

"I'm sorry, Sid. I didn't mean to snap there. It's just, you know how our Marie gets about bleedin' home improvements and bleedin' decorating."

Sid asked the million-dollar question. "You ain't changing the inside of The Miner's?"

Kev looked genuinely offended. "God no. I let her have her own way in everything, Sid. I'm a good husband, but she'll never alter the inside of this fine public house."

The Miner's Arms hadn't changed since Kev took over from his old man in '67. Not even the breweries had managed to convince the stubborn landlord to decorate, and even Kev's own failed arson attempts hadn't warranted a lick of paint.

It was a small pub. A pub for locals. Only one student had ever ventured into the public house, but that was because he'd been thrown in through the window. Tonight, it was relatively empty, like every night. Apart from Sid and Brian, only the lads were in. They sat round a small black-and-white telly near the bar watching a repeat of *Who Wants to be a Millionaire?* They were silent apart from the odd shout of: "Tarrant, you twat."

Walking into The Miner's, the first thing that hit you (if you were lucky) was the smell of stale beer and cigarettes. The smoking ban was paid no heed in these parts. Most patrons thought the ban was make-believe, like Father Christmas, paying taxes, or safe sex.

No pictures adorned the nicotine-stained wallpaper. Three flying ducks and a postcard from Great Yarmouth were the only decoration inside. The only other feature was the dartboard. The Miner's had a wicked team that inspired fear in the opposition, and not just because of their good *arras*. As you walked to the bar, the next thing you noticed was the infamous carpet, terribly worn, and with a pattern indistinguishable from the cigarette burns, chewing gum, beer spillages, and other stains of bodily origin. If the carpet was hung on the wall, you could walk up it.

There was a mismatch of furniture on the way to the bar with not a single chair or table alike in the entire pub. The bar, however, was immaculate, and Kevin Ackroyd was very proud of it. Bar stools were placed equidistantly along its length, which occupied the entire left wall up to the toilet door. That's where the flies were.

Only one toilet was originally built in The Miner's: the gents. It comprised of two urinals and a flushable toilet (unless Sid was caught short, in which case, it became a non-flushable toilet). The pub had undergone one small alteration since Kevin took over from his dad. The new landlord had designed The Miner's only refurbishment himself. In what was deemed at the time to be a crazy venture, he'd installed a ladies' toilet.

The venture only took an afternoon. He merely wrote "Ladies" on the Gents cubicle door in a permanent marker and put a mirror over the washbasin so the fairer sex could apply their war paint. It was still acceptable for gentlemen to use the ladies' loo. After all, it was not an uncommon sight to see the ladies using the urinals, and this was the age of equal rights. A regular Ladies' Night of variable vigour had been held periodically since the refurbishment, an event that had proven hugely popular with the locals. On the wall to the right of the bar were the remains of The Miner's Arms' jukebox. It had never been fixed since that ill-fated night when Sid had pressed the wrong buttons and ended up playing "Club Tropicana" on repeat.

Sid took the beers and returned to sit next to his friend.

"Cheers, Sid," said Brian, taking down a large draft of ale. "Now then, what do you say about giving this doggin' a go?"

Sid shook his head. "I don't know, Brian. It's a lot of hassle, and you never know who's going to be there, like. If I'm that desperate, I can always go and see that prossy, Lizzie, who lives down road."

"No, Sid. I won't let you pay for it again. Anyway, Lizzie has weathered since you last saw her, and she was never exactly a looker in the first place. I heard that you can get *the lot* for three cans of Skol."

Sid looked around. There wasn't a female in sight. "Guess I could give it a go, like."

"That's the spirit," said Brian beaming. "Tomorrow night up at Middlesbrough Memorial Park, they're having one of their regular meetings. Don't worry. It's a one hundred per cent heterosexual spot. After Charlie told me about it, I looked it all up on Internet."

More proof that Brian was the brainiest man on the Smithson Estate: He'd used a computer.

"Shit the bed!" said Sid slightly in awe. "If it was on that computer thing, then it's got to be reet."

Brian spent the night explaining to Sid what he'd found out on the World Wide Web and about the etiquette of the dogger.

The two friends smoked, supped ale, and chatted until Kevin Ackroyd kicked them out because he wanted to go to bed. The walk home was exciting for Sid, as tomorrow, after two years of waiting, he was going to get lucky.

"Howay, the lads!"

2

HE KICKED OPEN THE DOOR AND STOOD IN THE DOORWAY, *silhouetted against the moonlight. A howling wind whipped snow into the log cabin. A child playing in front of the fire screamed when she saw him, and a middle-aged man ran through from an adjoining room to check on his daughter. The father yelled, but his cries fell on deaf ears.*

Bloodlust had devoured the senses.

In a moment he crossed the room and picked the father up by the throat so that his feet dangled six inches from the floor. He sunk his teeth deep into the neck of the struggling victim. Blood sprayed onto his face and gushed down his throat, satisfying his thirst; the pure pleasure of it, every molecule of his body emanated life. These mortals could never experience such a feeling. Sex? Love? This was everything.

He let the limp body drop to the floor, and the senses returned with the wailing of the young girl who sat hugging her dead father. Her cries ceased the instant he snapped her neck. She wouldn't have felt a thing. Not that he cared. He was simply tired of the noise.

HE HELD THE HUMAN'S THROAT IN A VICE-LIKE GRIP. *Eyes looked back at him with the utmost calm. No fear. No panic. No emotion at all.*

"You bastard. Your mother should never have dropped you from her putrid womb. Look what you are. You're nothing, and you've taken everything from me." His voice matched the human's gaze, complete calm. Rage had subsided. Nothing he could do to this man could possibly match the debt the man owed him.

He tore the human's throat out and watched as his eyes glazed over. The human's pain was a moment. This pain, however, would burn for centuries. This would hurt until the very end.

GUNNAR AWOKE IN A COLD SWEAT. Those two events had haunted his dreams often of late. That log cabin had saved his life. He'd been trapped in an avalanche in Canada, starved of blood for weeks on end. A tragedy if he'd died that way—the great Gunnar Ivansey killed by a snowball. The absurdity of it all! It'd taken weeks to tunnel out of that drift, and then, he'd wandered around in a daze, unaware of time or space. Stumbling across that cabin had been pure luck. Blood had never tasted so good.

The other dream...it was hard to put aside such despair.

He quickly left his resting place. The room was pitch black, but he could see perfectly. There was only one door to this secret room, and he closed it behind him when he exited, climbing the stairs into a massive circular hallway, both grand and utterly extravagant. The mahogany staircase meandered round, and it was difficult to see any imperfection in the carpenter's work. The marble floor and the rosewood furniture from the seventeenth century would've thrilled the gentry. But he was so bored of grand and extravagant. Gunnar noted the time on the grandfather clock standing next to the huge oak front doors: quarter past eleven. He'd never been good at keeping time.

The bathroom was a vision from nineteenth century France, the likes of which would've been celebrated by humans, a shrine to money, a shrine to success. Things. Objects. Nothing more. He ran water in the sink close to boiling. He lathered soap between his hands and applied it across his face and scalp before shaving with a cut-throat razor. After showering, he left the bathroom and walked through to the next room. An entire wall was a mirror. To each side of the room stood open wardrobes that contained suits and shirts of every fabric and hue. He picked out an outfit with no hesitancy and dressed quickly but impeccably.

Gunnar admired himself in the mirror for several minutes. It wasn't just his size that made him stand out in a crowd, it was those ageless eyes, steely blue. They'd inject fear into any human. He turned on his heels and headed for his enormous underground garage. Out of the dozens of cars, he looked longingly at a black Porsche GT3. He should really drive a more inconspicuous vehicle to tonight's destination.

"Fuck it."

The garage opened automatically, and Gunnar raced the Porsche up the ramp and out onto the driveway. It was a significant distance to the front gates, which opened automatically when he reached them. He didn't have to slow down to pass onto the country road. Once on it, he raced around the twisting roads like a rally driver. After the kill, after war, driving was his next love. In this modern age, speed was the only thing that held his attention.

He was ten miles from Newcastle's city centre and it was time to meet an old friend. Ricard was the complete opposite to Gunnar. He was not a vampire of modern technology. Gunnar had taken him out in his Aston Martin DB5 in the 1960s and even that amazing machine didn't impress the old fool. *"We have an eternity to travel the corners of the world, and we have an infinite number of things to observe and behold. If we travel at one hundred miles an hour, we'll miss something."*

They say opposites attract, and it was the only explanation for their close friendship. Ricard was at least three thousand years old and had been a keen politician and an influential thinker from a young age. He was a true gentleman and a scholar of unprecedented intellect. However, the two fervently disagreed on the status of mankind. Ricard treated humans with respect and with a kindness that disgusted Gunnar. To him, they were less than cattle. Ricard was also one of the major contributors to the formation of the human-vampire Agreement, the abomination that kept vampires on a leash.

Ricard was a wiser vampire than he, and certainly a better creature. Nevertheless, Ricard's compassion would certainly lead to his eventual downfall. *Respect humans?* Gunnar thought to himself. *If they knew of us, would they show us the same courtesy?*

He bared his fangs at nothing, his instincts demanding the kill. Demanding satisfaction. Demanding vengeance.

Always demanding vengeance.

"SNAP OUT OF IT!" he screamed.

Gunnar reached the city centre. Tonight, he'd meet with others of his kind. He'd relax, unwind, and talk to his heart's content throughout the night and safely through the day if the need presented itself. This was the time for happiness. Tranquillity.

Peace and tranquillity.

He backfisted the driver's side window out.

He arrived at his destination, Rapunzel's Nightclub. It was full of human vermin who entertained themselves by drinking, fucking, and fighting; seemingly all they could manage with their brief spell on this Earth. How could Ricard hold any feelings for this race as a whole? They were disgusting, meaningless, shallow, selfish, despicable.

The door to the club's underground garage opened as he drew near. He drove through the dimly lit parking lot, appreciating the other vehicles. Was one of them Ricard's? Had he finally invested an insignificant portion of his immense wealth in a car? He laughed again at Ricard's disdain for speed, although on some occasions, the old goat was right. Gunnar could remember, all too well, the look on the paramedic's face after Gunnar had emerged from the wreckage. It was not in their basic training to deal with car crash victims that could walk and talk with half a windscreen protruding from their heart.

Gunnar parked the car and climbed the stairs situated in the centre of the garage. At the top of the stairs was an imposing black door with no handle. It opened slowly as Gunnar approached, and music poured through, heavy bass booming off the grotesque lilac-coloured walls beyond.

A giant of a doorman stood on the other side of the entrance in front of a short staircase leading to a similar door to the one Gunnar had just passed. He was as tall as Gunnar himself, about six-foot-eight and must have weighed twenty-five stone, all muscle. He was bulkier than Gunnar, but his muscles were the result of years of steroid abuse. Farther down the hallway, Gunnar could see humans dancing, drinking, and making complete fools of themselves. They deserved to die. He paid the doorman no heed and started to climb the stairs. A huge arm barred his path.

"Where do you think you're going, son?"

Gunnar halted but didn't look at the giant. "Move your arm and never bother me again." He held his composure for this was one of Richmond's pets.

"Who the fuck do you think you are, you little prick?" yelled the doorman, steroid-induced rage racing through his bloodstream. "Do you know who the fuck I am?"

Some of the drunk humans noticed the commotion, leering, jeering, adding fuel to the giant's anger....as for Gunnar's...

The bouncer curled up into a ball, hitting the floor, a dead weight. The doorman struggled for breath after the punch to the solar plexus, turning a shade of blue through lack of oxygen.

Gunnar hadn't meant to strike. He hadn't meant to lose control. "Has Richmond not told you that all guests who enter through the garage door can use the facilities at their leisure? I was trying to stay calm," he said, his words escaping through bared teeth. "Trying to stay—" he landed a boot in the ribs, delighting in the cracking of bone, "—fucking calm!"

He spat on the doorman before climbing the stairs. The door at the top opened automatically like the last. A fire roared inside, radiating a tremendous amount of heat. It was the only source of light, adding to the ambience of this small, antiquated room full of tapestries, paintings and sculptures of the last two millennia. A drinks cabinet on the far wall contained whiskies and brandies, centuries old. The decorator of this room certainly appreciated the finer things in life. Large, comfortable armchairs were placed around the room and a small table accompanied each chair, which held a selection of fine cigars. In an armchair nearest the fire sat Ricard.

"Good evening," said Gunnar.

Ricard turned from the fire. "Good evening, Gunnar," he said affectionately. Ricard showed a slight receding of his hairline, and his thick black hair was streaked with grey at the wings. His face would have resembled a man in his fifties if it was not for his ageless green eyes. Although he looked old for a vampire, he was still incredibly handsome. He was large compared to a human but of medium build when compared to his brethren. Gunnar's hand completely encompassed his as he shook it warmly.

"Was one of the cars downstairs yours?" Gunnar asked with a grin as he poured himself a brandy.

"Yes, actually. It may surprise you to know, I purchased a hybrid that's economical, and thus, the least polluting of your favoured smog-wagons."

Gunnar raised his eyebrows. "Smog-wagons?" he teased. "At least you've realised their necessity in this modern age. Who knows, you may even enjoy driving one day?"

"I'll have a suntan first."

"And how are you feeling, Ricard? Three thousand years must be taking its toll by now? Surely knees as old as yours can't take more than a brisk walk?"

Ricard appreciated the jest. "I feel the same as I did two thousand years ago, but then, I've never been the most athletic of our kind. I was born to use my head, dear boy, and if the need arises, rent muscle-for-hire like you. And what about you? I'm sure your body copes with everything you throw at it?"

"My body gets stronger every day, but..." He rubbed his hands awkwardly over his shaven scalp, "my head does not hold the same strength, no matter how hard I try." Gunnar trembled as he finished the sentence, his emotions betraying him as always.

"What bothers you?"

"Dreams," said Gunnar, as he stared wistfully into his brandy.

"Of your mother?"

Gunnar looked up from the glass. "That obvious?"

Ricard smiled sympathetically.

"Bah! Five hundred years ago. What is the point of hating yourself over the death of a low-life whore!" spat Gunnar. "She deserved everything that happened to her, Ricard, everything."

Gunnar's mother was executed in 1503, beheaded after a trial by the vampire council, the Lamian Consilium. Her crime was to fall in love with a human. It was punishable by death, and rightfully so. They should never have changed the damned laws.

"She left me for him, a mortal, only a century after a bastard hunter slew my father. How can I forgive her? How can I forgive *them*?" He remembered looking into the human's eyes, remembered his fingers tightening around his throat and slowly, so slowly, tearing out his windpipe.

"Love, Gunnar. Love is the world's ultimate power."

"Fuck you, Ricard! Everything is taken from us! How many decades of happiness can be rendered meaningless because of one action, one incident, one night? How can you sit there so calm, so righteous?" Gunnar stood up and punched the wall, shaking the room, leaving knuckle marks in the plaster.

Ricard wasn't affected by such displays. "We're all different, Gunnar. Your heart has ruled you since the day I met you. I, however, have always been ruled by this." Ricard tapped his head. "I admire your fire. I admire your spirit. But you're in danger of burning out. The pain you desperately hold on to will kill you. You punish yourself and mankind for your mother's death."

Gunnar sank to his knees, tears streaming down his face. "It's over five hundred years since I took her in for trial. I took her in! Five hundred years of guilt. Humans killed my father, and that slut took one into her arms, into her bed! She was all I had. I still hate her!"

"So much rage, Gunnar. So much hate and anger combined with so much power. I'm starting to worry your fury is insurmountable." Ricard poured another brandy and placed it next to Gunnar's armchair.

Gunnar stopped his sobbing in an instant. *Don't be so weak*, he thought, chastising himself. He got up and sat back down on the chair. He sipped at the brandy after regaining his composure.

"Thank you, Ricard. You've been a father figure to me for nearly half a millennium. I'm sorry I spoke out of turn."

"Don't be silly, dear boy. I've heard far worse profanities in my three thousand years, and from people for whom I felt a lot less love."

Gunnar was lucky to have such a good friend. He didn't have many. "What news do you have from our beloved Consilium, and their dealings with your precious humans and *their* Coalition and *their* Agreement?"

"A little hostility I sense there?" said Ricard with a wry smile.

"I'll never understand why Michael set up the Coalition. All it does is benefit humans."

"I'm the one you should blame."

"Michael's the one who rules."

"Because of my foresight. With modern-day surveillance, the Agreement is an absolute must for our survival. If it is jeopardised, the world will be plunged into war. The Coalition links vampire and man. Both races have their own organisations. The vampire has the Lamian

Consilium and man has the Hominum Order. The Agreement binds us together."

Gunnar dismissed it with a wave of his hand. "Have you any news which might affect me? Any nasty surprises on the horizon?"

"As you ask, yes, there's been a sharp rise in the number of humans killed in this region over the last year, and all were killed in a rather gruesome manner."

Gunnar smirked before raising his hands in defence. "It has nothing to do with me." He put a hand on his heart. "I can't believe you would suspect me of such a foul deed."

Ricard smiled. "Forgive me for judging."

This time, Gunnar laughed out loud, a rare sound to his ears. "And what of you? What does our all-knowing Lamian Consilium have you occupying your time with of late?"

"Oh, this and that. I'm too old for political games, especially those that affect mankind and not just our own people. I'm there to offer my advice when it's needed. I only wish for harmony between the species, although I accept that this harmony cannot be absolute. Michael rules the Coalition and the Lamian Consilium with an iron fist. Unfortunately, I believe it to be the only way."

"Michael Vitrago," Gunnar mused. "He'd put fear into the Creator himself. Gabriel and I followed him for decades, possibly the best decades of my life. Let's hope he regains his senses one day and puts an end to the *truce* between us and them."

Ricard shook his head. "It will be a dark day for the world if he does."

The door to the study opened and Richmond entered the room with a beaming smile for his guests. As always, he was elaborately dressed and wore an immense, white fur coat, which covered his broad, muscular shoulders. A matching fur top hat held in his long dreadlocks.

"Hey there, boys!"

RICARD STOOD UP TO GREET RICHMOND, HIS HOST. There was no one who disliked the massive African. The first impression that Richmond gave was that he was the epitome of happiness. The first impression was the right one. Moods were eased wherever he went.

Nightclubs: the perfect business for Richmond. He didn't need to work; no vampire did, for they amassed great wealth over the centuries. In this room alone were enough priceless historical artefacts to live a life of luxury. Richmond was in the business purely for the enjoyment of it all. He owned nightclubs all over the world, and each club had a room similar to this where he'd entertain his guests with his famous hospitality.

It was possible he didn't have an enemy in the vampire world. If he were human, things would be different. Many would hate him for his African origin. Vampires were different. There was no sexism, no racism. The main divide was the Agreement, and with all species, the lust for power.

"My friends, how has it been, apart from the terrible weather?" Richmond complained about the weather whenever he travelled outside of the West Indies, the place he adopted as home.

"Where to start, Richmond?" posed Ricard. "It has certainly been lacking a certain something without you around for the past twenty years. I'm sure you're up-to-date with the Coalition's dealings?" Ricard considered his question. "Or perhaps you've found other, carnal distractions?"

Richmond let out a deep bellowing laugh. "I think you know me a little too well."

"That I do. It's been a strange twenty years," said Ricard. "The technological advancement of the age changes our lives with every blink of the eye. I can't imagine what another twenty years will bring. Nevertheless, I'll watch with interest as events unfold and do my best to help us move forward."

"And you, Gunnar?" asked Richmond.

"I've driven some fast cars," said Gunnar, with a grin.

"And I've ridden some fast women," bellowed Richmond, laughing.

Richmond loved women, whether it was a lamia or a human, it mattered not, he'd pursue them all. Sex was a strange thing in the vampire world, and Ricard was thankful that most of the race were asexual. Most would never have sex of any kind throughout their lifetime, because reproduction was not a straightforward affair. The oldest living vampire was five thousand years old and had the appearance of an eighty-year-old man. There was no biological urge to procreate.

Procreation wasn't as simple as in humans. A male seed was still required for the female egg, but the female lamia required huge amounts of the male's blood to sustain the life of her and the child. Throughout history, this had often led to the male's demise and was a natural deterrent. The process kept the vampire population to a relatively low number when compared to their prey.

Sleeping with a human was once punishable by death, which was the crime Gunnar's mother committed. In this modern age, there were no constrictions, as conception between the species had been proven impossible. However, if a vampire of either sex raped a human, it was best practice to kill the human. Vampire DNA samples would create interesting problems down the line. This was another reason why the Agreement couldn't stand without the efforts of Sanderson, a human member of the Coalition assigned to hide vampire activity.

"Although the world changes around us," continued Richmond, "the three dinosaurs in this room do not." He raised his glass, and his companions followed suit.

The night continued into the morning and well into the daylight hours. Ricard and Gunnar would enjoy the hospitality of their host until the safety of nighttime returned. That would bring a reunion of a different sort, for Gunnar would be reunited with his closest friend and, for mankind, his most dangerous ally.

3

IT WAS A BEAUTIFUL, BRIGHT SUMMER'S EVENING. Sid had shaken off his hangover by mid-afternoon and was bright as a button in anticipation of adult entertainment. He was parked in Middlesbrough Memorial Park in his 1987 maroon Montego Estate and applying the finishing touches to a look that would guarantee action of the filthiest form.

Sid pinned on the Dambuster medal, which a bloke down the pub, Peter Rathbone, had sold him. Women never turned down war heroes. According to Brian, women never turned down anything, but then, he was a swordsman, possibly the finest. Sid got out of the Montego and applied a final splash of *Male* aftershave, which Rathbone had also sold him. Rathbone had said it was the manliest scent devised by scientists. Sid thought it smelled a bit like piss and was starting to question the authenticity of his purchases.

Reaching inside the car, he took out a dog lead. He had one of them guide dog leads with him, because he thought the ladies would love the sob story of him losing his blind dog. There were a few other cars in the car park, and they were empty. Obviously, the desperate, nubile, young females had left their cars to seek a jump out in the wilderness.

"They're gonna be gaggin' for it." Sid rubbed his hands at the prospect and pushed on.

Middlesbrough Memorial Park was a beautiful place mostly set on a hillside with views of the surrounding valleys and the sea in the distance. All of this was wasted on Sid, because Sid thought hills were shite. The fifty-yard trek up the shallow incline took all the fire out of his loins, taking Sid's personal hygiene to a bad-place, or, rather, a worse place. The Male Body Spray wasn't helping, in fact, it was taking on an even pissier odour.

Luckily, Sid's leather jacket hid the sweat rings that were growing at an alarming rate. Like the Germans of Sid's nightmares, the sweat rings from his armpits were invading the surrounding territory with ruthless efficiency, threatening to drown the tiger on his Esso Tiger Token T-shirt. Even a zipped-up heavy leather jacket couldn't disguise the smell the sweat rings would start making in the next ten minutes, nor would snorting bleach.

Sid continued along the path, huffing and puffing and smoking "Al Persio" Iranian cigarettes. He'd picked up four hundred of these full-tar, no-filter, carcinogentastic bad-boys as reward for finding Middlesbrough's only Iranian tobacconist, Isha Majeera's, dog.

The tree-lined car park had been left behind, and Sid walked around the hill on one of the nature trails. The first bench he came across was structurally tested when his considerable backside hit it with force. Sweat poured off him. He must have walked at least—he weighed up the trek—three hundred yards!

"Shit the bed!"

Who would've thought this doggin' malarkey would be so strenuous...and he'd not even started yet! He regained his breath after going through an Iranian per minute. From where he sat, he had a beautiful view of the surrounding countryside and woodland, marred only by the presence of Seal Sands' Chemical site in the distance.

Sid's lust waned. He couldn't see any ladies anywhere and the scent of the Male Body Spray was...evolving. If he left now, he could still get a gallon of ale in before The Miner's closed. However, a little voice in his pants said, "Keep trying, please! Not another cosy night in, just the two of us!"

The out-of-shape Casanova got to his feet. Another few hundred yards around the hill, and if nothing came of it, The Miner's was calling. Sid psyched himself up and set off around the hill of hidden passion. He took two steps and then stopped.

He could hear something up ahead. His mind raced. Unfortunately, Sid wasn't very imaginative when it came to the bedroom department, or any other department for that matter. He focused on....his old school teacher, Miss Stevens. Absolutely cracking set of jugs. Cracking. He imagined her...

He imagined her...

Err...

He imagined her flicking through a copy of *Tits*.

Imagery sufficient.

Sid's sex drive pumped blood towards a much underused appendage, which was shocked but pleasantly surprised. He strode forward, reached the brow of the hill, and...

This wasn't part of the plan.

In front of him was a well-dressed, middle-aged gentleman with a Scottish Highland Terrier.

The colour drained from the big man's face, which took a significant amount of time considering how red it was to start with. His mouth dropped open. The power of speech evaded him.

There was but one explanation: this was a *them lot* hill.

Before this moment, he didn't even know what a *them lot* hill was. What if he was German?

Oh God.

"Good evening, squire," English, thank fook, but wait...*squire*? This was worse. This one was Southern, possibly from London. Sid remembered back to Brian's lecture on how Londoners hadn't produced a straight man in their history and that the entire Cockney population was maintained by two Scouse dockers and a lorry driver from Hull.

"Are you all right there, old boy?"

Sid's eyes widened. *Old boy!* He mentioned his old boy! They were so forward! So forward!

The Southern *them lot* clocked the lead in Sid's hand. "Lost your dog?"

A cold, clammy sweat covered Sid, the type only raw fear can induce. Sid thought fast...(thirty seconds later)..."No."

"O...K....," replied the gentleman. "Well, good day to you." He nodded his head and walked on.

Sid waited until the man was well out of sight before heaving a sigh of relief. That was close, too close. He was going to have serious words with Brian when he got back to The Miner's.

"Ah fook this!"

If this was a dogging area for *them lot*, he was getting out of here. He smoked another Iranian and began the three hundred-yard marathon. His only saving grace was that the journey was downhill. Approaching the car park, a flash of yellow caught his eye. A man from the 'boro could spot blonde hair from space.

The blonde hair quickened Sid's pace...

The low-cut top doubled it!

"Fooking 'ell! Right, Sid, it is time, my son," he murmured to himself as all memories of the *them lot* hill floated away, literally with the fairies.

The peroxide blonde wore blue jeans that appeared painted on. How she got the waistline of the jeans over her massive buttocks could only be explained by forty-ish peroxide blondes who refused to accept they were getting old. She wore a vest, which didn't do much to conceal her impressive cleavage or the offensive tattoos on top of each breast.

Sid was in love.

Contact.

"Good evening, young lady." Sid Tillsley miraculously transformed into a fat, Northern Roger Moore.

"Y'alllllrrrrrriiigggght?" It took a good two seconds for the word to be completed. The strong Leeds accent went from his ears to his loins at the speed of light. She was from Leeds, she was blonde, she was forty plus, and she had tattoos on her titties. Sid Tillsley was certain he'd be getting down to it in a matter of minutes, possibly seconds. In fact...

Sid looked down at his old fella, just to make sure he wasn't already having sex.

"I'm very well, thank you, my dear." said Northern Roger Moore. He tried to raise a seductive eyebrow, but only succeeded in letting go of a little wind. "What is the reason that I come across you this fine summer's evening?"

"Walkin' dog, mate," she replied, then bellowed, "C'MON, ENRIQUE!" A red setter bounded from a cluster of trees. "Catch ya later," said the Northern rose, and began to walk past Sid.

"Hang on there, love." Northern Roger Moore disappeared. Sid didn't know what to say to initiate sexual contact, and his earlier innuendo had clearly failed. Sid looked down at his lead. He'd have to make a more obvious innuendo to entice the Jewel of the North into letting him give her one behind the bushes. "It's such a beautiful evening, and my dog is out...shagging."

The lady looked at Sid blankly. "Oh, that's grand," she said, slightly bewildered. "I think I'll be on my way." She turned to follow the red setter that had disappeared from view.

Sid didn't know what to do. She hadn't taken the bait, but he was so close. Shit or bust, he decided. "My dog's off shagging and I was thinking maybe...erm...I could give you one behind the hedge over there?"

The real Roger Moore would've had his kecks round his ankles by now. Northern Roger Moore was kicked square in the knackers.

4

IT WAS ALL SO DIFFERENT NOW. A planned kill. What was the point? "The Golden Age," they called it. At least Michael Vitrago, for all his hypocrisy, did. He was responsible for the massacre of tens of thousands of humans, all unnecessary and all for the pure fun of it. Michael was the most powerful vampire of the last two millennia, a force to be reckoned with, and a beast of a lamia. Who could have predicted his fall from grace?

Gabriel was his second in command during the true Golden Age, the tenth century. It was a time when humans lived their lives in righteous fear of the vampire. It was not hunting, it was feasting. Lords, ladies, there was no one powerful enough to avoid their fangs.

And now, thanks to the Agreement, Gabriel was to endure an organised hunt in the arsehole of the world: Middlesbrough. Now, vampires hunted local criminals who didn't deserve to die of leprosy, let alone be taken by an immortal. Nevertheless, if you didn't move with the times, then you died. That was the way of the world.

Gabriel was to meet Gunnar in a local public house after his meeting with Ricard and Richmond. Three completely different characters, all dear to his heart, but Gunnar was his kindred spirit. Born thousands of miles and hundreds of years apart, the same desires drove them. They were predators born to hunt and rejoice in the kill. This modern age was for the Ricards of the world: artists, philosophers, musicians. But the good times would return. Everything travels in cycles and the balance would be restored one day. How Gabriel lusted for war.

He watched the locals pour out of the pubs and clubs. Witnessing it made him nauseous. They drunkenly shouted at each other and threw punches, while others vomited on their own streets. If vampires had sunk in stature, humans had plummeted. He took in his surroundings. It'd be almost worth his death slaughtering the whole godforsaken town. He turned down an alleyway leading to the back of the Wolf's Head free house.

Gunnar was waiting outside.

"I thought we were meeting inside the pub?"

"We were," said Gunnar, "but I cannot waste time with you,

drinking and reminiscing. After fifty years, we can finally hunt."

Gabriel embraced his closest friend. "Then, let us hunt."

SHE AWOKE, AND HER THROBBING HEAD TOLD HER TO GO BACK TO SLEEP. When she opened her eyes, the world spun, so she shut them tight again. God, she was still drunk. Too much booze. Always too much booze. She'd lost her friends in a bar. Then, those lads had kept her company, buying her drinks. They'd been so friendly, but then…everything was hazy after that, like a dream. Like a—

That stench: alcohol, weed, a hot breath on her face. She opened her eyes again and—He was on top of her!

She was in…She was—Oh, God, her top had been pulled down! She was in a car. Where was she! Her fight or flight instinct kicked into overdrive. She erupted into a rage, clawing and yelling at her attacker as he tried to grab her flailing arms and legs. He slapped her hard, but she kept fighting for her life. He was hideous: a pock-marked face, greasy hair, and a stained baseball cap. She kicked him hard, and he flew back, and he kept flying, twenty feet away from the car door.

"What the…?"

A face, just as ugly, just as evil, loomed. He sat in the front seat, mouth and eyes wide open. He stared at her and then at the car door where her attacker had disappeared. Suddenly, a face filled that doorway, a face which couldn't have been more different.

"Are you OK, girl?"

She nodded but couldn't speak, not because of the alcohol, but because of the beauty of the man before her. Dark hair blew across his perfect skin, and she couldn't escape from his transfixing brown eyes. He took off his coat to reveal powerful, broad shoulders and gave it to her. Suddenly aware of her nakedness, she quickly wrapped herself in it. The ordeal was sobering her up, fast.

"My friend and I have to deal with these two young gentlemen, so please, shut your eyes. Whatever you hear, do not open them. You're safe now."

She struggled to shut her eyes and stop looking at this angel, but she had to obey. There was the sound of a car door opening as the man in front seat screamed. The door slammed shut and then there was nothing.

STEVE WAS DRAGGED TO WHERE DAZ LAY MOTIONLESS. By the dim light of the moon, he could see Daz was still breathing, but Steve couldn't make up his mind if that was a good thing.

These men were tall and heavily built, one a skinhead who looked mental, and the other one with dark hair. They had to be the police, and he knew which one would be bad cop. This was all Steve needed. He already had two cautions, and this was serious stuff, probably a jail sentence. Fuck, it was just a bit of fun. The girl was on her own, pissed out of her head. A few more drinks and it wasn't tough to coax her out of the club and into the car, and then, it was just a short drive out of town into the countryside...

The dark-haired copper touched Daz's neck and he came to, coughing and wheezing... What the hell? It was like someone had thrown a cold bucket of water over him. "You were going to force yourself on her," said the copper to Daz.

Daz couldn't speak. He couldn't even breathe. Man, they'd messed him up bad.

Steve broke in. "We weren't, copper! She asked to come out here with us. We met her in town. She was well up for it."

The dark-haired one said, "What makes you think I'm a policeman?" He reached down and grabbed Daz by the throat, picking him up with ease until Daz's feet dangled a foot off the ground. Steve's eyes bulged, and he struggled to control his bladder.

"My acquaintance is Gunnar Ivansey. I am Gabriel. I was born in Hungary centuries ago. Do you know what we did to rapists in Hungary?" His stare caused Steve to cower. "No? The education system today..." He sighed and shook his head mockingly. "We ripped off their genitals until they bled to death." He reached down, grabbed Daz's crotch, and said to him, "You're going to relive the past."

Daz screamed in pain, but Gabriel drove his thumb into his throat quenching his cries. Daz's mouth distorted into a silent scream, and Steve vomited. Daz's eyes closed as he lost consciousness but this thing, this devil, Gabriel, shifted his grip and Daz's eyes bolted open.

"Don't worry. Soon, you'll sleep forever." The torturer lifted his hand so he could show Daz his own dismembered, blood-dripping genitals. "You value these tiny little things so much, don't you?" He shook his head at Daz. "It is true what they say, 'Those who live by the sword, die by the sword.'" He threw Daz to the ground, who screamed for a second before the pain took him. Gabriel threw Daz's genitals at Steve who didn't dare move for the terror that bound him. "And you..."

This time, Steve *did* lose control of his bladder. He couldn't take his eyes off Daz whose breathing was slowing.

"Were you going to rape that poor, defenceless girl?"

"No...I..."

"Do you wish to share the same fate as your friend or maybe your punishment should be more severe?"

Steve's gaze was ripped from Daz's dying body at the mention of a more severe punishment. "Mister, I...I..."

"Were you just going to watch? You don't look the sort who could force himself on a woman, but you would've sat there and watched wouldn't you? I have another punishment for you."

Gabriel reached down and thrust a forefinger into Daz's eye-socket, hooked the finger once inside, and ripped out his left eye. Daz didn't move; he must have passed out. Steve wept. His stomach had no more to give, nor did his bladder, but he'd never stop crying. He shut his eyes tight, hoping it was all a nightmare.

"I'm going to give you a chance, rapist. You can walk away, a free man and with everything intact. Aren't you the lucky one?"

Steve nodded, nervously trying to go along with the situation, doing his best to survive.

"There are two things you have to do to walk away. Number one." Gabriel held Daz's dripping eye and rubbed his stomach. "Dinner time!"

"Wh-wh-what?"

Gabriel threw the detached eye to Steve, and it hit him in the chest leaving a bloodstain over his white T-shirt. It bounced to the ground in front of his knees and stared right back at him. The oozing blood from the optic nerve and the limp extra ocular muscles caused him to dry-heave incessantly.

"Oh, poor show, poor show." Gabriel looked away in disgust. "Pick it up," Gabriel ordered.

Steve reached down slowly towards the eye, his hand shaking unrelentingly. He paused millimetres from the sickening object.

"I...I can't," he whimpered in between tears.

"Do you have your wallet with you, young man? Do not answer, just listen. If you have, then I have your address. If you do not do as I ask, then I can play these games with your mother and father. Perhaps your little brother would like to eat parts of your little sister? Your choice?"

Steve picked up the eye and placed it in his mouth. He bit down on the soft tissue and liquid exploded inside his mouth, and poured down his throat.

"Good boy! Now just one more thing to eat. What was the other thing I took from Daz?"

"HAVE YOU FINISHED PLAYING JUDGE, JURY, AND EXECUTIONER?" asked Gunnar.

Gabriel stood over the dead bodies of the men, looking down with a smirk on his face. "I do like to teach them the error of their ways before sending them on their journey to the afterlife."

"Have you ever let one live?"

"What do you think?"

Gunnar nodded and then gestured at the car where the girl still sat with her eyes tightly shut. "She's waiting for her Knight in Shining Armour."

Gabriel strode towards the car. He opened the door, grabbed the girl, and yanked her out of the vehicle. A reassuring crack indicated a dislocated shoulder. She screamed as he dragged her by her useless arm. No more games. Bloodlust consumed him. He fell upon her and gorged himself on her neck.

Gunnar joined him and savaged the other side.

The girl went into spasms and blood gushed from her mouth as her arteries and veins were ripped to pieces.

As one, they stepped back, their faces covered in blood that glistened in the moonlight.

Gunnar held his hands aloft and roared.

Gabriel fell backwards onto the ground, satiated. A minute later he said, "The moment after the rapture, we realise we live in dark, oppressed times."

Gunnar spat on the ground and pulled out his mobile phone. "Three to clean up as expected." He hung up without waiting for a reply, shaking his head. "Poor Sanderson. It must destroy him knowing he has to come and clean up after us. Shall we leave the place in a state?" He ripped off the girl's dislocated arm.

"No, let's not play games. Let us hunt, for the night is young. Let us hunt, Gunnar, for old time's sake." He tore off the girl's other arm and held it up as if making a toast. "To old times."

"To old times."

They ran through the night. They jumped from tree to tree, sprinting, diving, embracing free running, leaping over hedges as if they weren't there. This was what their lives used to be. Every vampire's life had been about running; either running to catch food, or running away from a lot of food. These two, however, had never run away from anything.

Gabriel hadn't been united with Gunnar since World War II where they travelled across France. They'd killed at will, and to them, it was the greatest time in the past century. Now was a time to taste blood and remember a better life. Neither cared about the consequences of the crimes they were about to commit. Nothing could come close to the sixty years of boredom since the war. Up ahead was the north car park of the Memorial Park and human activity was unusually high.

The two ran at pace until they reached the outskirts of the clearing.

"Like old times, Gunnar?"

"Not quite the same. There are no arrows or bullets flying past our ears." He vaulted a small tree. "Same old man in the moon smiling down on us, though."

"Better that than the sun."

They both stopped on a sixpence and were unrecognisable in the shadows. From where they lay, they could see three cars.

"There is a young couple in that Astra, early twenties," said Gunnar. "They are intimately entangled, and she's a very friendly young lady." He smirked. "In the Land Rover are a couple in their early thirties; two attractive young women enjoying each other's company."

Gabriel grinned. "Perhaps this is the 'Golden Age,' after all?"

"Yin and Yang. There's a fifty-year-old man being intimate with himself in that Volkswagen Beetle."

Gabriel's grin turned to a look of disgust. "Humans, bah! What's the plan?"

Gunnar raised an eyebrow, "My plan? This is a turn-up for the books."

"Yes, I don't know what I was thinking." Gabriel surveyed the car park and looked at the Beetle. "I want that man dead."

"As you wish." Gunnar gave a mock salute and disappeared into the night. A moment later, the door of the Beetle opened and the man's head fell forward. Gunnar was back by Gabriel's side in a matter of seconds.

"Very good, assassin."

Gunnar flourished the black blade. "It didn't deserve me to touch it. That leaves us with a choice of two. The females or the more conventional couple?"

"We'll kill the boy and the girl." He grinned. "And then we'll have our fun."

After two relatively quick murders, Gabriel nodded towards the Land Rover. He and Gunnar surrounded the car. Gabriel opened the passenger's door while his companion opened the driver's door. They were rewarded with the sight of two attractive women, kissing and touching each other passionately. The two vampires grinned at each other. The girls didn't look up, but they became increasingly intimate, turned on by their audience.

"Do you just want to watch? Or do you want to join in?" asked the more dominant of the girls without even pausing to look at her captive crowd.

"What do you think?" asked Gunnar.

"I think I'm hungry." He climbed into the car and shut the door behind him, Gunnar following suit. Gabriel bit the first warm piece of flesh he reached. He ripped into an arm and blood sprayed onto the windshield. The victim screamed and clutched at her wrist. She thrashed pathetically, trying to rid herself of the bite.

Gunnar went straight for his victim's neck, killing the girl instantly. He'd always struggled reigning in his killer instincts. Gabriel, however, wasn't finished. His hunger satisfied, now was time for fun. He grabbed her wrist tight to quell the blood loss. He wanted his game to last as long as possible

"Ask me to kill you," he said.

The girl thrashed harder, kicking and screaming.

"Ask me to kill you, and it will be over. Only then can you join your friend." He grabbed the girl's dark black hair and pushed her face into that of her lover's. Lifeless eyes stared back, and she stopped struggling.

Gabriel persisted. "Ask me to kill you, and it will be all over." He pulled back her head and kissed her, smearing her own blood across her face, but suddenly, her eyes deadened and she fell limp. He looked up to see Gunnar spit out a hunk of the girl's neck.

"Why did you do that?" he asked with calm annoyance.

"That car flashed us." Gunnar pointed at the car on the opposite side of the car park. It must have arrived moments ago. "There's no time for games if there are witnesses. Have your fun with them."

Gabriel frowned. The occupant would pay dearly for the interruption. The two left the Land Rover and crossed the park until they drew near to the car. A fat human jumped out and shouted obscenities at them in an inaudible language. He was a horrible wreck, even by human standards. They could sense his diseased veins from metres away and the smell of the man's unwashed body was overpowering. He stank of urine.

Gabriel circled the man, leaving Gunnar to attack the front. The man was petrified and fear oozed from every pore of his clammy skin. Gabriel could sense his pulse racing through clogged veins. With a nod towards his comrade, Gabriel leapt.

And then, there was nothing.

5

SID ENTERED THE MINER'S to find it almost empty except for a few lads watching Tarrant. Brian was about, entertaining a forty-ish-year-old redhead and was "in the zone," as he normally described it. Seeing the master was at work, Sid bought himself a pint of Bolton Bitter, took a seat near the dartboard, and lit up an Iranian. It'd been a terrible day, but a few ales would sort him out. A few ales sorted everything out.

Sid enjoyed his ninety-first, second, third, and fourth Iranians of the day, watching his friend work his magic. The master gracefully moved in for a kiss, and a less graceful tweak of the breast. Brian was Middlesbrough's answer to Lionel Ritchie.

After a couple of reloads at the bar, Sid caught Brian's eye and waved a paw at him. Brian gave him a nod and excused himself from his date.

"What you doing here, Sid? You should be getting ready for a night of shaggin'."

"I've been, Brian," said Sid dejectedly. "It went pissing terrible." Rubbing his swollen genitals to emphasise the point. She'd managed to connect with both of them.

"What do you mean, 'you've been?' It's only quarter past ten. It's only just got dark for fook's sake. The only people up there in daytime are bird-watchers and dog-walkers!"

For Sid Tillsley, many things fell into place.

Brian looked over his shoulder at the redhead who was playing with her hair in, what some would consider, a seductive way. "Look, mate, I'm on for one here. She's a dead cert, and she's fooking gagging for it, like."

"Who is she? I thought you were servicing Charlie's missus tonight?"

"Charlie's done his knee in. Banged it on the bonnet of a Peugeot 406 the other night. Had to phone his missus from the dogging site. Told her he was bat watching and she bought it. Anyroad, he won't be going out for a few weeks, so I canna go round." Brian gave a shrug and then nodded towards the redhead. "That there is a new cleaner from work. And Sid, I'm going to give her something to clean up!"

"She's a bit young for one of your cleaners, ain't she?" said Sid. Brian, being a scholar, worked in the town. He was the manager over half a dozen cleaners at Middlesbrough General Hospital.

"Yeah, but she just got out of nick, and they set her up with a job. She don't speak much English, like." He looked over again and tapped his chin thoughtfully. "And I don't think she's foreign. Anyways, I've got to go, mate. I don't want to lose this one. Give the car-park thing a go tonight. I told you: it don't start till 'bout midnight. Remember, keep your interior light on and flash your headlights twice. What can go wrong?"

SID TILLSLEY, FORTY-SIX, GSOH, LIKES: TITS, DISLIKES: COCKS, sat in his maroon Montego Estate. The back seats were down and the radio was turned up. Status Quo bashed out riff after riff of unadulterated *Manrock*.

His Montego was a well-known vehicle around the streets of Middlesbrough. Local legend has it that the maroon estate was the first one of its kind. Mr. David Montego was the mastermind behind the ultimate human-transportation device. The idea had come to him after he was struck by lightning one afternoon while playing golf. He said that God himself had told him to build a machine worthy of the almighty. David took fifteen years to design the Montego and helped build the very first with his own hands. He put his heart and soul into his creation. When he finished, he passed away mysteriously. Some say that he'd sacrificed his own life-essence in creating the car. Others say that God punished him because the car was shit.

Sid's Montego did, however, exhibit some strange attributes. It always passed its MOT and never obtained speeding tickets or parking fines either. This was most likely because the majority of the people in Middlesbrough knew of Sid and of Sid's devastating right hand. Therefore, rumours of David Montego haunting the car to ensure that no ill befalls his beloved creation were, like most pub rumours, bollocks.

There were three other cars in the Middlesbrough Memorial car park. No streetlamps meant Sid could only see by the moonlight. The other cars consisted of a Land Rover, a clapped-out Astra, and a new Volkswagen Beetle. Sid had his eye on the VW Beetle. After all, it just had to be a lady driving it, and if it wasn't, then it was best he kept an eye on it. He assumed the Astra was a young lad with his girlfriend, and that the Land Rover was probably a businessman looking for some action, just like him. He didn't consider that the driver could be one of *them lot*. They could never handle such a big car.

The Beetle's interior light hadn't been set to "Howay the lads!" The Land Rover and the Astra were both unlit and motionless too. Sid had been here for fifteen minutes now, nervous yet excited. His nerves had the upper hand at the moment. He'd not plucked up the courage to turn on his own light.

How things had changed since his heyday. He remembered the days of wining and dining girls, not meeting them in car parks. Brian had changed with the times. Sid hadn't. He was an old romantic at heart.

Sid flicked through the copy of *Tits* he'd bought at the local newsagent. All he wanted was a gigantic set of breasts in his face. Was that too much to ask? It really was tough being a romantic.

He looked up.

Movement! Near the Land Rover. Maybe a lady had gone over to the lad in the 4x4. Sid's heart rate increased. He could see a couple of shadows either side of the car.

"Where have these horny lasses come from?" he said, curiously.

Both front doors of the Land Rover opened simultaneously, and the two shadows entered the car, which instantly began to rock up and down.

"Fookin' hell!" Sid rubbed his hands together and looked down at his crotch. "Tonight, son, you end the biggest drought of your life!"

The rocking of the car stopped when the big man flashed his lights over-enthusiastically at the Land Rover. The doors opened and the two ladies jumped out of the car, turning to face the Montego, edging slowly towards the erect Sid. The moon shone behind the two girls and Sid couldn't see their faces, but he'd decided on the way down here that it didn't matter what they looked like. In fact, he'd decided when he was fifteen that it didn't matter what women looked like. They continued slowly towards the car.

It dawned on Sid that the two girls were a little bit on the large side, not fat, more...Amazonian, but that was OK. Sid had slept with big women before, some unbelievably big women, but he'd certainly never slept with any as tall or as broad as these two.

"They've got their titties out!" said Sid with glee, although he wasn't happy about how small the ladies' breasts were, although they were incredibly pert, even though the hair was a little off putting. As the two young, desperate, nubile nympho sluts walked in front of the headlights, a horrible realisation dawned on Sid. The young, desperate, nubile nympho sluts were actually blokes...

And of course that meant...

"Them lot!"

The two men were now ten feet from the car and the only way Sid could get away was through them, and that caused him a lot of discomfort. He went for the keys in the ignition, but the sheer terror of having *them lot* just feet from his Montego Estate caused him to drop them. One of the blokes stood directly in front of the car and placed his hands on the bonnet, staring through the windscreen at Sid.

"Aw fook, where have his hands been!" said Sid, fearing for the Montego's polish. Fight took over from flight, and he jumped out of the car.

"Right, yous twos. I'm a fanny man, so fook off!" He clenched his fists, the equivalent to taking the safety off a gun.

The threat didn't bother them and both snarled back at him.

"What the fook have you done to your teeth? They're pointy! I didna realise you fookers had different teeth! Ain't wearing ironed clothes and shaving your plums enough!"

Slowly, the two circled Sid. They were sly fookers, which meant he could only see one of them in his field of vision. They both entered striking distance.

"You ain't getting any, ya bastards!" He recalled a conversation the night previous. *What was that there fairytale thing Brian was on about?* he thought. *Ah!* "Rumpledforeskin! Rumpledforeskin!" he cried desperately trying to rid himself of the unwanted male attention.

Suddenly, the man outside of Sid's vision leapt at him, but Sid's *Pink Alert* gave him eyes in the back of his head *and* his arse. Spinning around with a speed that defied his size, he unfurled the right and connected fully and firmly with the airborne attacker. He continued his spin until he faced the other fairy. Sid knew the first one was out cold. When he dealt his right hook, they always were.

"Now then, Tarquin, your turn."

Sid's attacker was not looking at him. He was staring behind him to where his fallen comrade lay. Sid knew it was a trick, because they never came round until morning. The young man turned his gaze to Sid. Terror filled his piercing blue eyes. He somersaulted backwards and twisted in mid-air to run at full speed upon landing, sprinting across the car park and out of sight.

Sid looked down at his right and smiled. "Won't be trying that again will you, Shirley?" He turned around to look at the fallen fairy.

But he'd gone.

GUNNAR RAN LIKE THE WIND, NOT CARING WHO SAW HIM. What he just witnessed added more pain, more suffering, and more anguish to a soul already saturated with hatred and vengeance. He stopped dead on the edge of the cliff tops, having covered thirty miles in what seemed like a moment. The North Sea crashed below, unrelenting as his woe. The moonlight shone beautifully on the water.

He leapt.

The wind whistled past his ears, and he plunged deep into the icy water. His foot shattered against a rock. It'd heal in minutes, not that he cared. He floated to the surface and gazed at the moon. That same beauty he'd looked upon when he lost his mother. Why must something so beautiful remind him of something so terrible?

6

BEN EDRIC WAS IN OVER HIS HEAD. He tried to calm his breathing and stop his foot tapping manically on the floor, but he was on the verge of a nervous breakdown. He forgot the danger at hand when a beautiful, slender woman stood up and took the floor. Flowing raven-black hair spilt over the shoulders of her black suit. She was immaculately dressed, although it was difficult to notice anything apart from her face. Unblemished pale skin encompassed high cheekbones, a small, perfect nose and luscious red lips. She appeared to be in her thirties, until he fell into her eyes. They were a vivid emerald green; stunning, yet there was something more to them. Looking into them, he could see something more sinister hiding beneath, like the thorns lurking beneath the petals of a rose. Deep into that unblinking stare, he fell until everything else around him was...

He shook his head clear. That's how they got you. And they always got you.

"Last year, the total harvest was twenty thousand and ninety-seven, twelve per cent over quota." Ben leaned forward, hanging on her words. Her voice was enchanting. "This is slightly unexpected, but it didn't prove to be a problem for—"

"No, it wasn't a problem, but only because of our fantastic team of Cleaners."

The hoarse voice snapped Ben out of his trance. Charles' interruption had brought him back to reality.

Charles was a portly man in his fifties, with thinning grey hair combed desperately over his balding scalp to give the impression of substance. Ben hated the way he stared over the top of his small half-moon glasses. The fat, pompous toad continued, "But, Lucia, twelve per cent over quota is the worst year we've had since records began. This, I think you'll agree, is a cause for concern?"

The other councillors nodded in agreement, all except the monster, ever looming, ever dominating; the most terrifying thing that had ever walked the earth. Ben's fear returned. He must be insane. He should have fled when he had the chance.

The beautiful Lucia continued with her magical tones. "Are you saying we're not doing enough?"

"Two thousand people were killed unnecessarily," said Charles. "This puts a huge strain on our resources and incurs a huge cost, which eventually comes out of your pockets. We need to deal with this now."

Lucia sighed. "There's no need to make a mountain out of a molehill. I've seen these events many times before."

Caroline quickly followed up. "I appreciate we haven't seen these events in person, but our place on the Coalition is well earned."

The tension mounted, and Ben was glad of it. The attention turned away from him. Caroline was involved now, and she was one hard-nosed bitch. She looked almost motherly, like she wouldn't say boo to a goose, yet he knew the truth. The cream suit she wore contrasted starkly with her dark black skin. Surely she struggled sleeping at night because of the decisions she made, siding with the vampire, the lamia. She never wanted Ben on this council to start with. Now, a year later, he wished she'd had her way.

"No disrespect was intended, Caroline," said Lucia, "but we've been at peace for hundreds of years. We have the expertise and resources to deal with anything."

"But that twelve per cent isn't all, is it, Lucia?" said Charles, who looked over to where Augustus sat, lounging in one of the great chairs surrounding the table. "Now would be a good time to present the details of the vampire population, Augustus."

"As you wish." Augustus sat up straight and yawned.

Jealousy ripped Ben's heart in two. *I fucking hate you*, he screamed from inside. His heart banged against his ribcage again. This meeting was an emotional roller coaster: fear, lust, hate, all in a minute. He reached into his pocket for a pill that would take away his anxiety. He drew it out and popped it in his mouth. He was only thirty-two, but he needed them, especially now. The pill took instant effect, but was he drawing attention to himself?

He looked around as far as the monster, but daren't look up to see if he held his gaze. This was a monster unlike Augustus.

Michael Vitrago.

Just the thought of the name saturated Ben's shirt with sweat. Vitrago knew what Ben had been up to...he had to.

Ben tried to concentrate on Augustus whose shirt was open to halfway down his chest, revealing bulging pectoral muscles on which a large, gold crucifix lay. He wore it to laugh in the face of every man and woman here. His blonde hair hung roughly in a ponytail down his back. He didn't have to try to look good. He looked just like the vampires from the novels written for simpering teenage girls. If they only knew the truth. Those sapphire blue eyes of his...

Was that what she *saw in him?* Ben thought. *Was that why she did it? Either way, you're going to pay, you bastard!*

"One thousand nine hundred eighty was the registered vampire count at the end of April," Augustus drawled. "The following figures are only an estimate; we're not kept on a leash as some may wish. About a third of us are permanently based here in London, while half reside in the cities: Glasgow, Manchester, Belfast, Birmingham, and Bristol.

"The remainder work in our industrial services such as Dover, for import/export, and Seal Sands, Middlesbrough, in our chemical sector. Two per cent of our permanent residents are either abroad or living the peaceful, nomadic life nature intended. How quaint," he mocked. "The nomads amongst us populate the Highlands and the North Yorkshire Moors. I hope that's sufficient information for you all." He slouched back into his chair. His arrogance was sickening.

"Thank you, Augustus," said Charles. "Can I please ask how the population densities match up with the harvesting statistics?"

"I can deal with this one, sir,"

Jeremy Pervis, you snivelling, arse-kissing snake. Ben hated Pervis. They were both raised to councillors at the same time, and Pervis had seen it as his duty to outdo him at every opportunity. Pervis's clothes were expensive, yet they didn't suit him. He was tall and gangly, awkward even, like he struggled to control his limbs. His ginger hair was gelled back over his head. Strands broke free and he swept them back over his head in between nervously pushing his glasses up the bridge of his nose. For all his brains, he had no place here. Ben would've put his house on Pervis still living with his mother.

"Do not call me 'sir' at these meetings, Jeremy." Charles sighed. "We all stand equal here on the Coalition."

Ben pressed his lips together. *Stand equal? Who are you trying to kid?*

"Yes, sir," Pervis said before turning to the others. "Good evening, ladies and gentlemen. I'll get straight to business, shall I? I have statistically analysed the data, and we have one anomaly: the Northeast, England. The harvesting in the Northeast is abnormally high."

Charles asked, "What made up the harvest?"

"Nationally, five per cent through the Prison Justice Programme. As for the Judicial Programme recently introduced, it has accounted for approximately forty-two per cent of the harvest this year. Known rapists, paedophiles, drug dealers, pimps, and prostitutes were taken from the streets. Some key figures in organised crime have met an untimely, and also, rather grizzly end."

Ben loved that one. Sure, a few criminals were wiped out, but how many innocent victims were killed when the executioners became a little too enthusiastic?

"Thirty per cent were harvested in the Euthanasia Project, which incidentally saved the National Health Service thirty-four million pounds. Our contacts in Parliament were delighted. The discreteness of the cleanup operations carried out by Sanderson has meant that no untoward questions were asked. Another fantastic job, sir."

Sanderson ignored Purvis entirely. Sanderson was a soldier who hated the little office-jockey as much as Ben did.

"Twenty-three per cent were unplanned, unsanctioned murders. Although this figure is high, it remains within the confidence limits, considering the economic and demographic factors. However, this is where the Northeast raises alarm bells." Jeremy offered the floor. "Sanderson?"

Sanderson stood up. A tall man in his forties, casually well dressed, with grey streaking the sides of his short brown hair. He was probably a handsome man once, but his face didn't suit his relaxed appearance. Lines of worry were etched heavily on his forehead, and Ben could understand why. The horrors this man witnessed every day...

Ben felt safe when Sanderson was around, but a thousand Sandersons wouldn't help him here, not if they knew.

"I've been in the team for twenty-five years, and this is the most stretched we've ever been. It's not just the number of incidents that we've had to deal with; the ferocity of the attacks in the Northeast has been sickening. I've had to move my office to Newcastle to help, and I've been doing dirty work new recruits should be doing. That thirty-four mill saved on health care has not even scratched the surface of the extra finances we've had to call upon." He didn't share his colleague's well-spoken accent as he was raised in a rougher part of town. It was hard to pin his accent down. This man, this soldier had never settled for long.

"More officers have been drafted in, and recruitment ain't easy. Kids have got no balls any more, and if they have, then they've got no brains. If it keeps going like this, then we're fucked!" Sanderson wore his heart on his sleeve and didn't try to put an act on in front of his fellow councillors. "In an attempt to cover up the savagery, we've had to make most of the victims look like goddamn burn victims. Some of the things I have seen over the last year..."

Ben tried not to think about it.

"Is there a pattern to all this?" asked Lucia.

"None," barked Sanderson. "None except everyone gets ripped apart, men, women, children, even the goddamn family dog." The veins of his neck protruded with the pressure. "It's a fucking war zone up there."

"Have the hunters been involved with the Northeast at all?" asked Charles. "Augustus, I believe you have a report on their activity?"

"Yes, Charles. The number of hunters is at an all-time low, which is good news—depending on your point of view."

Ben's blood boiled as Augustus chuckled to his own joke. *We'll see how funny you find it!*

"We've had seven losses this year. Three were almost certainly killed by the hunters."

"Three?" asked Charles. "Is that all? Have they given up?"

"If a lamia is weak or foolish enough to be killed by a mortal, they deserve death."

It was the first time the monster had spoken this meeting. A giant with heaving shoulders and a neck as thick as a man's leg, his elbows were on the table, his chin resting on giant fists. Tribal tattoos ran up the back of his neck to the top of his completely shaven skull. Ben didn't dare look into his eyes. Looking into his eyes was not like looking into the eyes of the monster's brethren. Michael Vitrago was a lion amongstst cats. He was a vampire who'd put fear into God himself.

With the sound of the voice, Ben's world dropped from under him. He wanted to empty his stomach. He wanted to lose consciousness and never wake. Why did he come here? Why didn't he run? Revenge wasn't worth this.

"Who was lost?" asked Charles.

"Viktor Kretzig was taken, in London, by Jonathan Russle, who died performing the task. Elizabeth Gray from Whitby was taken in her sleep by Donald McSteel, who..." Augustus let out a small laugh. "Died earlier in the year, ironically from skin cancer."

Keep laughing. Ben grimaced.

"Finally, Steven Windmar, killed in Newcastle, while working in the chemical sector. We believe Reece Chambers was responsible. He's someone we'd like to get hold of."

Don't worry, you'll see him soon enough, Augustus. Ben suppressed a smile.

"We believe he's hiding in the Northeast. It cannot be coincidence that takes him there. We know very little of this man. There are no records of him even existing until he graduated from Oxford. He's nothing compared to the hunters of yesteryear, but he has eluded us for well over a decade."

"We should make every effort to get rid of this man," ventured Charles. "Every year brings thousands of extra surveillance cameras into the country. We've enough to hide without having some bloody idiot running around on a personal vendetta."

"Let the man get on with it, is what I say," spat Sanderson.

The air sizzled.

"And please tell us why?" demanded Lucia.

Sanderson's firey temper got the better of him. "Perhaps Chambers will find out what's causing the mess up there? Maybe he'll try ending the merciless mutilation of whole fucking families, of children, of babies, of fucking pregnant mothers!"

"That's enough, Sanderson!" Caroline shouted. "We've had enough profanities from you for one evening. This is a place for impartiality. You should know that by now."

Sanderson continued unabashed. "Whatever's out there isn't normal. We haven't seen anything like this before. What I've seen in the last few months..." He paused before turning his gaze on Vitrago. "What's out there?"

Ben couldn't believe his eyes. Sanderson had balls of steel.

"What the fuck is out there!" he screamed, before standing up and smashing his fist into the table.

"Sanderson!" yelled Caroline. "Control yourself!"

Sanderson fell into his seat, shaking. He'd punched the table so hard, he'd cut his knuckles.

"Go and sort yourself out," she growled under her breath.

He staggered to the edge of the hall with the weight of the world upon him. A slit of light appeared on the wall and then expanded, revealing the dark stone corridor beyond. Sanderson walked through the light, and darkness immediately closed in on him.

How Ben wished he could've gone with him.

"I must apologise, Michael, members of the council," Caroline began. "He'll beg for forgiveness when he's of sound mind."

Michael smiled. "Caroline, you need not apologise. He blames me because I'm the one with the history which will never be forgotten. However, that was a different age, a savage age. We should not dwell on the past. There is business to attend."

Ben stared into the table, praying that he didn't mean him.

"The Northeast needs investigating," said Caroline. "Something is out of our immediate control and needs rectifying. I suggest we set up teams from both parties."

"Agreed," finalised Michael.

"Sanderson would be my first choice, but I believe the dear fellow could use a holiday. Pervis, you'll assist in the matter."

"I would be honoured, ma'am." Pervis beamed smugly at Ben, who, for once, didn't care.

"Good. Which vampire will reciprocate?"

Michael answered without a pause. "I'll inform Franco Stoloni of his new role."

"Very well. I believe we've dealt with everything on the agenda. Is there any other business?" Caroline waited for a shake of the head from each councillor.

Ben tried to look as confident as possible when it came to his turn.

"Meeting adjourned."

Ben breathed a sigh of relief. One more meeting, one dangerous meeting, and then a one-way ticket to Tahiti was the order of the day. He rushed to his office and gathered as many of his possessions as he dared. Time was of the essence. Once he was out of this damned building, he at least had a chance. He filled his briefcase with papers, vital papers that, if he did find himself in a sticky situation, would be good material for negotiation. He was done. The only personal item he left was the photo of a beautiful woman. He picked up the frame.

She smiled at him, like butter wouldn't melt in her mouth.

"Whore!"

He threw the picture with all his might at the wall, resulting in the satisfying breaking of glass.

"Temper, temper."

A mass filled the door of his office. Ben's life flashed before his eyes. "Michael, what brings you here?" Ben tried to stay calm when his basic instincts screamed at him to run and hide.

"Going somewhere?"

"No, just taking some work home, that's all."

Michael didn't say a word. He walked over to the broken photo frame and picked out the picture of Ben's ex-girlfriend. "She's very pretty. I can see why you're...upset."

Ben couldn't deny his rage, not after Michael had witnessed his outburst. He tried to bluff instead. "With my best friend, who wouldn't be?"

"I didn't realise that you and Augustus were so close."

Ben's knees buckled, but he kept his feet.

The massive vampire walked around Ben's desk and took a seat on his comfortable desk chair and poured himself a whisky from a crystal decanter.

"I know why I'm not trusted; I'm Michael Vitrago, or as I was named, 'The Bloodlord.' That's why people suspect me of the upheaval in the Northeast. Three hundred years ago, it would've been me. Three hundred years ago, rivers of blood flowed and the carnage was wondrous. How things have changed. Even the wildest animal can be tamed, and now, I'm a simple bureaucrat, a politician." He took a sip before continuing.

"It's a common saying: move with the times. It affects humans in their business, fashion, and everyday life. For us, who are here for millennia, this saying is life or death. If we don't adapt, then we bring attention to ourselves. If we bring attention to ourselves, then we die. You're our food and that won't change. We cannot survive without you, but you can survive without us. If war broke out between the species, you would win. Your numbers are too great and technology too advanced."

Finishing his whisky, Michael poured himself another.

"Can you imagine the losses? Can you imagine the firepower needed to bring a lamia like myself down? However, the human loss of life would be insignificant compared to the scientific and cultural demise that you would suffer. Where would the human race be if vampires didn't walk amongst you? Would humans have walked on the moon? Would humans have discovered the Earth revolves around the sun? Can you imagine facing the next millennium alone, without thousands of years of knowledge to guide you?

"The Agreement that was made between vampires and humans two hundred and eighty-four years ago must be upheld. Do you think I would imprison the animal inside me for three hundred years just because I wanted to save your pitiful lives? Do you think I would deny my instincts and sit on this council—the so-called *Coalition*—with you monkeys, as *equals*, because of my love for mankind? The only reason I uphold the Agreement is because the vampire needs it to survive."

The whisky tumbler shattered in Michael's hand.

All Ben could hope for now was a quick death.

"The sole purpose of the Coalition is to vigilantly uphold the Agreement. The vampire has disappeared into the shadows. Our kills are sanctioned, arranged. We were born to kill you, and now, we are on the end of a leash, and that leash keeps us alive. Do you really think I'd let you break it because of a filthy wench who lusted after a vampire, a god compared to your worthless flesh?"

Michael got to his feet and advanced.

"I...I...wasn't going to..."

"What insults me is that you even tried. We know everything about you. You're our puppet. You're my puppet, but the strings are now broken. You were going to tell Reece Chambers all he needed to know about Augustus's movements so that he could kill him. Augustus fucked your girllfriend and she begged him for it. You were willing to destroy us all because of it. It's lucky we intercepted the information you tried to send. It's lucky the information in your briefcase didn't reach the public eye. If it did, your end would've been...more interesting. Still, it'd be wrong not to set an example."

With one hand, Michael grabbed Ben by the collar and lifted him off his feet. Ben had avoided staring into the eyes of the monster for the entire meeting, but now he'd no choice and stared into the eyes of Death itself.

Ben snapped his eyes shut. "Please, please make it quick!"

The warmth of Michael's breath as he laughed in his face washed over him. Behind the whisky, there was no mistaking the smell of blood, and the imminence of agony.

"I think you know me a little better than that."

7

"PINT OF BOLTON, PLEASE, KEVIN." Sid lit up a Turk. He'd acquired four hundred "El Kebabo" cigarettes for delivering a case of dodgy meat to Jock the Turk's Kebabateria. It was the closest Sid had ever been to delivering meat around the back.

Kevin poured a perfect pint. "You all right there, our Sid? You look a little peaky."

Sid shrugged. He didn't reply but instead guzzled half the beer in one manly draught, finishing the rest with an equally manly second. "Same again, like."

"Coming up."

Sid took his beer to an empty table. They were all empty except for a few lads watching a re-run of Tarrant on a TV in the corner. Sid lit up another Turk. It was eight o'clock, the day after his confrontation. Yesterday wasn't a good day for Sid Tillsley: a shot to the stones, a *them lot* confrontation, and a bizarre fight that ended with someone actually getting up.

Brian entered the pub and ordered a pint of Bolton. Clocking Sid, he took his ale over to the table to join him. "All right there, Sid?" He asked, giving the big man the once over. "You look a bit peaky."

"I'll be reet," said Sid, dismissing the unwanted attention. "How did you get on with that piece last night?"

"Nailed her, like," said Brian with a fist pump. "Easy really. She's been inside with all them lasses, so she was just gaggin' for some Middlesbrough meat."

"Class!" said Sid, momentarily forgetting his woes. "What did you get out of her?"

"Well, not quite as much as she got out of me."

Sid's brow furrowed. "What do ya mean, like?"

"She nicked me stereo on the way out," chuckled Brian. "She was inside for burglary."

"What you laughing about, mon? Go round there and get the bastard thing back. Surprised you stood for that, like."

Brian gave a knowing smile. "You see, Sid, I work closely with her parole officer. She's now in me debt, and anytime I fancy a quickie at work, she'll have to put out or I'll send her back to nick."

"That's brilliant!" said Sid in awe. Brian Garforth was truly the most intelligent man on the Smithson Estate. Sid doubted whether Poirot was sucked off as much as Brian.

"Give it a few weeks and I'll grass her up anyway. They've got to learn that crime doesn't pay," said the righteous scholar.

Both men sat for a while, quiet, contemplating, both satisfied that justice would be done. It was Brian who eventually broke the contented silence. "Well, Sid, what happened last night, then?"

"*Them lot*, Brian," said Sid in deadly seriousness. "*Them lot* happened."

"Are you sure, mate? I know you can be a little over-cautious when it comes to the gays." Brian flinched and hoped that Sid wouldn't think he was gay because he knew the word.

"I swear on my Dambuster medal that it was *them lot*. That's not what I'm worried about though. *Them lot* are always after a bit of me. I realise that I'm a bit of a catch, and in some ways, I canna blame them. It's just...the one I hit...he got up."

Brian dropped his pint and glass smashed all over the floor. Beer sprayed up his burgundy suit, not that he noticed. Kev did.

"What the fook you doing, Garforth? They cost bleeding money you know?"

"Shut up, Ackroyd, I spend enough in here," said Brian dismissively. He turned back to Sid, and whispered in disbelief, "He got up? You sure?"

"I turned around and he was gone."

"I guess...I-I don't know, Sid, you're forty-six, now, perhaps you've lost a bit of the power you used to have." Brian didn't sound convinced though.

"That's what I thought, so I tested it out, like. Stopped off by a bunch of cows on the drive back. Put some big, bastard bull out with a fooking jab. It's still there." He kissed his fist.

"I'll get the beers in, have a think about it, use me intelligence, like." Brian went to the bar. At the same time, a scruffy character walked into The Miner's. Sid and everyone else turned to stare. Strangers always received funny looks in The Miner's Arms.

The newcomer had long grey hair tied into a rough ponytail, which instantly inspired distrust. Long hair was for hippies or *them lot*. His attire didn't help his cause, either. A long wax jacket and filthy hiking boots gave him the look of an outdoorsy type. Sid and all council estate pub goers didn't trust the outdoorsy type; normally health-conscious and not man enough to drive home after fifteen pints. Scum.

The stranger took a seat at the bar and waited to be served.

Brian returned with the purchased beers. "Busy tonight," he said nodding towards the traveller. "You seen him before?"

"No, and the fooker keeps looking over here at me."

"Nah, mon, you're just being paranoid after what happened last night. Forget about it. More importantly, what do you think happened with that fella? You catch him wrong or summat?" Brian was grasping at straws. When Sid hit people, they went down. Always had, always will.

"Caught him perfect. Awesome connection."

Kev kept glancing over in Sid's direction while speaking to the stranger. It was making Sid nervous. "He's talking about me, Brian, I know he is."

Sid was on edge. Someone getting up from his right hand was unheard of. Sid could knock out a camel, which he proved, Blackpool Beach, Miner's Summer Excursion, 1994.

"Sid, give us a fiver and I'll get another round in, check it out." Sid handed over the note without question. Brian held the note up to the light. It was real!

"You *are* spooked, ain't ya?"

Brian sauntered over to the bar. "Two pints of Bolton, please, Kev." He nodded at the stranger. "Evening, mate." The stranger ignored him. His pint of beer was untouched. "Not a fan of the beer?" Brian asked.

"Just here for the atmosphere." The stranger's voice was deep. It wasn't a Middlesbrough accent either. Brian tensed up. It would have taken all his restraint not to punch the stranger in the face.

"What brings you to the 'boro?"

"Just passing through." The stranger still hadn't made eye contact. Brian's knuckles turned white, gripping the bar.

"Don't say much, do ya?"

"Who's your friend?" said the stranger, nodding towards Sid.

Brian pulled himself up to his full height. "Why the fook do you want to know?"

"Just wondered." The stranger's calm only sparked the Northerner's natural aggression.

"Well stop fooking wondering?" said a seething Garforth. "Who the fook do you think you are? Stepping into a pub you've never been to, thinking you're fooking Shadow from *Gladiators*?"

Sid, realising that trouble was afoot, got up to assist. "You OK, Brian?"

Kev ran over as Sid rolled up his sleeves. "Sid! Pack it in! I'm not having my pub smashed up again." Kev wanted to calm the situation, but Brian, who was now jumping up and down with rage, wasn't helping.

"Knock his fooking head off, Sid!"

Sid went to grab the stranger by the coat.

"Where were you in the early hours of this morning?" The stranger's voice, calm and steady, knocked Sid for six.

"Eh?"

"I was merely enquiring to your whereabouts. I believe I can answer a few questions that may have been troubling you since."

Various scenarios raced through Sid's mind. Was he a copper looking for doggers? Was he one of *them lot* thinking he could try it on because Sid was at a *them lot* dogging site? Was he a Benefit Bastard who saw him deliver the meat to the kebab house? Every single option ended up with Sid in shit. There was one option: Sid headed for the door.

"Wait!" Desperation crept into the stranger's voice. "I'm not looking for trouble. Hear my story and I'll buy you a beer!"

Sid turned a neat 180-degree pirouette. Fraud squad or not, there was no way they could get a free beer back unless he pissed on them and no one wanted that...unless he was one of them Germans.

Kev, banging a pint of Bolton Bitter on the bar, made the decision. Sid hammered it down. "Better make it one more, you know, to keep my concentration."

The stranger nodded at Kev who set about pouring Sid another ale. "May we talk in private?" The stranger looked at Brian and then at Sid.

"Can I have a quick word please, mate?" Brian took Sid to one side and whispered so no one could overhear. "Look, Sid, he could be anyone, fooking anyone. He could be a Benefit Bastard for all you know. I don't like the look of him."

Sid held his beer up to the light and gazed upon its clear magnificence. "Brian, this is my second free ale. I canna turn down free booze, and I could be on for a five-pinter, 'ere."

Brian sighed, "All right, mate, but I'm only letting it lie 'cos of the beer." Brian took his place at the bar a few yards away, giving the mystery man filthy scowls.

Sid took a seat near the broken jukebox and the stranger sat opposite. "What's your name?" he asked Sid.

"If you want to keep me talking then keep these beers flowing, OK?" If he was getting arrested, then he was going down pissed.

"OK. What's your name?"

"Sid."

"Sid who?"

"Me glass is empty."

"Landlord," the stranger called, "keep this man's glass full." He looked at Sid. "If you stop talking, you'll stop drinking."

"Tillsley. Sid Tillsley"

"What do you do?"

Here it comes, Sid thought. The Benefit Bastards thought they could get him this easy? No chance. He coughed a couple of times for effect. "Me? I canna work cos of me angina and me back. Oh, what cruel fate cursed me with these dreadful diseases...'nother beer, please."

The stranger didn't look impressed. It wasn't Sid's best performance as the ale was kicking in.

"I'll level with you, Sid. I was tracking two men last night, and you bumped into both of them in Middlesbrough Park in the early hours. I saw you fighting, and I want you to tell me what happened."

Sid didn't think the guy was one of *them lot* because a) he'd ordered himself an ale, and b) he hadn't tried it on yet. That left Benefit Bastard or copper. "You a copper?"

He grinned. "Not the sort that you'd know of."

"You a Benefit Bastard?"

"A what?"

"Do you work for the benefit office?"

The stranger laughed. "God, no. Sid, the two men you fought have a violent history and are wanted by the authorities. It's an extremely delicate matter; local constabularies haven't been informed yet."

"Shit the bed!" interrupted Sid.

The stranger continued. "Sid, you're not in trouble. You won't need to give any statements or have any connection with the law, I promise you. Just tell me what happened during the fight," the stranger almost pleaded.

"Where were you when all this kicked off?"

"I was in a tree in front of your car. I knew those men you fought were going to be at the park. I was waiting for them." He offered his hand to Sid. "My name's Reece Chambers. I'm one of the good guys. Tell me about the fight, please."

Kev walked over with a fresh pint. "You better be paying for these bastards," he threatened.

Reece reached into his pocket and pulled out a plump money clip. An awed hush would've filled the room if there were enough people to make the effect work. Reece flicked off a twenty-pound note and gave it to Kevin. It was the first twenty-pound note to ever enter The Miner's Arms' till. "Keep them coming."

"Yes, sir, right away, sir." No one had been called "sir" in The Miner's Arms before.

"Twenty quid! Flash bastard! Who the fook does he think he is coming in here with his fooking twenty quids?" shouted an outraged Brian from the bar.

"Please continue, Sid," Reece said loudly over the commotion. "Any information is useful."

"Are they criminals?" Sid asked. He knew lots of criminals. All of his mates were criminals.

Brian wasn't letting up. He was like a Jack Russell. In the background, he could be heard putting on a voice of mock aristocracy. "Look at me, look at me! I can pay for things with my mighty twenty-pound note! Am I not the biggest wanker in the land?"

"Shut up, Garforth!" said Kev.

Sid was used to it, but the stranger was struggling to ignore the commotion. He put a finger in one ear. "Murder. Mass murder. They are animals. Just tell me what happened and I'll be on my way."

"How dare you?" Brian yelled at Kev. "How fooking dare you? I spend hundreds of pounds a month on this shit beer, Ackroyd, and you have the nerve to treat me like this? You, sir, are a penis and a twat!"

It was the second time the word "sir" had been used in The Miner's Arms.

Sid contemplated what harm it could do telling this stranger what happened, but as always, it was best to say nothing.

"Penis?" replied an outraged Ackroyd. "Twat? You're barred, Garforth! You are barred!"

"Please, Sid?" begged the stranger, leaning forward so Sid could hear over the uproar. "Just tell me what happened."

"Barred?" screamed Brian. "You can't bar me!"

The stranger jumped at the sound of breaking glass. Sid and the other locals didn't; they were used to it.

Sid gave in to the begging as it made him uncomfortable. "*Them lot* surrounded me. The dark-haired one circled behind, which was his first mistake. He jumped at me, so I hit him. I turned to face the other one, but he legged it. The first one must have done a runner as well 'cos he was gone when I turned round."

"I won't be threatened in my own home!" yelled Kev, who had picked up an antique musket from under the bar. "Have at thee, sir!"

"And?" said Reece. "That's it?"

"Yeah." Sid shrugged.

"Make your move, sir!" Kev held the antique rifle out, bayonet pointing at Brian's heart.

"That thing don't work. You got that when you were an extra in *Sharpe*, ya fat bastard. That gun's a fake! If I make it past that bayonet you're a dead man!" Brian flourished the broken bottle.

"Got up again?" asked Reece.

"Yeah, well, he weren't there when I turned round."

"What did you hit him with?"

The stranger clearly wasn't from these parts or he'd have heard of Sid's infamous right, so he held it up. "This."

Kev screamed, "Make your choice, you worthless dog! You're dead or barred!"

Reece looked desperate. "But surely you were holding something? Were you wearing any rings, holding any weapons?"

"*AAAAAAAARRRRRGGGGGHH!*" Brian let out a deafening war cry.

"Nope, only need this." Sid kissed the right.

"*For King and Country!*" Kev let out the battle cry he had to shout when he was an extra in *Sharpe*.

"This can't be!" Reece grabbed Sid's right hand.

BANG!

Several things happened at once: Brian made a courageous charge at Kev who fired his antique musket. Sid, not used to his hand being grabbed by another man had let loose his left. The bang from the gun coincided with Sid's left fist cracking bone. Smoke filled the air...and then nothing.

When the smoke cleared, both Brian and Kev were lying unconscious on the floor. The musket had exploded and the resulting force had knocked out both duellists. Reece lay unconscious on the table. Sid stood above him wondering if he was OK. After all, Sid still had seven or eight potential pints to drink before he passed out. The remaining patrons of The Miner's still sat round watching the end of Tarrant.

"What a fookin' mess," said Sid, shaking his head. He felt an itch at the back of his head. He turned around, perplexed, and The Miner's bar was before him, the unattended Miner's bar. He edged slowly towards it. The gravitational force of the Bolton handpump was impossible to ignore, impossible to fight. He may as well turn back the tide, may as well deny the calls and wants of Mother Nature herself.

And besides, it didn't count as stealing if you were pissed.

KEVIN AWOKE WITH A START when Sid mercilessly vomited into his face. Kev jumped up, wiping his eyes and then grabbed his throbbing head. "Jesus wept!" he moaned. Gunpowder had blackened everything within a ten-foot radius. Sid lay in a heap with a string of sick connecting his mouth to where Kev had lain; the mess was spreading towards the box of Seabrook crisps on the floor. "You bastard!"

"Nnnnnggghhh." Brian acknowledged he was alive. He lay spread-eagled on the floor, his face blackened, his tie burnt off up to the knot, and his little beard completely missing.

"You bastard!" said Kev.

Reece lay unconscious on one of the tables. The lads who watched Tarrant had passed out in front of the telly. Empty pint glasses and tumblers were strewn where they lay. There was an empty bottle of rum in the optic.

"YOU...*bastards*," he tried to shout, but his pounding head prevented him from raising his voice.

Kevin remembered the musket Sean Bean had autographed personally that now lay on the floor, blown into two. "You *bastard*!"

Sid groaned and slowly got to his feet, rubbing his head. "You all right there, Kev?"

"You bastard!"

"What do you mean, mon? I was knocked out when the gun went off! I could've been killed!" Sid argued, unconvincingly.

Kev pulled regurgitated pork scratching from his cheek. It actually looked more appetising than usual. "You bastard!"

"Concussion, it makes you sick!" Sid pretended to go dizzy for effect.

"Who's shit 'emselves?" Brian had got to his feet.

"Worse things happen at sea, Brian," said a filthy Tillsley.

"You bastards!"

"Kev, we need to talk about this," Brian began. "Some events took place last night that are best forgotten. Everyone drunk a little too much, like."

Kev surveyed the damage with his head in his hands.

Brian said, "You did try to shoot me, for fook's sake!"

"WHAT THE FOOK IS GOING ON HERE!" A high-pitched shriek tore through the men's abused bodies to shred at their nerves.

Standing in the doorway was Kev's missus, home from her mother's. Things had gone from bad to worse. Much worse. "Get out, you arseholes! Kevin Ackroyd, what have you done!" She laid a less-than-ladylike boot into one of the lads who'd been watching Tarrant. "Fook off, you worthless pieces of shit!"

Everyone was scared of The Miner's landlady, none more than The Miner's landlord. The lads made remarkable recoveries and began to exit before she could really get to work. She noticed the stranger unconscious on the table and poked him with her umbrella.

"Erm...excuse me, ma'am," ventured Sid guiltily. "I think he's a little bit knocked out."

"Oh, Sidney," she said disappointingly, but with a sign of affection that riled Kev. "Could you and Brian be so good to escort him off the premises, please?" She smiled at the two as they picked up Reece, Sid taking the arms and Brian taking the legs.

"And Sidney...?"

"Yes ma'am?"

"Go change your kecks, son. It is not right for a grown man to shat himself."

"Yes, ma'am."

The forced grin faded. Her stare found a distant place a thousand yards distant. She turned, her face ashen grey. "Now, Kevin dear, me and you are going to have a chat..."

SID AND BRIAN, with the comatose Reece suspended between them, made it through the door before it was slammed behind them. Fresh cries of pain and anguish echoed from the closed door. No man wanted to witness the beating Kevin was now taking from his wife.

They took Reece down a passage and into an alleyway that ran down the back of The Miner's where they dumped him in a skip outside one of the adjoining houses.

"When will he come around, Sid?"

"About midday I reckon, mate." Sid could judge his punches to perfection.

"What did he want? He was a reet wanker."

Sid looked at the stranger curiously. "He saw what happened with them *them lot* the other night. He was amazed I used me bare fist to smack one of 'em. Strange lad. But there are more important things to attend to." Sid set off at a brisk pace down the alley. It was the closest he'd been to a run for years.

Brian called after him. "What is it, mate? What's so important?"

"Hangover dump!" Sid yelled in mid-stride.

Sid Tillsley abruptly stopped his sprint at the end of the alleyway. "Ah well, worse things happen at sea."

REECE CHAMBERS OPENED HIS EYES. They burned with the bright midday sun shining down on him. The smell of rotting vegetables and dog excrement filled his nose. His jaw ached and his head throbbed.

What the hell happened? he thought, realising he was sitting in rubbish in a skip. He recounted the evening, the monster of a man who'd done the unthinkable, the annoying weasel, the greedy barman, and the filthy pub. He'd tried to conduct himself with all the composure he could muster but needed to see if the oaf was wearing any rings or amulets.

Ah...the punch.

He didn't even see it coming, and he was a black belt in five martial arts. It was certainly a mighty blow, more powerful than anything he'd been hit with before. Nevertheless, surely it couldn't have killed a vampire?

Impossible! The oaf didn't even know what he was fighting.

Reece pulled himself out of the skip. One thing was certain: he needed to find Sid Tillsley again. And that wouldn't prove difficult.

8

RICARD OPENED THE DOOR OF HIS COTTAGE and witnessed a sight he thought he'd never see. Gunnar Ivansey stood before him, but not the vain, self-obsessed vampire Ricard had grown to know and love. Instead, a dishevelled character, unshaven, and soaked from head to toe, slumped pathetically against the door. The once beautiful and noble predator now looked like a drunk that had fallen asleep on the beach and been awoken roughly by the tide.

"Come inside, dear boy," Ricard ushered him in and sat him down by the fire that blazed in the hearth. "Have you fed recently?" Ricard didn't wait for the answer but hurried from the living room, returning a minute later with a tankard of blood. "Drink!"

Gunnar took an insignificant draught before sobbing uncontrollably, the blood bringing forth all the emotion from his troubled soul.

Ricard knelt beside him. "What is it? Tell me what ails you?"

Through the torrent of tears, Gunnar managed to say, "He's gone."

Instantly, Ricard knew: Gabriel. His fall was the only thing that could turn Gunnar into this shadow of his former self. Ricard took Gunnar's head in his hands. "How?"

"At the hands of a mortal," Gunnar spoke as if he didn't believe it himself.

Ricard spoke slowly and meticulously. "Gunnar, how? Was he taken in his sleep?"

Gunnar shook his head.

Ricard left him and paced the floor in front of the fire. This was an unexpected event, indeed. Gabriel was one of the most physically dominant vampires of the age and had been for the last two millennia. A human couldn't take an animal like him.

Gunnar continued to weep. Centuries old and still unable to control his emotions. That's what made him so dangerous. He was a threat to everything around him: vampire, human and the Agreement. Ricard feared what the younger vampire might do.

THE FIRE ROARED AS RICARD REFUELLED IT WITH MORE WOOD. It had taken an hour for Gunnar to regain his senses, and now, he sat expressionless in the armchair. "We were hunting. We hadn't ran together in decades, and it was as if I was alive again. We stumbled across a car park where human scum go for sexual gratification. We killed all there, all unsanctioned." He held up a hand, wearily. "Do not lecture me on that, not now!"

Ricard remained silent. Gunnar continued.

"One car was left. A single human male, tall and broad, but fat and grotesque. He was a hideous mess, even for a human. I could sense his clogged arteries, his damaged lungs, and failing liver and kidneys. He was the bottom of the barrel, even by their standards.

"Gabriel," he grimaced at the mention of the name, "circled to the rear and I stayed in front. The human muttered something, but his accent was so strong and his voice so slurred that I couldn't understand him. Gabriel moved first and leapt at the human. The man turned with speed I was not expecting. He punched Gabriel square in the jaw and that was it."

"What do you mean, 'that was it?' What was it?"

"That was it. He was gone." Gunnar's voice was empty.

Ricard's mind raced. How could a punch kill a vampire? A bullet would only kill a vampire if it took the head clean off. So what killed Gabriel? Perhaps he was struck with a force so great the spinal column severed. He doubted even a vampire could unleash such power. "Gunnar, whom have you told of this?"

"Nobody. Who is there to tell? Who is worthy enough to hear of Gabriel's demise...to a *human*." The last word he spat. "I will find him, Ricard," he said through gritted teeth. Gunnar's tears were done. His eyes blazed. "Nothing will stop me. You know what this means."

Ricard gripped Gunnar by the arm and tried to talk sense into him. "You're not to tell anyone about this, do you understand? Gunnar, listen to me and listen to me carefully. You're not to pursue this man."

"Do not get in my way," threatened Gunnar.

"Listen! A human has killed a vampire with his bare hands. Not any vampire—Gabriel. This matter is more important than your revenge! Do not be foolish. You cannot jeopardise the Agreement!"

"Revenge will be mine, Ricard. I will break the world for it. Fuck the Agreement. For centuries, the world has been spared my wrath. No more." He leapt up, breaking Ricard's grip on his arm, and bolted out of the door and into the night.

"So be it." Ricard shut the door to the warm summer night breeze and poured himself a whisky from the drinks cabinet. Whisky, a human invention and one of their finest.

Gunnar wouldn't tell another soul. He couldn't cope with the shame of a human killing Gabriel. Rage would cloud his judgement for a while, and this would give Ricard time to work.

Ricard raised his glass in toast to Gabriel. His kind would not be seen again. But it was best that he was gone. It'd make Ricard's work a lot easier.

9

SID LOOKED IN THE MIRROR OF THE MINER'S ARMS' TOILET and adjusted his *Question of Sport* tie. Around his massive neck, it would've almost passed for smart if he wasn't wearing his *Porky's* T-shirt.

He took out a comb to tend his scalp but paused and took another look at himself. "Aaaaayyyy." The comb went back in his pocket.

Sid went back into the bar, hoping some ladies had stopped by. He was looking his Sunday-best and they wouldn't be able to resist. Disappointed with the lack of talent, Sid consoled himself. "Pint of Bolton, Kev."

Kevin pulled the pint of best bitter. He had a shining black eye and his eyebrows were singed. The musket blast was not as damaging as the beating his wife had given him. "You're lucky you ain't barred, too, Tillsley. That's £1.98."

It was like a dagger to Sid's heart.

"£1.98? Shit the bed! 2p on a pint? That's highway fooking robbery you shortarsed, fat, Dick-Turpin bastard, you!"

"Now then, Tillsley!" Kev winced as he lifted his arm to point threateningly at Sid. "A lot of damage was caused last night, and a lot of booze has gone missing. I can't prove it's you, but I *know* it's you. That will be £1.98. And you can tell that scrawny little bastard, Garforth, he's barred—for life!"

Sid paid up with a scowl, and Kev went to sit at the other end of the bar, sulking. Kev only talked to people when he was in profit.

The front door opened, and the one and only Arthur Peasley entered the building. He joined Sid at the bar. "Hey, man, I heard there was a hoedown in here last night, everything cool?"

Sid shook his good friend's hand. "Aye, mon. I had to knock one client out, but that was n'owt. Kevin and Brian had a bit of a scrap, like. They're both sulking at the moment, but it'll blow over in a few days—in time for Ladies' Night."

"Oh yeah, man, Ladies' Night!" Arthur slicked back his perfect, black hair. He, like Brian, was a devil with the fairer sex, but he didn't employ Brian's "cloak and porkdagger" technique because Arthur Peasley was, without a shadow of a doubt, the most handsome man in Middlesbrough.

Kevin walked over and banged a pint of Bolton in front of Arthur, spilling it over the sides, "£1.98."

"Hey man," Arthur started. "Don't you take your grievances out wit—" Then, it hit home. "£1.98? That's highway fucking robbery you shortarsed, fat, Dick-Turpin bast—"

"Blame Garforth!" shouted Kevin, before storming back to the end of the bar for more sulking.

Sid lit up a Nigerian "El Deserto." He'd picked up eight hundred by helping Areed Nafal, a local Nigerian market trader, transport a load of fake designer wear to Doncaster Market. "Aye, Ladies' Night," he said. "You definitely coming then?"

"You better believe it, man. I wouldn't miss it for the world. You know me, baby!" Arthur threw out a catalogue pose, a catalogue that specialised in sequin jumpsuits. "Sorry I didn't mention it earlier, Sid, but you're looking mighty fine today."

Sid could never take anything that Arthur Peasley said in a *them lot* context due to his unparalleled skill with womenfolk. He even made the tassels on his jumpsuit look hetero. Sid straightened his tie and smiled. "Cheers, pal. It's time for the Benefit Bastards interview, again."

"That's a tough break, man, a tough break. I hope they don't catch you. You've been dodging them sons of bitches for so long now."

"Aye, but old Wally Harwood is interviewing me."

"Shucks, man, why didn't you say?" Arthur raised his glass to Sid and gave him a knowing wink over the top of his Foster Grant sunglasses.

Wally Harwood was a man of the people. Born on the Smithson Estate, raised on the Smithson Estate, due to retire in a year's time on the Smithson Estate, and almost certainly due to die on the Smithson Estate. He was the most racist man in the North, which by default made him the most racist man in the universe. He took racism to the next level by hating everyone who was born outside his council estate.

Wally wasn't really a man of the people. It just so happened that virtually every single member of the Smithson Estate were born on the Smithson Estate, and they were white...except all the men over forty, who were generally a deep, red-purple colour. And the fairer sex who were more of an orange colour. And a fair few patrons of The Miner's Arms, and similar pubs, were a sickly yellow because of their poisoned livers.

The reason Wally was loved by the people was because Wally was the most crooked benefit officer in the whole of Teesside. Wally was the main reason Sid had got away working for thirty years while claiming benefit. He'd set Sid up with work since he was a young nipper, including jobs that were a little less savoury. Sid had done his share of debt collecting, bare knuckle fighting, and a one-night-only role as a donkey in a pantomime, which resulted in Sid's only ever kicking. Meeting with Wally was the only reason Sid wasn't shitting himself over the Job Centre visit.

THE JOB CENTRE WAS JUST OUTSIDE THE SMITHSON ESTATE BOUNDARY. It was a modern building; accidental firebombing had burnt down the last three. Sid had to psych himself up before entering, because this place crushed his soul, plus there were loads of stairs. Through the front door he ventured. Despite the fires of Hell, a cold shiver ran up his spine as every employee turned to stare at him, Britain's most infamous benefit fraudster.

You've got no proof, ya bastards, thought Sid.

He gave a nod to all and sundry before joining the nearest queue. There were five queues to five desks where five Benefit Bastards, given the Herculean task of processing Middlesbrough's finest unemployed into Middlesbrough's finest employed, awaited.

There were two people waiting in front of Sid. The lad in front was only a bairn. Sid, being the friendly fellow that he was, tapped the lad on the shoulder. "How old are you?" he asked when the lad turned round.

The young man looked Sid up and down suspiciously. "Why do you want to know?" He hadn't heard of Sid Tillsley...yet.

Sid was rather taken aback by the reaction. "I'm just asking. How old are ya?"

"Nineteen," he said, pushing his glasses up and narrowing his eyes.

Sid blew out a sorry sigh. "It's terrible the evil bastards get their claws into kids so early."

The scrawny teenager puffed out his chest, not very far, but as far as it would go. "I want a job. I'm studying History of Art at The University of York, and I require a summer job to fund my studies."

Sid was confused. He'd never spoken to a student before. "Where are you from?"

"Well, I'm here in front of you, aren't I?" he said patronisingly. He raised his nose and peered over his glasses. "Therefore, chances are quite high that I'm from Middlesbrough."

"Are ye fook!"

The young student gave an annoyed sigh. "I'm from Middlesbrough, but that doesn't mean I have to talk like an uneducated ox." He turned his back on Sid and tapped his foot impatiently.

"History of Art? Why the fook would anyone give a shit about that?

How the fook are you gonna get a job if you're so keen on getting one?"

The student turned to Sid again, his face reddening. "What do *you* think I'll be able to do? Oh, I can't wait to hear this."

Sid scratched his head. The action caused a considerable amount of armpit odour to diffuse into the student's spotty face, and he recoiled as if struck. "Fook all?" Sid ventured.

The bespectacled nerd was almost as red as Sid himself. "You *townies* do not understand that university is not just about learning a subject. It is about learning people skills and about interacting with your fellow man."

"Why are you such a wanker then?" asked Sid innocently.

"How dare—"

"Next!" yelled the Job Centre employee.

The student gave Sid an evil stare, turned on his heel, and went to the waiting bureaucrat.

Sid chuckled. Students! The legends were true. Absolute bell ends.

"Name?" asked the Benefit Bastard of the student.

"Gareth Wigglesworth."

Sid's ears pricked up. *Wigglesworth?* "Ain't your ma'am Sharon Wigglesworth?"

Gareth turned around, looking furious at the interruption. "What has it got to do with you?"

"Because I'm best mates with your Uncle Brian!" Sid gave the biggest smile his pearly yellows could manage.

Gareth screamed a war cry and threw himself at Sid, punching and kicking with all of his worthless skinny might. History of Art may teach something, but it certainly isn't fighting.

Sid looked confused. "What's he doing?" he asked of anyone who might answer. Watching a nine-stone nerd laying into Sid with the effect of an annoying fly while screaming and crying simultaneously was a sight no one wanted to witness but had to watch. Finally, after some moments, the young Wigglesworth wore himself out before running out of the Job Centre, stopping briefly to take a puff from his inhaler.

"Next!" shouted the Benefit Bastard, unfazed.

"Tillsley, Sid Till—"

"I know who you are. Room Twenty. You know the one."

SID KNOCKED ON THE DOOR OF ROOM TWENTY.

"Come in."

Sid obliged. Behind the desk of room twenty sat the beaming Wally Harwood.

"How do, Wally?"

"How do, Sid? Good to see you again." Wally was getting on in years but still had all his hair, even if he was completely grey. He had a paunch, which came with the cushy office job. "Sit yourself down, lad."

Sid wasn't often referred to as "lad," but he'd a lot of respect for Wally. He didn't agree with some, or rather most of his views, but he was a good man at heart because he found Sid tax-free jobs.

"What you been up to then, Sid?"

"No proper work, like. Done the odd job here and there, bit of courier work and that sort of thing. Was hoping you could sort me out like, Wal'." Sid asked hopefully.

Wally blew his cheeks out. "To be honest, lad, I'm in no position to offer you anything at the moment. Been getting a lot of attention from the powers above 'cos I'm retiring next month, and they're doing their best to get rid of me and me hard-earned pension."

"Bastards!" said Wally and Sid in unison.

Wally continued. "They waste all the council's fookin' money on them fookin' immigrants, then they take it out on the hard-working folk like you and me. Taxing us up the arse so we can pay for Jonny Foreigner to go on bloody holidays and buy them bloody cars to go out and find jobs. Aston Martins, someone down the pub told me."

Sid gave Wally a comforting pat on the arm. "No worries, Wally. You've been bloody good to me over the years. There's always work for a big fella around these parts. Summat will turn up."

Wally smiled. "You're right, Sid. Made a fair few quid from them hams of yours meself." Wally threw a couple of mock friendly jabs at Sid, but then the smile faded. "I'll still keep you informed of any jobs that I hear of. I like to look after me lads. Not many old-school like yourself any more. Smithson is being overrun with every fooking race under the sun: Hispanics, Chinese, blacks…"

"What, not ol' Winston?" asked a surprised Sid. "He's been here man and boy, and his old man has! Top fella is Winston. Lovely family too. You don't mean him, do ya?"

Wally dismissed the comment as if Sid were mad. "Don't be stupid, Sid. Winston's old-school like yourself. He don't bleedin' count. He's one of us!"

"What about Rodriguez? He's been here thirty year!"

Again, Wally acted surprised, "No! He's a bloody living legend, that man. Finest bullfighter in all of Cuba he was, until he retired to Middlesbrough."

"Surely you don't mean Lau. Best fookin' food in the Northeast."

Wally was starting to get annoyed. "Of course bloody not! He don't count. Lau's been a good friend to one and all. Does all that Jap-slappin'-Kung Fu-kickin', too, don't he?"

"Aye, reet handy little bastard. Me and him have been in a few scrapes together. His hands move as fast as lightning, like." Sid tried to do a karate chop and knocked Wally's mug of tea over the floor. Wally shook his head. There were a lot of tea stains on the floor of Wally's office.

"Sorry, mon," said Sid. "Anyway, who do you mean?"

"Eh?" asked a lost Wally.

"Well, you said all them foreigners have moved in to the Smithson Estate. I can only think of three and they're our mates."

Wally paused, scratched his chin, looked out of the window and then came to a conclusion. "Well, Sid, time you were on your way." He got up and opened the door for Sid. "Next time you're here, though, it won't be me interviewing you, mate. You're gonna have a proper Benefit Bastard, so make sure you get your story straight. Rumour has it, there's a right ball-buster coming to the 'boro and you're her number one priority."

Sid shrugged his shoulders. "I'll be reet. Don't you worry about me."

Wally gave Sid a hearty slap on the back.

"Oh yeah," said Sid, "do you know Sharon Wigglesworth?"

"Aye, nice looking lass. Fine set...well, until recent years," replied the forever politically correct Wally.

"Her lad was in the queue for a job. Reet little wanker he was. Anyway, I mentioned to him his Uncle Brian and he went fooking bananas, he did."

"Sid, you're a naïve young lad sometimes. Garforth was knocking her off when her old fella was away." He laughed. "Garforth's wrecked more homes than that Lawrence Llewelyn-Bowen."

Sid gave him a blank look.

Wally sighed and explained. "Garforth's an arsehole."

10

"RIGHT," SAID THE TWENTY-FIVE-YEAR OLD with a pseudo-mullet, wearing a dinner jacket with scruffy T-shirt and jeans intentionally made to look dirty. Sid knew he'd be a jumped-up little wanker from the moment he set eyes on him. "Don't let anyone down this hallway. Most importantly, don't question anyone who comes from either of the staircases. Actually, do not even look at them."

"Why's that then?" asked the inquisitive Sid Tillsley as he lit up a Russian. He'd obtained six hundred "Vlad the Inhalers," by helping Nickov the Russian sell a batch of ex-KGB bugging equipment. There was a definite gap in the market out there and Middlesbrough husbands and wives, suspicious of their loved ones, had snapped them up.

"Don't ask questions, either," the jumped-up little wanker added.

Sid had little experience of the new breed of trendy type. After his meeting with young Wigglesworth, and now this arsehole, he was starting to wonder whether he'd lost touch with the younger generation. According to Brian, there were loads of these little shits around these days. Sid was struggling to understand the lad because the young Geordie was trying to put on a cockney accent. *Why would anyone want to change their accent?* Sid wondered. *Apart from Scousers.*

"Right. You can get changed in the gents' locker room. The club opens at nine, and you need to be here for ten-to. OK, now you can ask questions." He waited. "Well?"

Sid scratched his head. "Get changed?"

The jumped-up little wanker rolled his eyes. "Into your tuxedo. You didn't think you'd be working in that, did you?" He looked Sid up and down with disgust, which greatly confused Sid. What was wrong with his brand new Tarantula Bitter T-shirt? He'd won it for drinking two crates in an evening without throwing up, and he looked the business. "This is what I always wear, like," said Sid.

"Yes, I imagine it is. Listen, you're a last-minute replacement and were employed because you're meant to be fairly handy. Tonight, you're getting paid extremely good money for an extremely easy job. Do as you're told and you may make a few extra quid in the near future, OK?" He didn't wait for Sid's answer. "Terry, who normally works this patch, is off with a punctured lung. He didn't do his job properly and he asked too many questions. I suggest you do your job properly."

"Not a problem, lad."

"His tux is in the gents' locker room. Terry was in better shape than you, so do your best to fit into it."

"When do I get me money?"

"You get your money after you've performed a decent job," said the jumped-up little wanker.

"Fookin' hell, mon. I've been doing this job since you were sucking on your mummy's tats. You run along and don't you worry yourself. I can do this job standing on me 'ead."

The jumped-up little wanker stood speechless before blowing his top. "I am the assistant bar manager. I don't need to take abuse from fat, drunken—" He broke off. Closed his eyes. Regained himself. "I am professional, and I expect you to act the same way."

"I'll be reet. You can run along now, lad." Sid lit up his seventieth Russian of the day.

"You...you can't smoke here!" The assistant bar manager's composure flew out of the window.

Sid was getting tired. "And why the fook not?"

"Listen here." The jumped-up little wanker started to go red. "This isn't some dirty little pub in smogland 'boro," he said. "This is a high-class superclub, and punters expect you to be polite and to do your job professionally. They do not expect some—"

Sid's fist absorbed the rest of the young man's sentence.

"Jumped-up little wanker." Sid shook his head and threw the unconscious twat over his shoulder. He needed to dump him where he wouldn't be seen until morning. Sid looked around.

"Where the fook am I?"

He was in Rapunzel's nightclub in Newcastle, doing the type of work that suited him down to the ground: a bit of security work out of the public eye, and out of the way of the Benefit Bastards. It was one night of work, cash in hand. Perfect. One of the lads down The Miner's who often did a bit of door work put him on to it. And here he was, Saturday night, trying to dump an unconscious body. It wasn't the first time, and it was unlikely to be the last.

He mentally retraced his steps: through the entrance, through a long corridor, cloakrooms, pay booths. No good, as there would be people around. Through to the massive circular main room, through the corridor to the main pissers, and then through...

"Fook it."

It had been a trek and he wasn't going back. He looked around.

There were two staircases: one that went up and one that went down. He picked the downward staircase to conserve energy. There was a door, but no handle.

"Shit the bed!" He looked back. There were at least ten steps. "Fook!" He forgot he'd have to climb back up. Eventually, he made it to the top, working up a hell of a sweat in the process. He looked up the other flight of steps. "Fook that."

Sid ambled down the corridor until he saw another door labelled CELLAR.

"Aha!"

Voices could be heard down the corridor, so he ambled quicker and made it to the ale cellar, avoiding any detection. He was ninja...sweaty ninja. Steep stairs descended into darkness, and he made his way down carefully, ignoring the jumped-up little wanker's head, which banged heavily off every stair.

"Perfect." There was many a good hiding place to stash the little arsehole.

Something caught Sid's eye: four crates of Tarantula Bitter, Hartlepool's finest. He grinned. This could be the finest stitch-up ever! If he did this properly, he could get the jumped-up little wanker sacked for stealing and also have a tipple himself.

"Sid Tillsley, you could've been in the *A-Team*." But then something else caught Sid's eye. Next to the bitter sat four crates of Stockport Ice, a cheap rip-off of Smirnoff's lemony girly drink. This was a conundrum and a half. This jumped-up little wanker would almost definitely be a Stockport Ice drinker. A student type would never drink proper ale. Never. Should Sid complete the perfect plan and actually drink the ladies' favourite?

Yes. Yes, he would. Sid unceremoniously dumped the jumped-up little wanker like a sack of spuds and set to work on his flawless plan.

SID TILLSLEY WAS VIOLENTLY SICK.

"Blaaaaaaaaaahhhhhhhhhhh...mmmm, lemony." He was still standing, but only just.

The perfect plan was almost complete. Twenty-eight bottles of Stockport Ice in forty-five minutes had to be a world record, but he'd heavily underestimated the beverage designed for the feminine drinker. Now, all he had to do was get into his tuxedo, stand in the hallway, and the plan was complete.

The alcohol would hinder him, but surely a lady drink couldn't possibly thwart his master scheme, and the jumped-up little wanker wouldn't wake up until at least mid-morning. "Actually–*hic!*–better make sure. Always better to be safe than–*hic!*–something."

Sid lined up his big right foot, and connected with a devastating toe-punt to the wanker's groin.

"Thatsh better."

He considered the mess he'd made, and "mess" was an understatement. He picked up the jumped-up little wanker and laid him carefully in the sticky, multicoloured pool of sick. *Voila!* Innovation at its best.

He made for the stairs, but although *he* wanted to go, his legs had other ideas and he hit the ground hard. The perfect plan was now in jeopardy, but with the will of a prizefighter, Sid got to his feet. It was a staggering eight count, and the fight should have been stopped. However, the big man didn't quit easily, especially as he hadn't picked up his wages yet.

He managed to get to the top of the stairs and stumbled along the corridor towards the changing rooms. Fortunately, most of the bar staff had arrived and the doormen weren't on duty yet, so there weren't many people going to-and-fro. Sid was going to need a lot more luck in order to get away with this little scheme. He was in a hell of a state, and one of his eyes wasn't working any more.

Meandering through the club, he bounced from wall to wall, knocking everything over that wasn't nailed down. He made it to the changing rooms and fell through the door.

"Fook!" That fall hurt. His hands didn't make it out in time to break his descent and his chin hit the floor. Luckily, his belly cushioned most of the fall.

"Fook!" said Sid again, getting back to his feet and commenting on the general state of affairs. There were lockers along the left and clothes hangers along the right of the small changing room. Three or four tuxedos hung neatly for his perusal.

Sudden panic rose with a feeling of impending doom from somewhere deep in his intestines.

"Oh, fook!"

He set out with pure desperation for the toilets. The acidity of the lemons in the Stockport Ice had caused a lot of movement in his lower bowel, and bad things were travelling south, fast.

Very fast.

He ran as best he could, clenching his buttocks with vice-like intensity, a practised skill. The toilet was near, but so was an anal explosion that would be picked up on global seismographs.

Sid was within six feet, the toilet door was open, the lid was up and the seat was down. Thank God. He felt a rumble that was indicative of

Armageddon. There was only one option left, and that was to perform a manoeuvre that only hardened drinkers could perform, and only then at times of pure peril.

If he didn't make it in time, he'd end the night in the worst possible predicament. If he made it in time, there would be a plumber in the worst possible predicament. If he got halfway, there would be a team of cleaners in the worst possible predicament. No matter what, someone was going to have a really shit time. When he was within five feet, he leapt. Sid had never made the manoeuvre from more than four feet before. This was going to be close.

Only a slow motion, *Matrix*-esque rotating camera could do the move justice. The simultaneous act of undoing your belt, pulling your pants and trousers down, turning around in mid-air, landing on a toilet seat, shutting the door, and then defecating at rate deemed fatal for a hippo was not the work of a man.

It was the work of a pissed-up god.

"FFFFFFFFOOOOOOOOOOOOOKKKKKKK!"

KAAAAABBBBBBOOOOOMMMMM!!!!

He made it...God damn it, he made it!

Sid's almost nuclear-like excretion had instant sobering effects, which he was not thankful for when he realised there was no toilet paper.

SID CHOSE TO FORGET DISCOVERING THERE WAS NO TOILET PAPER but did spare a thought for the cleaner who would eventually find his kecks, rolled up and stuffed behind the bog. It was time for Sid to get ready. He checked the four tuxedos to find the biggest size.

"All these bouncers are fooking midgets!" he exclaimed. He couldn't find a size forty-eight inch waist. He squeezed into a pair of forties that were available and had to wear them low so he could do them up. It left ten inches of trouser leg that needed turning up and three inches of bum crack exposed proudly to the world. He put on the shirt, but left it unbuttoned because it was impossible to do up. The jacket was skintight. Doing up the bow tie up proved useless, and he made a complete mess of it.

Sid checked himself out in the mirror. "Lookin' good!" he said with a devilish grin. With only a few staggers, he left the changing rooms and headed for his post. Some miscalculated corners later, he made it.

Mission accomplished.

It was nine o'clock and the club was now officially open, although it only tended to get busy after about ten thirty. Some top DJs from the North were playing, and it was going to be a busy night, so he'd been told. Rapunzel's was a high-class nightclub. There was hardly any trouble, and the doormen had strict guidelines as to who was let in. None of this bothered Sid. All he had to do was stop anyone from the nightclub passing by him. Everyone who came the other way could do what they wanted. It was that simple.

A doorman approached Sid. He was short for a bouncer, well under six foot, but he was as wide as he was tall. His head was shaven and he had a heavily scarred face. To anyone apart from Sid, who didn't care about such things, he'd look menacing. "Hey, you seen Miguel?"

"Miguel?" said Sid with the same facial expression he pulled when he once tried health food. "What kind of a name is that?"

"The assistant bar manager. He showed you around. Have you seen him?"

"N-no, no." stuttered Sid. He wasn't a good liar. That was, unless he was confronted by the Benefit Bastards or the police. He was an even worse liar after a few ales, and worse still after twenty-eight bottles of Stockport Ice.

"You been drinking?" The doorman moved closer and reeled back quickly as if punched in the face. "Your breath stinks! You're a disgrace!"

Sid couldn't afford to lose this job, especially after what had befallen in the last half hour. He staggered back accidentally but regained himself with dignity. "How dare you!"

The bouncer gave a look of disgust. "You'd be sacked if it wasn't club-opening time. Aren't you Sid Tillsley?"

"Why?" Sid never liked to admit who he was, especially when out of the 'boro.

"Thought so." The bouncer shook his head. "Word is you're the best fighter in the town, if not the whole of the Northeast. The doormen round there are always telling stories about you."

Hardest man in the Northeast? Sid had never given it a second thought before because he couldn't give a shit. He'd got along just fine with the mantra: if someone plays silly buggers, punch 'em in the face. Sid merely shrugged.

"You're just a drunk though, aren't ya?"

"How dare—" Sid cut off his outburst, recalling the last hour. "Well, I can't say that I don't enjoy a tipple now and then."

The doorman shook his head once more. "If you see Miguel, tell him I'm looking for him."

"No problems, boss." Sid gave a salute. As long as he was paid, he couldn't care less what anyone thought of him. He'd already knocked someone out tonight and didn't want to add another to the list. Nothing could go wrong now. Absolutely nothing.

11

SID WAS BORED SENSELESS. A few clubbers partied down the far end of the corridor, but his orders were simply to stop people going any farther, so he ignored them. With every second, he was sobering up, and a hangover was looming. The music of the club pounded through his skull incessantly. How could these young'ns listen to this garbage? And why so loud?

Four hours to go and no one had discovered Mig...Mick... Michelle—?—yet. What a stupid name. No self-respecting Geordie parent would ever name their bairn Michelle. He must have changed his name, the jumped-up little wanker.

Click! The door at the bottom of the stairs opened. A man in a long coat wearing a wide-brimmed hat walked up the stairs. He didn't look up or acknowledge Sid but walked down the corridor, head bowed, into the club. Sid made a mental note. *Right. That fella is allowed to go anywhere, so best remember him.*

Partygoers ebbed their way down the corridor as the night progressed, just to cool off or chat. It was quarter past eleven and still no one had tried to get past him. Sid's alcohol levels had metabolised to take him to the "merry" stage, a stage reserved for the middle classes, a stage reserved for arseholes who'd never thrown up over a prostitute in their lives. Sid had developed a serious headache and was in a bad mood because of it.

He spotted the guy with the wide-brimmed hat walking down the corridor with a young lady wearing practically nothing. "Ah fook! What do I do now?"

As the man approached, Sid moved into the middle of the corridor, and rubbed the rolls on the back of his neck awkwardly. "Erm, sorry, mate, I was told to let you through because you came through that door," he nodded to the basement, "but, I canna let the lass through unless I get the go-ahead from one of me bosses, like."

Sid couldn't see the man's face from under the brim of his hat, but the voice spoke quietly in an accent Sid didn't recognise. "I'm friends with the owner. I assure you, any guest of mine is allowed through. Be co-operative, and you'll be rewarded at the end of the night."

Sid didn't see the guy move, but a twenty-pound note had appeared in the top pocket of his tight tuxedo.

"Go right on in, sir." Sid bowed as the couple passed. He watched them go up the stairs. His professionalism wavered when he ducked down so he could see up the girl's skirt.

He almost fell over when he saw what he saw. "No knickers!" he cried. That was, without a doubt, the best twenty quid Sid Tillsley had ever earned. He went back to guarding the corridor with a renewed sense of vigour and tried to put on a doorman's face by looking like a miserable twat.

A group of girls walked up to Sid after seeing the encounter with the couple. All three were about twenty years old, all three wore very little. Sid got excited both emotionally and physically. After all, ladies love bouncers.

"What can I do for three beautiful ladies?"

"What's up them stairs?" asked a brunette with a lovely set of jugs.

Sid talked to the lovely set of jugs. "It's the VIP room, my young lovely."

"VIP lounge is other side of club, mate," replied a blonde with an even greater set of jugs than the brunette.

Sid continued with his lack of subtlety by bending forward for a better look. The breasts acted as a fantastic painkiller for his quickly receding headache. "This is for the real VIPs, pet. Proper Real Important People. That's why I'm guarding the door." He gave the blonde's breasts a winning smile.

"Who's in there, like?"

Sid turned around to face a flat-chested blonde. He ignored her.

"Can we go in there then, mister?" asked Best Jugs.

"Well, that depends?" said Sid, abusing his power.

"On what?" asked the Second-Best Jugs.

"On what you ladies can do for me? I could murder a brandy."

"Fook off!" said Flat-Chest. "They're about three quid a shot in 'ere," she said.

Sid really didn't like this girl.

"How about you let us in there, and I'll suck ya off?"

Sid was prepared to forgive and forget.

"That method of payment will be quite acceptable, young lovely. Will any of your friends be joining you in your adventure?"

"Will we fook," said Second-Best Jugs. Hurry up, Cheryl, so we can go get ourselves some footballers."

"Where we going then?" Cheryl asked.

"Ah, fook...yeah...err..." Sid paused. Where to go? The downstairs basement had no handle, and there were people upstairs. He'd been sick all over the ale cellar. Fook! There was nowhere else to go. He was now torn. Did he walk away, take the twenty quid, take the ladies' offer, and call it a day? Alternatively, did he work for the next couple of hours and pick up the eighty-five quid promised to him?

Sid was stumped with a question that had plagued man since the beginning of time: was a blowjob worth eighty-five quid?

"I'm sorry, love, but I canna leave me post."

It was like winning the lottery and losing the ticket.

Cheryl gave the big man a filthy look. "Fooking 'ell. How many offers do you get from a lass like me? You must be queer or summat? Come on, girls."

The girls departed. Sid put his head in his hands. That was the closest he'd come to some action for two years, but then, eighty-five quid was a lot of money. He could subscribe to *Tits* for three years with that sort of wedge. Sid made peace with his decision.

Midnight came. The jumped-up little wanker had said that someone would bring him a cup of tea at half-eleven. Sid now had a hangover mouth and was desperate for a slash. Twenty-eight Stockport Ices is a lot of liquid for one human to consume in forty-five minutes. It'd be pretty impressive for a camel to drink twenty-eight Stockport Ices in forty-five minutes.

Another half an hour passed, and the club was at full capacity. So was Sid. He was now dying for the toilet. Moving around awkwardly, he tried to numb the pressure build-up in his waterworks. His irritation showed in his work.

"What's down the corridor, mate?"

"Fook off."

Clubbers meandered their way as far as the ale cellar, which meant he couldn't open the door and piss down the stairs. The only option was to try upstairs. If there were people there, surely they'd understand. Jesus, he only wanted a piss. Gingerly climbing the stairs, he found the door slightly ajar. He knocked. Nothing. He knocked a bit louder, still no response. Sid's nether regions screamed for relief, so he opened the door and walked in.

The room was beautifully decorated, proper classy, with all them antiques those rich folk who live in Scarborough have. Sid could even appreciate some of the artwork on the wall: pictures of grapes and apples and people and stuff. Aye, beautiful....but not as beautiful as the...

Drinks cabinet!

Whisky! he thought. A man always feels thirsty after a few whiskies. Maybe a few whiskies would dehydrate him a bit. Then, he could have a few more whiskies before he'd need a piss again. Yeah, that made sense. It made absolutely perfect bloody sense.

Sid picked up the first bottle he reached. The bottle was very old and the label had mostly perished. He uncorked the top and took a sniff. "Fookin' hell, that smells grand." He poured himself an extra large glass.

Sid took a large mouthful of the golden liquid. "Oh, aye." Never, in his thirty-two-year drinking career, had Sid savoured the taste of every drop of alcohol. This was not the whisky that MacTavish the Glaswegian made from de-icer and weak tea down the estate. This was very special indeed. "No wonder Scotsmen are drunks," said the drunk.

Sid Tillsley, whisky connoisseur, picked another bottle. He examined the bottle, uncorked it, sniffed it, and drunk a lot of it. He nearly savoured every drop. This particular brand he savoured slightly less than the one before.

"One more and I'll find a pisser. Just one more..."

Three triple whiskies later and Sid Tillsley had found danger.

"Right! Time for a toilet." Sid went for the door; Sid fell through a coffee table. "Fook!" said Sid, struggling to his feet. Too much noise. "Must be like ninja. Ssshhhh..." he said to...he wasn't sure. The ninja staggered into a large, floor-standing plant next to the broken coffee table. He fell backwards with it and screamed, "It's a fooking Triffid!" before once again hitting the floor.

After realising the plant wasn't trying to eat him, and considering his circumstances, Sid reasoned that he'd be stupid *not* to piss in the plant pot in front of him.

IT HAD BEEN A BAD NIGHT FOR JACQUES JEREAUX. He hated England almost as much as he hated humans. This nightclub was not a good place for his mental wellbeing. All this way to meet up with the Lamian Consilium, who were third on his list of hates. At least he was meeting Richmond. Not a soul in the world could dislike Richmond, a vampire of the old code. Unfortunately, Richmond hadn't arrived yet. He always slept more than usual for an immortal.

Jereaux had arrived an hour ago and decided to pleasure himself on a young girl. Human females were at least good for something apart from feeding. He'd found himself a particularly pretty specimen and bought her back to the safe house. Richmond had a number of spare rooms allocated for this very carnal purpose. The fat oaf on the door had tried to stop him but was bribed with a small amount of money. Humans had no honour. Not that Richmond would mind him bringing this girl back.

Unfortunately, she decided to run off when the going got too rough for her. What did she expect? Did she think someone like him would be bothered about pleasuring her? He would've ripped her head off if he were outside his guest's house. He'd run after the girl to calm her down and ply her with some drink. The fat imbecile of a doorman had his head buried in his hands as they went past. As for the girl, she was bought easily. A bottle of champagne had convinced her that everything was fine. She'd pay the price later.

Jereaux took in the sights and sounds of a thousand humans playing their music at a level damaging for their delicate ears, drinking ethanol and taking narcotics until they were ill, fighting, or fucking. It made him sick that he had to eat them, but they did taste exquisite. Walking back to the safe house, he pushed aside partygoers as he went. The idiot had left his post.

"Useless bastard." He pushed open the door, and in front of him was the overweight oaf, inebriated to near-unconsciousness, sat in the shards of a Jacobean table, and urinating in a plant pot. As Jereaux entered, so did Richmond. "What's going on here!" he cried.

SID SAT, COCK IN HAND, COFFEE TABLE SHARDS STICKING IN HIS ARSE. "Thanksss God you ladshh came in time!" he slurred.

The hostility in the air was thicker than that of the average war.

"Who are you?" asked the big Jamaican fella through gritted teeth.

If Sid were wearing a cap, he would've taken it to hand. "Sshir, I'm bouncing the corridor downshtairs, shir! I...errr, heard a commotion up here and investigated. I think there's been a shtruggle?" Sid indicated the mess with a sweep of the hand.

"Why is your penis in your hand?" asked the Jamaican.

It was a fair question. It'd take an extremely intelligent man to think of a good explanation. "There...was...a fire! Yes, a fire. I put it out, be...because...because...fire." Sid was that intelligent man.

"Richmond," said the fella in the hat, "would you give me the honour of disposing of this scum?"

Sid got to his feet on the fourth attempt. "Gentlemen, gentlemen, there'sh no need. I have averted the danger. I ssshall continue to perform my duty downstairs. Good night." With that, he bowed and continued to bow until he fell into an unconscious heap on the floor.

THAT TEN SECONDS AFTER WAKING. After the night before, halfway between the land of sleep and the dawn of the new day, there is a life which has no memory of the past and no thought for the future. That place is peace...

Until the hangover kicks in.

Sid Tillsley migrated from that state of "peace." Flashbacks attacked him with unrelenting brutality. Twenty-eight bottles of Stockport Ice and a bottle of malt whisky attacked. Sid was sick over the side of the bed.

No...there was no bed. It was a cold, hard surface, and it wasn't doing his piles any good. He opened his eyes expecting to see the streets of Middlesbrough, but no, a tin roof.

Where the hell was he?

He sat up, although "rolled around a bit and ended up in a sitting position" was a more accurate description. He'd had water thrown over him. Five men stood around him in a large warehouse full of computer equipment. He recognised a couple of the men: that big Jamaican who'd seemed a little peeved at him drinking his whisky, and the angry bloke in the hat who'd also seemed a little peeved at the whisky drinking. Sid didn't recognise the other three. They were big lads, well dressed, and they looked a little bit peeved too.

"Now then, lads," said Sid clutching his head, realising he was going to have to talk himself out of some shit, "about the whisky. I only had one to sort out me cold." He sniffed for effect. "Look, I'll get you another bottle," he lied. "Not a problem."

"Whisky should be the last of your worries," said one of the men.

Sid beamed. "Well, that's very kind of you, mate. You're all right, you." He looked at the Jamaican fella. "Now, there is the small matter of me getting paid for me evening's work."

"You should be more worried about your life," said the lad who'd caught him with his cock out.

Sid considered this. "Well, I guess I do eat too many saturated fats."

"Look at yourself, human. Pathetic, too stupid to know your fate," said another. "We're going to rip you to shreds. We'll keep you alive as long as possible and make you suffer."

Sid was rather confused with the whole affair. How could one of them be worried about his health and the other want to kill him?

Then one of the big lads said, "Your ass is mine!"

PINK ALERT! PINK ALERT! PINK ALERT!

In milliseconds, Sid was on his feet and ready to go.

"Keep away from me, you dirty bastards! I won't be having any of it!"

"So you know of our kind, human?" asked Richmond.

Sid turned to face him. "Yes, I bloody do. I've seen your kind before, bloody everywhere, these days. Every five seconds on bleedin' telly, dancing on that fooking ice. I fooking hate that ice dancing shite!"

The *them lot* looked at each other, looking confused for some reason.

"And in them toilets down the park. Them toilets are for pissin', not for you lot! Brian told me about them holes you drill in the cubicles. Say if I'd had a look through! SAY IF I'D LOOKED!"

"What?" asked the Jamaican *them lot.*

"Could've had me bloody eye out!"

"You have no idea, do you?" mocked one Sid didn't recognise. "Your simple mind cannot comprehend what we are. It's best we put you out of your short-lived misery. We are the vampire." And with that, he launched himself at Sid with cat-like agility.

But Sid had seen cat-like agility before. And not just in cats. He'd fought a few of them poncy, martial arts fannies in his time, spinning around in pyjamas screaming things in foreign. Bloody idiots.

All the cat-like agility was wasted. The vampire had attempted a double-back-shadowless-spinning-axe kick, while Sid had attempted—and succeeded with—a big punch in the face. The vampire crumbled into dust, making Sid cough and splutter. "What the fook?"

The remaining vampires stood motionless, eyes wide, mouths gaping.

"I knew you lot weren't made of the same thing we are!" said Sid. "Come on then, ya bastards!"

The fight was over in seconds. The one who caught him with his cock out and two others attacked Sid simultaneously. Sid went for the biggest one, as the others in a group normally backed off when the big lad went down. He caught the one who caught him with his cock out with a straight right, turning him into dust. The other two jumped back, but Sid caught one on the way, which meant he had one attacker left to deal with, who made the mistake of pausing. Sid's right didn't.

Sid paused for breath, hands on knees. Pointing at the big Jamaican fella who had stayed well back, Sid said, "You son...will get yours...as soon as I get...my breath back... Otherwise, fook off!"

Sid didn't know it, but for the first time in six hundred years, Richmond ran.

12

RICHMOND PACED ANXIOUSLY. He hasn't stopped pacing since...since the impossible. In all his centuries, he'd never addressed the Lamian Consilium. They'd never requested anything from him, and he'd never had reason to seek their help. This was different. How could a human do what the fat man had done? Was he even human?

"Richmond? Would you join the Consilium, please?" A young male vampire called him into the meeting.

Richmond didn't recognise the young and serious vampire, no doubt already trying to network himself up the ranks. Surely, he'd better things to do with his youth than get involved with this political, back-stabbing bullshit.

Richmond followed the vampire into the room.

Archaic torches lit every corner of the vast chamber. Hundreds of gargoyles stared down at the centre of the room in grotesque poses. Fifty vampires sat in a circle of ornately carved throne-like chairs. Grouped together opposite the entrance of the hall sat the founders of the Consilium.

Michael Vitrago sat amongstst them. He appeared younger than the other elders, some of whom had receding or greying hair and lined faces. Augustus and Lucia were present. They, along with Michael, were the only members of the joint vampire-human Coalition that sat on this group.

"So, we've come no closer to establishing what is feeding incessantly in the Northeast?" asked an elder, a small, wiry vampire, but still large by human standards.

"No," answered Lucia. "Franco Stoloni is tracking through the moors as we speak. He's recruited a few lamia, good trackers, but they've come up with nothing."

"What have the Hominum Order discovered?" asked a female vampire.

"The same as us, it seems," said Lucia. "Caroline heads the Hominum Order, and she'd share any information. Whatever is making a dent in Middlesbrough's population is as silent a killer as our best assassins. It's hard to believe, considering the mess it makes of its food. The brutality is...impressive."

The comment brought heated discussion throughout the group.

"Richmond, it has been a long time." The other vampires stopped talking amongstst themselves as soon as Michael spoke. All eyes turned to Richmond who was waiting outside the circle.

"Yes, Michael, it has. I never thought we'd meet under this roof."

Michael gave a rare laugh. "Nor did I. But, Richmond, I believe you have something to tell us, something urgent?"

"Yes, my friends, I have. This is my first time in front of you all, and it will, hopefully, be my last. The news I bring is, indeed, urgent." He gathered his thoughts as he walked into the circle. "Vampire hunters have been a joke to us for centuries, shadows of their forefathers...until now. This morning, I witnessed something infinitely more powerful. I watched a human kill four vampires in thirty seconds with nothing more than his hands."

The revelation brought forth a tirade of questions from the congregation.

"Are you sure?"

"How do you know they're dead?"

"Were they really vampires he killed?"

Richmond raised his hands. "Brothers and sisters, please! I've told you the truth, so enough with the stupid questions." He looked at them pointedly. He really had no patience for this, but the situation was critical. "When his fist landed, it was as if the sun took them."

Michael sat with his head propped up by his massive hands. "What do you think this means, Richmond?"

Richmond shook his head slowly.

"What was he like?" asked another member of the council. "What could possibly take one of us?"

Richmond recounted the tale. He included every detail. "The man was in a bad state from a serious hangover, and, physically, he was in terrible condition. I could taste the cholesterol in his veins from the other side of the room. However, when he moved, he was like one of us, and the power...you could sense the power explode from inside him. It was almost supernatural. He killed Jacques Jereaux."

A gasp went up from several of the congregation. Jereaux was an extremely powerful vampire. Richmond listed the rest. "Stefan Kahn, Winston Montero and Terence O'Hara. Not easy pickings."

A female elder stood. "Could the humans have a new weapon?"

"Possibly, but why would they give this weapon to a wreck of a man?" said a younger vampire. "Still, the threat in the Northeast is the greatest problem, for both races. We need to get to the bottom of that first."

"I agree," said another elder. "Whatever's killing humans is more dangerous than a man killing vampires. If he goes to the press, no one will believe him. However, if the news of horrific killings is leaked, I do not want to think of the consequences. The Agreement always comes first."

"Richmond, what do you know about the man himself?" asked another council member.

"He was hired for one evening's work. We were down a man because Gunnar injured one of my door staff. He was hired on a whim, the same way I hire all of my temporary staff. His name is Sid Tillsley. He's in his forties and has a hard-man reputation in a rundown council estate in Middlesbrough. He smokes and drinks heavily, living his life in a pub. He was adamant about getting his money paid, cash in hand. We told all the staff that Tillsley got drunk, so we sent him on his way with a few quid in his pocket."

"How could this man perform these deeds?" asked an elder. "He sounds like he struggles to take care of himself. Time will solve this problem in due course."

"Perhaps, the Firmamentum is upon us?" said the oldest member of the assembly whose eyes had lost part of their characteristic agelessness. "This hasn't happened for two millennia. That was the last time a human killed a lamia in hand-to-hand combat."

Richmond recognised him: Pontius. Richmond never spent time with him because he was too boring.

"The Firmamentum?" said Michael surprised. "It cannot be, Pontius. That would be impossible to hide."

Pontius considered his comment. "I'm often mocked when I speak of the old days. Our so-called scientists describe the Firmamentum as 'a spike in genetic evolution,' but I see it as a reminder of what it is to be a true lamia."

Richmond wasn't bothered, but the other vampires, spare a few, sat captivated by the ancient's words.

"The Firmamentum is a phenomenon to celebrate, both in battle and in blood. It is a time to rid ourselves of mankind's petty bureaucracy and rely on our feral instincts and our lust for violence. The Firmamentum has always brought unity to the vampire race. We cannot hide away like scared vermin when the monster is set free!"

"What monster? What's the Firmamentum?"

Pontius looked up and down at the young vampire who had interrupted, closed his eyes, and shook his head. "We have fallen so far.... The Firmamentum is when the most powerful, bloodthirsty vampire is born onto the world. Every two thousand years, this magnificent vampire—this beast—strides across the land, decimating everything in its path. However, in nature, there is always a balance, and the Firmamentum is no different. A human, too, is born with awesome power, far greater than our own, the Bellator. This human is as fair and beautiful as the beast is brutal and vile—and the two are always born simultaneously. The Firmamentum brings the beast and the Bellator.

"We've grown weak over the last two millennia. We need a Firmamentum to show us what it means to be a vampire, a real lamia. This modern-day *arrangement* we've made with the humans will shatter as soon as the animal reveals itself. Politics do not control the mind of a beast whose instincts are as terrible as they are deadly. How will petty words control an animal that doesn't kill to feed but kills for nothing but the sport?

"If the Firmamentum is here, there is but one chance of peace, and that is the human—the Bellator. However, kill the Bellator..." Pontius cast a sly glance around the assembly, "and the beast is free to bring sanity back to the world, end the Agreement, and the ridiculous charade of the Coalition!"

"Enough!" Michael banged his fist on the arm of his chair in an unusual sign of frustration, which Richmond couldn't recall seeing before. "Things have changed, Pontius, possibly beyond the limit of your council. We cannot live like we did in the old age. Such talk is madness."

Most vampires cowered in Michael's presence, but Pontius was not affected. He chuckled to himself, amused. "Sparle was born from two vampires of Russian descent, a hardy couple that migrated to Italy out of interest in the Roman Empire. The two vampires were nothing special. She was plain to look at and not a powerful being, yet her thirst for killing bordered on the abnormal. The male didn't share his partner's lust for killing, but did thrive on torture, whether it was human, vampire, or animal. He was a natural sadist, and the only thing he ever loved was his wife, although it was probably her lust for murder that he loved." Once more, Pontius chuckled, but this time at the sadism and torture he described, a love he shared.

"Sparle's mother died during childbirth, which always happens when a monster of the Firmamentum is spawned. It is the same for the Bellator. Sparle's father blamed him and tortured the baby from birth. When it was two years old, the child killed its father. Five years later, our good friend Ricard was the next lamia to come into contact with the child. It had killed everything within fifty miles of the house where it was raised. By eight years old, it was six-foot tall and hulking with muscle. Sparle possessed no conscience, and the only thing he inherited was his mother's desire for murder and his father's lust for sadism.

"How Ricard survived, he—as usual—kept secret, but I believe it shows how dangerous the old bastard is." Pontius scowled. His contempt for the scholar was apparent. Richmond couldn't fathom how anyone could hold a grudge against his friend. "He spent fifteen years with Sparle, a name which he gave him. He tried to teach Sparle how to live and hunt humanely. He watched him grow to an immense size, knowing what he was. The Firmamentum has existed since vampires and man have walked the earth, but that stupid bastard thought he could change Nature's monster.

"Nevertheless, if anyone could've done it then, although it pains me to say it, Ricard would've been the one. Sparle, at the age of twenty-three, grew tired of the old man. How the old man escaped death is another mystery. The monster wandered for two years and killed all in its path. Lamia, animal, human, he'd drink the blood of anything. It was after attacking a Roman garrison that Sparle's future was decided. He attacked the camp of fifty soldiers and killed all except one scout who managed to escape and take word to his commanding officers. With the exception of Ricard, he was the first, man or beast, to escape Sparle's murderous intent. Armies were sent against him, and he relished the battle. He destroyed everthing that opposed him."

Meanwhile, in Rome, a gladiator dominated the games. Remo Elscachius, the Bellator, was a human who was beautiful to gaze upon. His body was sculpted out of rock and his eyes carried the same luminescence as the immortal. I watched him kill a vampire, with speed, grace, and nobility in the Coliseum. It was he who the Emperor sent to fight the monster, and it was the most incredible battle I have ever witnessed." Pontius' voice quickened with every mention of bloodshed.

"With two swords, Elscachius danced around Sparle and cut him over and over again. The earth was soaked with blood and Sparle screamed in pain and delight at the challenge he'd found. Sparle was cut hundreds of times, and his body struggled to heal. Then, he landed a backhand on Elscachius that sent the man fifty feet in the air. The human landed hard and didn't move from what looked like a fatal strike. Sparle was no tactical fighter, and he ran over to feast on his newest victim. As he knelt to feed, Elscachius stuck two daggers through his eyes, deep into his brain. It enabled him to withdraw the weapons and decapitate Sparle, ending his magnificent life."

"Remo Elscachius, the Bellator. What happened to his line?" asked Richmond.

Pontius laughed. "Oh, for the vanity of humans. He sired many bastards from the hundreds of whores he cavorted with. His bloodline was diluted and died out centuries ago. He became a hunter until his life was ended by the son of the vampire he'd defeated in the Coliseum...Isn't that right, Michael?"

Michael sneered at Pontius. "As well you know, Pontius, as well you know. I witnessed my father's death at the hands of a human and sought the revenge I saw fit."

"How did you?" asked Augustus.

"That is of no concern to any, except Remo Elscachius and I. He could not be classed as human. He and Sparle did not belong on this Earth. The Firmamentum can damage the very structure of our civilisation. As for its reoccurrence, and for all of Pontius' stories, it is absurd. If one of Sparle's power walked the earth, then we'd know within hours of him coming to age. I do not think that a human like Remo Elscachius will be born again. From what Richmond has just told us, the man, Sid Tillsley, does not even appear to be in shape!"

Richmond nodded. "Yes, you're right, but his power matched ours. He was no normal human, I promise you."

"An anomaly of any kind requires our full attention," said Augustus. "I would be astonished, as I think most members of the council would be, if he turned out to be the Bellator."

Michael nodded. "I do not believe he's the Bellator. Nor do I believe the bloodshed in the Northeast can be attributed to an animal like Sparle. The Firmamentum is not here. If it was, the vampire race would be on the brink of extinction. The Firmamentum is not something to celebrate. It never was. The Agreement is in place for our survival. If it falls, we fall. The Firmamentum would be the end of us all." He gave Pontius a disgusted look. "I'll contact Franco Stoloni who's investigating the massacres in the Northeast. He won't struggle tracking this human down. We should not kill him immediately. We need to find out exactly what he is and how he performed such feats."

"Are you suggesting we capture him?" asked another elder.

Michael nodded. "I think we'd be foolish if we didn't. But first, we should determine his movements. There may be something more sinister behind his actions."

A murmur of agreement went up around the hall.

"Should the Hominum Order be informed of these matters?" asked Augustus.

"Of course they should," answered Michael. "We work in harmony with our sister council for the benefit of both species."

Richmond was impressed. Michael had somehow managed to sound convincing.

13

"SO THERE I WAS IN MIDDLE OF THIS ROOM, and the undead were upon me!" Sid lit up an Embassy Number One. One of the lads had donated the cigarette to Sid, and it was his first legal cigarette for nigh on ten years. It was eight o'clock on the Sunday night. Brain Garforth (reinstated drinker of The Miner's Arms—Kev could never turn down a dollar), Kev, Arthur, Peter Rathbone, and the lads watching Tarrant, surrounded Sid, listening to his tale of courage and drunken haymakers.

"I'd had a few ales, like, as you do when you're working the door. Lucky I had a few, like. It warmed me up for a scrap with them vampires."

A man, not too dissimilar to disturbed, three-day-old dog shit, piped up, "I kicked a zombie in the bollocks when I was smacked off my tits, once."

Every eyeball rose to the roof simultaneously. Every pub had a certain character, and that character was an arsehole, a complete and utter arsehole full of the shittiest shit. Peter Rathbone was that arsehole, the greasiest, dirtiest, filthiest little arsehole going.

"Shut up, Rathbone," said Brian. "Let the man tell the story. No one wants to hear your bull."

"Prick," said Rathbone.

Sid continued. "As I was saying—" He stopped mid-sentence. "Hang on, Rathbone, you know that *Male* aftershave you sold me."

"It wasn't piss," said Rathbone, immediately.

"Oh, reet, that's all right then," said Sid. "As I was saying, I was in the middle of the room, and the undead were upon me!"

"Where were you, man?" asked the handsome face of Arthur Peasley.

"It was in some warehouse. I didn't really know where the hell I was. I just woke up 'cos some bastard had thrown water over me."

"How did you get there?" asked Brian.

"That's the thing, mate, I ain't really sure. I was at the club, and then, I went for a slash 'cos I'd had a few too many. Must have slipped and banged me 'ead." It all genuinely puzzled Sid. Booze is wonderful at taking the memories away.

All heads nodded simultaneously and gave that "aaaaarr" sound that people make when the penny drops. Sid often passed out through alcohol abuse, and once from eating crisps, but that was for a bet, which he won.

"Anyroad, I'm in this warehouse thing, like, and there're five of these big bastards surrounding me." Sid described it like an everyday occurrence. "I knew it was gonna be trouble, mind."

"When studying karate, my daddy could cope with four men simultaneously!" exclaimed Arthur. "Maybe not towards the end, with all the extra weight and all. I followed in my daddy's footsteps, and I could never take more than three good men, even with my best stuff used on 'em. Sid, you fought the undead. I'm surprised you're here to tell the tale, baby."

Sid gave a dismissive shrug. "They had shit jaws, like."

"Sid?" asked Kev. "How do you know they were the undead?"

Sid lit up another free Embassy. "At first, I thought they were *them lot*, which was their first mistake. They had big, pointy teeth, like that fooker I knocked out when I was trying that doggin' lark out."

It was now common knowledge that Sid was experimenting.

"Anyroad, one of 'em said summat like: 'we're fooking vampires,' or summat along them lines. I like to keep an open mind on things, you know?"

"That include gays, Sid?" volunteered Rathbone.

A horrible silence followed...and kept following.

The big man's face indicated that thoughts were racing (well, gently traversing) from one side of his massive, yet limited, brain to the other. The thoughts slowed, got a little sidetracked, and were forgotten about. Full *Pink Alert* avoided, all thanks to his Gay Defence System.

"Anyway, lads," his mind finally back on track, "I'm out of pocket until benefit day. My beer and tab supplies have dried up, so I bid you good day." He headed for the door.

"One more beer on the house," said Kev.

Sid turned on a sixpence and returned to the arena. One of the lads passed him a free Woodbine.

"So, where was I? Oh yeah, the undead. Yeah, they were really pale and had them teeth thingies." He gestured with his hands like he was pulling mustachios. "And when I hit 'em, they exploded into dust."

There was a murmur around the group. None of them had experienced the undead before.

"So what are they like, these vampires, Sid?" asked Kevin.

"Well I don't know much about 'em really. I've only smacked 'em"

Everyone looked at Brian.

Brian let out a huge sigh. "Don't you uneducated fookers know anything?" He cleared his throat, indicating education was afoot.

"Vampires live off blood and need to drink it otherwise they die. They can be killed by sunlight, a stake through the heart, crosses, or garlic. They have been known to be extremely good at maths, and some of them love to count."

"Clever bastards," offered Kev.

Brian looked at Sid. "I don't know how you managed to kill them, mate." And there wasn't much that Brian didn't know.

"I canna remember it that well. I had the mother of all hangovers. Half me thoughts were of not being sick and shitting meself at the same time, cos that can kill ya!"

The group nodded in agreement. Drinking was a dangerous game.

"Anyway, they swore at me a bit. I think they were annoyed 'cos I drunk all their whisky and pissed in their flowers."

The group could understand the vampire's point, and Sid sensed their feelings.

"Which I was genuinely sorry for!" Sid shrugged his big shoulders, giving a puppy-dog look, making him look like a flushed scrotum. "I remember saying: 'I'm sorry, lads. I had a few too many last night. I'll get you another bottle of whisky and we can call it quits?' After all, I still hadn't been paid for me night's work. Then they started calling me names. They really were quite rude."

The group shared looks of disgust. The youth of today were bad enough, but for the undead to show that sort of behaviour was quite unacceptable.

"After a few minutes of them talking silly buggers, one of 'em jumped at me, and I caught him with a sweet right."

They all grimaced as one. They'd all seen the "sweet" right before. The only thing that it had in common with "sweet" was that both were bad for your teeth.

"He turned to dust in mid-air. A few others tried it on, and they got a bit of the same. The big black pansy just bolted. After I got me breath back, I left the warehouse. Turned out, I was in fooking Scunthorpe! Glad I pissed on their plants." Sid was offered another free cigarette, which he willingly accepted.

"What are you going to do then?" asked Kev.

"What do you mean?" said Sid, placing his empty glass on the bar.

"Last one. I mean it." Kev gave Sid a stern look. "It isn't every day that someone is attacked by the undead. Are you going to sell your story? I reckon there's a bob or two to be made."

Sid weighed it up. "Don't know, like. If I make a few quid off a story, the Benefit Bastards will have me. I can't afford to lose me allowance. Me 'eart canna take to work, and I got to think of the future."

"You've got to think of your fellow man!"

The group turned as one to see the grey-haired stranger standing in The Miner's doorway.

"It's that prick from the other night," said Brian.

REECE STRODE INTO THE PUB. *"You*, Sid, can put an end to this war that has raged for centuries."

"Who are you, man?" asked an extremely handsome man, inexplicably wearing a white sequinned jumpsuit and taking up a defensive karate stance. He looked strangely familiar...and looked like he could take care of business if the need required.

"Easy, Arthur, mate," said Sid.

"My name is Reece Chambers. I'm a vampire hunter. For twenty years I've hunted the very thing that hunts us. I've travelled the country looking for Hellspawn. I've put an end to many of their wretched lives and thus ended thousands of wanton murders. The undead you speak of, they have slaughtered children. When you hear on the news of women raped and killed, of children abducted and abused...it is the vampire who are responsible. Murderers, butchers, animals!" His voice shook with emotion.

"Not that twat, again," said the weasel Garforth, rolling his eyes. Emotions were not welcome in this pub. "Didn't you dump him in that skip, Sid?"

"Aye, but that was then, and this is now. Gotta let bygones be bygones. Let's listen to what the lad has to say." Sid took a seat at the bar. "After he buys me a couple of beers."

Reece nodded to Kevin, who dutifully pulled a pint of Bolton Bitter. "You fought and killed vampires. It may sound stupid, far-fetched bullshit, but the fact of the matter is, vampires are real." He waited for the gasps, but there were none. Some of the men turned away to watch the television where Chris Tarrant was presenting *Who Wants to be a Millionaire*. "There are two thousand of these creatures in the UK, alone. They populate the entire world!"

The man in the white jumpsuit said, "It's true, fellas. My momma told me that my daddy took down one of these sons of bitches down in Memphis once. He used his karate on him." He demonstrated with a flurry of karate punches.

Reece shook his head.

"So," said the most disgusting, greasy individual Reece had ever laid eyes on. "these vampires, are they actually baddies, then?"

"Shut it, Rathbone," said Brian.

The dishevelled, horrible, greasy little bastard Rathbone continued unabashed. "Well, I saw that *Dracula* film thing, and he was a baddy in that. Bit weird when that wolf shagged that lass, but you did see her tits, like. Then there was that vampire film with that short arse from that plane film, *Top Gun*."

Reece looked the excuse for a man up and down. "What the hell are you talking about?"

"I can get you them films on VHS, fiver for the lot."

Reece restrained his temper. He remembered his sore head after the night in the skip. Still, there was only so much he could take.

"I can get you *Lethal Weapon 2* and *3*, *Die Hard*, *The Last Action Hero*, *A Clockwork Orange Penis*, *The Load in My Ring* and—"

Reece couldn't take any more. "I think it's time you—"

"*Load in My Ring*? The missus wants to see that," said Kevin. "She's read the books and everything. Loves it she does. Thrives on it. This could get me back in her good books."

The pub went silent. Even Chris Tarrant was quiet.

"*Load in My Ring*...is, err...Mrs. Ackroyd into that sort of thing, like?" Rathbone asked.

"Aye. I saw an advert for it. It's got that fella with the big white beard interfering with them little dwarfs?"

"Yeah, that's the one," confirmed Rathbone.

"And that short fella thinks he can destroy that little dwarf's ring. He gives it everything he's got with one of the biggest weapons I've ever seen, and it doesn't even split the bastard."

"Yeah, that's the one."

"Then, they go down that dirty mineshaft."

"Yeah, that's the one."

"And they have to pull out 'cos it gets real messy."

"Yeah, that's the one."

"And they go and see that slutty blonde piece in the forest whose got a lovely ring already, but the little fella offers her his, and she ain't having any of it, like."

"Yeah, that's the one."

"At the end that fella goes a bit funny, and ends up with more pricks in him than that dartboard." He nodded at The Miner's dilapidated board. The pub turned to the dartboard, shuddered as one, and then turned to look at the landlord. "Aye, the missus told me all about it. I'll give you a fiver for it."

Rathbone took a copy out of his coat pocket and handed it over.

"If this gets me back in with the missus, then I may even get some afterwards!" The fat landlord ran out the back of the bar and up the stairs.

One of the locals ran outside to be sick.

Reece tried to gather his thoughts. He wasn't used to this sort of environment. He lived a solitary life, always on the run. He'd dealt with people before, but these weren't normal people. Sid Tillsley was something different. Was he what the prophecies spoke of?

"Sid...SID?" said Reece.

Sid jumped up, startled. "Eh, what?" He'd obviously been bemused by the *Load in My Ring* controversy.

"The vampires, Sid, remember the vampires? We have a duty to protect mankind."

"Well, in all fairness, Rich, them there vampires haven't actually done anything wrong to me, have they? They had a go at me while I was out doggin', but it's not like I was being an upstanding citizen. The second time they had a go, I'd drunk their whisky and pissed on their stuff. I ain't got no beef with them."

Reece had a sinking feeling, the one where the blood rushes from the head, inducing dizziness.

"You've got 'no beef' with them?" Reece was distraught.

"Aye."

"These murderers...You've 'no beef' with them?"

"Aye..." he said it a bit slower as if Reece was stupid.

"Tens of thousands of us...*us*...were taken last year!"

"Bloody hell!" offered Brian. "Who do we know who's gone missing?"

Sid scratched his head. "Jim Heathers?"

"In prison," replied Brian.

"Ricky Morgan?"

"He went to Thailand to find a bride."

"Jimmy Parsley?"

Brian paused. "I haven't seen that lad for bloody ages. Last time I saw him, he'd just grown himself a moustache like that fella out of Magnum."

Reece breathed a sigh of relief. He was finally getting through to these idiots.

"You see, gentlemen, they are amongst us. They are taking the lives of your friends."

Again, Brian cut him off. "He ain't my friend, like. He thinks he looks like fooking Magnum? Does he shite. Fook him. Twat."

Reece rolled his eyes. He walked in front of Sid so that he could have no distractions. "Sid, listen to me, please!" Sid's eyes left the television and centred on Reece. "You've managed to kill vampires with your bare hands. You don't understand what it means. Vampires are immortal."

"I thought they could get killed by sunlight?" asked Brian, which obliterated Reece's train of thought and sent Sid back to watching the telly. Tarrant had finished and there was a documentary on about parrots.

"What? Oh yes, they can."

"Not immortal then, are they?" Brian's smug smile made Reece feel sick.

"What?"

"If they can die, then they ain't immortal. It's kind of like the opposite of what they actually are. It's like me calling you a cock, when actually you're a cun—"

"My daddy said they're allergic to garlic," interrupted Arthur.

Reece looked at Garforth with disgust but answered Arthur's question. "That's a myth. They need blood to live. The plasma in blood regenerates their bodies. They can go without it for a couple of months, after which, they wither and die of starvation. They don't need to kill to live. They don't even need human blood. The only reason they kill us is because they choose to. They say they can't satisfy their bloodlust if they don't take human life. The needless suffering could end tomorrow if they had any sort of willpower."

"So, they're like them lasses from Diet Darlings who can't help but eat cakes?" asked Sid.

"If the vampire feeds, then they will age at an astoundingly slow rate. A vampire has never died of old age or illness. They can't turn us into vampires; they're a separate species. The legends and myths that talk of silver, garlic, and crucifixes are old wives' tales that have deviated from fact along the course of history. Vampires, I can assure you, can be killed. I know, because I've killed many of them myself. They can be killed by sunlight, and it remains our greatest ally. They can be killed by decapitation, but the blow needs to be powerful enough to cut through the spinal column, the fatal step.

"Sid, the point is they can't even kill each other with a punch, and they are incredibly strong. You've done something that hasn't been done before. With you on my side, we could end the bloodshed and live in peace. You could save mankind from the vampire."

Sid grimaced. "I canna be seen working, Rich, as I claim jobseeker allowance. I canna send that money down the shitter. I got to think of me future, like."

"I will pay you five times more than the dole." Reece argued.

"But for how long? I've worked hard to maintain that money. I put a little bit aside for a rainy day. I do little odd jobs, here and there, to wet me whistle."

Reece was desperate and desperate times called for desperate measures. "What would happen, Sid, if you were to lose your jobseekers allowance?"

Sid's beady eyes managed to narrow a little further. "What are you saying, like?"

Reece leaned against the bar. "Well, say for instance, that the benefit office were to get wind of you working? Say they caught you on the job?"

Sid started to get the gist of what Reece was saying. "They haven't so far. Why would they now?"

"Yeah, everyone in the whole bleedin' town knows Sid will do an odd job for the right price. Including kicking seven bells of shit out of some blackmailing scumbag!" said Brian.

The tension in the pub skyrocketed. Arthur took an offensive karate stance. Reece held up his hands.

"Gentlemen, I'm not looking for trouble. You've stumbled on to a world which will devour every single one of you. I must see humanity protected from the vile abominations that share our Earth. Sid, come out with me for one night, just one night. I'll pay you five hundred pounds."

"How do I know you ain't a Benefit Bastard?"

"Sid, if you don't come with me, I'll set you up for benefit fraud. It will be easy. How do you think you got the job working that nightclub?"

"You bast—"

Reece interrupted more abuse from Brian. He looked Sid directly in the eyes and held his gaze. "However, you come out with me for one night, and I solemnly swear that I'll never contact the benefit fraud investigators, or try to set you up. On my honour, I swear it."

"Can you give me five minutes for me to discuss this with my colleagues?" asked Sid formally. Reece nodded and left the pub.

SID WAITED FOR HIM TO WALK OUT AND CLOSE THE DOOR. "Five hundred notes? Fooking hell, I'm a millionaire! Stupid bastard, I would've gone out for two hundred Benson and Hedges. Kevin!" he shouted so Kev, who was still upstairs, would hear him. "Bolton all round!"

A half-arsed cheer when up.

"You could be on to a goldmine here, mate," said Brian.

"Aye, you're right. Someone get the stupid bastard back in here. He's got a round to pay for."

One of the lads knocked on the pub window and motioned Reece back in.

"Five hundred notes, one night, no killing, and you get these beers in." Sid offered out his massive hand.

14

As soon as Caroline heard about the death of four vampires at the hands of an unarmed human, she called the emergency meeting at a desolate cottage in the Buckinghamshire countryside. The Hominum Order were scattered across the country and included all the human representatives from the Coalition. This was the most central location allowing for this ad hoc meeting to be called. Everyone was here, except for Ben Edric. His fate was known to the Order, but no one enquired how it had happened. No one wanted to know.

Caroline's spies within the Lamian Consilium were always trustworthy and accurate down to the last detail. Humans had never had the luxury of a vampire spy before, and Caroline was the first leader of the Order to obtain one. She knew it was not her negotiating skills that built the bridge. Every passing year meant huge technological advancement in surveillance. It'd be possible to one day track every vampire across the world.

A vampire with an incessant passion for murder had approached her, promising to leak any important information, provided a blind eye was turned to her unsanctioned kills. It was for the greater good of the human race. Caroline tried not to think of the thousands of children murdered for the "greater good." This was a cold war, and war was never glamorous.

"Thank you for turning up promptly." Caroline said to the assembled council. "I can assure you it is for no light matter."

This put a stop to the puzzled murmuring. There were twenty people in the small, beamed cottage. "I called you to this remote cottage with news that could change the world." She looked at a young gentleman in a designer suit and glasses who peered into a laptop. "Ruskins?"

"There isn't a bug for 2.3 miles, ma'am," he said with certainty.

"Very good." She gave a smile that vanished in an instant. "Two nights ago, a human killed four vampires. A week before that, we believe this same human killed Gabriel." She paused to let the enormity of it all sink in. The stunned faces said it all. "He killed them all with nothing but his fists."

"Gabriel? He killed Gabriel?" asked Charles, flabbergasted. Gabriel's raw power had been unquestionable.

"Yes. We believe Gunnar Ivansey was there but fled the scene."

"Gabriel and Ivansey, together?" said Sanderson excitedly. "You'd need a fleet of tanks to bring them down, and that's if you were lucky. This is a time to fucking celebrate! A 'fuck you!' from the thousands of victims! Ivansey, fleeing the scene! What I'd give to witness that."

"Who were the other four?" asked Charles.

"The other vampires killed were Jacques Jereaux, Stefan Kahn, Winston Montero, and Terence O'Hara."

This excited Sanderson further. "All well-known bastards. I won't mourn the loss of Jereaux, the son of a bitch. The amount of his handywork I've cleared up." He spat. "How did it happen, Caroline?"

"I was informed this morning. The Lamian Consilium was informed yesterday, and they've sent a team out to investigate this phenomenon, as will we. I'm awaiting the official contact from them, which should follow shortly. Leaks go both ways, remember.

"Richmond witnessed the death of the four at the hands of Sid Tillsley; forty-six, born and currently living on the Smithson Estate, a poverty-stricken council estate in Middlesbrough. He has fraudulently claimed jobseekers allowance since he left school. The Benefit Fraud Squad has never been able to pin him down with anything."

"Is that all we have?" asked Charles.

"At the moment, yes. His name doesn't link any family members to any vampire activity. So, at present, we have no motives for him to become a hunter, and even if he did, his résumé does not infer that he'd scientifically discover, well, anything. We need to send a team pronto."

"Count me in, ma'am!" yelled Sanderson.

Charles snorted. "I don't think so, old boy. I think your temper could get the better of you. You've been under immense pressure, of late."

Sanderson's eyes flashed. "With all respect, I believe I'm owed this."

Caroline cut him off. "There is no *owed*, Sanderson. You, like every person in this room, are a soldier and are fully expendable. The job will go to the most suitable members of the team."

Sanderson gritted his teeth but held in his rage. He'd still be reeling from the tongue lashing she gave him last time.

"Rickson," called Charles.

"Yes, sir?" answered a man that could've been anywhere from late twenties to his early forties. Brown hair and brown eyes with an average height and build, he was difficult to describe, which was why he was in the team. He was recruited from MI6 for the sole reason of tracking and spying on humans. Rickson was a hardened serviceman.

"You know what to do, Rickson," said Charles.

"Yes, sir."

"Jeremy, I think it'd be a good idea for you to accompany Rickson on this field mission," said Caroline.

Jeremy Pervis looked on smugly. Caroline didn't like Pervis, a snivelling little shit. Rickson was good enough to do the job by himself, but a bit more hands-on field experience might toughen Pervis up. Rickson looked taken aback.

"Forgive me, ma'am, but I work best alone."

"I don't care, Rickson."

"Do you still want me to coordinate tracking whatever's causing the chaos in the Northeast, Caroline?" asked Pervis.

"Yes, but we'll send more help. There are difficult times ahead. We must remain vigilant, and the Agreement must be upheld." Caroline stood up and gave the group a curt nod. "Good day to you all."

15

IT WAS A WARM AND BALMY FRIDAY NIGHT. Two nights had passed since Sid made the deal with Rich, and he was under strict instructions not to drink anything at all. Not surprisingly, Sid could murder a pint or fifteen, so he took his mind off drinking by smoking a few more tabs than normal. He was on his hundred and seventh Alaskan of the day: "Eskimo's Friends." He'd helped Middlesbrough's only Inuit deliver three hundred-weight of salmon in the back of his Montego Estate and was rewarded with two hundred Alaskans, and then an extra fifty quid once Sid realised the smell of fish would be lingering in his car for the next few weeks.

Sid was to meet Rich outside the local corner shop. Apart from the beer rule, he'd been told to wrap up warm. This particular rule was ignored. Men from the Northeast didn't need to wear coats on a night out. He wore his leather jacket though, because it made him look cool.

"You turned up?"

Sid jumped, grabbing his heart. "Shit the bed! Where d'you come from? You know I've got me 'eart, Rich."

"It's Reece," he said. He was dressed in black, and his grey hair was tied back underneath a hood. "You have to move silently in this world."

"Silently? I nearly..." He rubbed his chin in thought. "I may have shat myself."

Rich held his nose. "You have to blend in with your surroundings or you die...if you're lucky."

Sid belched loudly. "Don't you worry. I can be as silent as a mouse, me."

"Walk with me, Sid."

"You never said anything about walkin', like!" This was going to be the hardest five hundred quid Sid had ever earned.

"Sid, tonight I'm going to show you how rife the world is with vampire activity. I'm going to show you their ferocity and their merciless disregard for human life. Tonight, I'm going to open your eyes."

"Is it gonna take long? I'm gagging for a dump."

Rich sighed. "Sid, I've killed thirty-eight vampires in twenty years of hunting. Thirty-eight. That's impressive, even by my ancestors' standards. You've killed five in a fortnight. I spend months planning each move. You kill one with a single punch."

"Aye, I've always had a good punch on me. I would've got into boxing, but getting hit in the head can slow your brain down." Sid couldn't understand why Rich was giving him a strange look.

"I can, to some degree, understand your reluctance to join in the battle against these monsters. You live every day in—" Rich stopped talking and looked back.

"Give me a sec, lad," Sid was wheezing, having parked his ample buttocks on a garden wall. He looked up at the smog. It was a beautiful evening. He hadn't seen a completely sober night for many a year, and he was getting a bit of exercise. It was all lovely stuff, apart from the exercise and the lack of booze. "Sorry, Rich, what were you saying?"

"It's Reece," he corrected. "I was saying, Sid, that in my business you live every day in fear."

Sid lit up another Alaskan. He could've sworn they smelled slightly fishy, but a tab was a tab. "Why do it then? Why hunt 'em?"

"Do you fear anything, Sid?"

"Oh aye, mon. Always got an eye out in case the Benefit Bastards are trying to catch me doing an odd job here and there. That and...*them lot.*"

"Them lot?"

"Aye, *them lot,* you know...*them lot* who are very close to their mothers."

"Homosexuals?" asked Rich.

The orange streetlights silhouetted terrace roofs and chimneys, every one outlining a Sky dish paid for by the council, while the smog danced magically in the moonlight. Maybe it was the beauty of his surroundings that made Sid comfortable enough not to knock out Rich at the mention of the word. Sid felt he could get things off his chest. Sid spat out a massive, black, Alaskan-induced spitball, and now that was off his chest, he could chat.

"Aye, I don't get 'em, like. Them and Australians. They have barbecues on the beach at Christmas. Something fooking wrong with 'em, like." He could get into this philosophy thing. "Anyway, how come you got into this vampire-hunting business? Why're you going round causing them trouble? Hating them for killing us and then doing the same back is a bit hyposhitical, don't you think?" Sid was high off the philosophy chat and decided to throw the biggest word he knew into the fray.

Rich sat next to him on the wall. "I was twenty-three years old, having finished my masters in criminology at Oxford, when a letter arrived through my door asking me if I wanted to know the truth about my past. You see, I was an orphan and never knew my real parents. I was bought up in a terrible orphanage in Sheffield. I was beaten, abused, and humiliated until I was eleven when I murdered the 'carers' who harmed me. I went through child counselling for my trauma, but I wasn't sick or disturbed. The people who mistreated me deserved to die. Then, I was put in a foster home. A loving, caring family took me in, but because of my past, I could never get close to them. Nevertheless, they supported me through school, college, and then university. Then, the letter came."

Sid sat smoking and listening. He was a good listener, as it didn't involve any work. "Who was it from?"

"My father. Turns out I wasn't an orphan, after all. My father was a vampire hunter. They took my mother just after my birth. My father put me in an orphanage to protect me from them. He said that he couldn't risk contact in case they found out I was his son. He'd never have made contact with me if I hadn't made it by myself. He was a hard man, and I absolutely hated him for leaving me, but they put him in that situation. They took my mother, making me go through years of hell. That is why I hate vampires. And here we are now, Mr. Tillsley, this is where it all begins for you."

Sid took another drag of his cancerous cigarette. "Now then, it may end here tonight as well. One night, we agreed." He waggled a sausage-like finger at Rich, which said, "No silly buggers, like."

"I'm a man of my word. You will get your five hundred pounds at the end of the evening. As agreed, there will be no killing...at least not by us."

"What happened to your old man?" asked Sid.

"Ah! He...he was taken from me." Rich stuttered.

Sid didn't pursue it. Not because he was concerned with Rich's feelings, but because he wasn't that bothered.

Rich pulled out a keyring from his pocket, pressed it, and walked over to a car parked adjacent to the pavement. It was black, but Sid couldn't decide what it was. It certainly wasn't a Montego Estate.

"What kind of car is this, then?" asked Sid.

Rich beamed as he opened the door and got in. Sid followed suit and sat in the passenger seat of the four-door hatchback. Rich started the engine, and the car was as close to silent as a car could be. The big man gave an impressed whistle.

"Made it, well, modified it, myself," Rich said. "It took me an age, but it was worth the effort. If you were to identify this car to the police, how would you describe it?"

"I didn't see anything, officer," Sid gave his monotone, generic answer.

Rich laughed, although Sid wasn't joking. "OK, pretend you're describing it to your mates. What kind of car is it?"

"Well, you made it, like. I couldn't really say it was anything."

"Exactly," said Rich with a touch of smugness.

"But, then again," added Sid "it's the only car like it, and that makes it pretty recognisable now."

Rich didn't look happy. He floored the accelerator and raced away.

Sid sensed tension in the air. He was sensing many things now; he wasn't pissed. "Can I put radio on?"

"There is no radio," was the icy reply.

"My Montego Estate has a radio." One-nil. Sid couldn't resist. He didn't have many opportunities to boast when it came to cars.

"This is not the kind of car you go cruising in, you know?" Rich had obviously never seen a Montego Estate before. "It's a weapon in its own right," he added, trying to sound cool.

"Class. Has it got missiles and ejector seats and shit like that?" asked Sid, a big fan of James Bond.

Rich didn't respond.

"What about a machine gun out of the exhaust?"

Rich scowled.

"Can it leak oil out of the back to make enemies skid?"

No answer.

"My Montego Estate can. The amount of pile-ups that bastard has caused!" He chuckled to himself.

"Look, just fuck off! Fuck off!" Rich shouted.

Sid shut up, worried about losing the five hundred quid. "Erm...the dashboard is pretty snazzy, isn't it? I'd love to have a dashboard like this in me Montego." He stroked it and gave an impressed whistle between his teeth.

Rich sulked for a few more miles. They were in the countryside, possibly ten or fifteen miles from Middlesbrough town centre. They turned off the main country road onto a bumpy dirt track, lined with large evergreens, which carried on twisting and turning for about half a mile.

Rich put his dummy back in. "The first night I saw you, you were seeking sexual gratification in the car park of Teesside Memorial Park."

"How dare you!"

"Shut up, Sid. We're nearer Sunderland now. This is a new spot for doggers." He talked louder as Sid protested at the outrage of being called a dogger. "It may get hit fairly soon. They never attack anywhere where there're too many people. New dogging sites are perfect."

Rich drove farther along the track until it opened out to a large car park, surrounded by woodland. He parked away from the other cars; a couple of them were already rocking.

"You're just a pervert, you!" said Sid, with a gleam in his eye. Little Sid had a gleam in his eye too.

"This place could get hit at any minute. Keep an eye out for anything untoward."

Sid screamed.

Sid screamed like he'd never screamed before. It was a high-pitched yelp that could shatter crystal and eardrums. Only desperate fear could cause a grown man to make such a noise. He was staring out the side window, straight into the eye of an erect penis that was being waggled at him by a middle-aged man in a Macintosh.

Sid covered his eyes and put his head in his lap.

"Relax," said Rich, trying to calm Sid down. "If I don't turn my light on, he'll go away. This must be a gay site."

Sid passed out.

"SID?" REECE GAVE THE MAN A SHAKE. "Sid!" Reece laughed. This man could kill vampires with a swipe of his hand, but being in the presence of active homosexuals was enough to make him collapse in terror. This was worth the five hundred pounds alone.

"Come on, Sidney, it's time you came back to the land of the living." He opened the glove box and took out a bottle of water. He opened the top to pour a little over Sid's large and uncharacteristically pale head. Suddenly, he stopped.

The car. Did it just move? A repugnant smell filled the vehicle. Reece sighed in disgust. He went to pour the water, but again, his hand was stayed. There was a definite vibration in the car, and one not caused by Sid Tillsley's anus. He looked around the car park. A couple of cars were still rocking while men stood outside watching, nothing troublesome considering the circumstances.

There it was again, but more intense, like the distant rumble of a train. He could see nothing past the light thrown from the parked cars, and the moonlight offered only shadows.

Was that movement? This could be what he brought Sid to see. He poured more water over Sid, but he didn't stir. Reece needed Sid to see this, to see the horror. Suddenly, a Volkswagen flew across the car park, airborne for fifty feet. It crashed into another car in an explosion of twisted wreckage. One of the spectators was flung backwards from the blast, while the other man was crushed by the soaring vehicle. A moment later, a tree followed, landing on the fallen victim, caving in his chest cavity, blood momentarily fountaining from the catastrophic injury. The men outside of the vehicles ran, fleeing for their lives.

"This isn't...right." Reece was transfixed. Vampire attacks didn't happen like this. Vampire attacks were cool and calculating. They weren't noticed until it was too late and there was no chance of escape. Then, the bastards had their fun.

A car's wheels screeched. A large saloon car parked on the edge of the wood was wheel spinning, the driver desperate for it to achieve traction.

"Idiot!" If the car was trapped in mud, then he was only making matters worse. The reason for the wheel spinning became apparent when the vehicle began to lift off the ground. There must be at least three or four of them! It would've taken a great number to throw that other car so far.

Shadows obscured the tormentors, but Reece remained calm. They wouldn't be able to break into his secured car, which was bullet, fire, and explosion proof. No matter what the vampires did, they wouldn't break in for hours, and daylight would be here by then. He switched on the headlights, and that's when fear took him.

For what seemed a lifetime, he stared into the eyes of the Devil himself, straight into the eyes of Death and into the world beyond. It took all of his will to start the car and slam his foot on the accelerator, performing a sharp U-turn that threw up a trail of dust. He tried to force the image of what he'd just seen out of his head and concentrate on the road, his escape, his only chance of survival. A deafening roar erupted from behind Reece's speeding car. Blood exploded across his windshield along with a body hitting the bonnet. The body rolled off almost immediately, but Reece noticed the extent of the mutilation.

The car automatically started the windscreen wipers after it sensed what it thought was rain. Reece, although temporarily blind, didn't move his foot from the floor. The vehicle began to shudder. *It* was following! They should be safe if he could make it to the main road, but how fast could this thing run? Surely, it couldn't beat him on tarmac?

"Where the fook am I?" Sid awoke with a start. He looked over at Reece. "You're as white as a sheet, mon! And fooking hell, slow down! What's a matter wit' ya?" He sniffed the air. "You haven't shit the car, have ya, ya dirty bastard?"

Reece didn't answer. The thing was getting closer; he could feel the reverberations through the car. It was actually catching up, and he was travelling at sixty.

"What the fook was that?" asked a startled Sid. Trees crashed everywhere around them, with the ever-present rhythmic beat of giant strides.

Through gritted teeth, Reece managed, "Look what hunts us."

Sid turned round in his seat, struggling to get his belly into position. "All I can see is dust, mon. Hang on. I just saw a few trees fall down. Fook me!" he cried as a tree flew over the car, missing it by a matter of feet. "That could be dangerous, that!"

Dangerous! thought Reece. What an understatement! It was running at sixty miles an hour while smashing trees down and throwing them like javelins. Vampires were not capable of that, not even Michael Vitrago.

"I think I can see summat, like." Sid squinted. "Aye, some big bastard is running after us. He's fookin' quick, like. You must have really pissed him off. Did ya cut him up at the roundabout or summat?"

Fear subsided and astonishment filled the void. "It's running at sixty miles an hour, Sid!"

"Aye, he's pretty quick, like, but I reckon Brian could take him over thirty yards. Brian's quicker than you think, Rich."

The beast let out another deafening roar, but the sound of falling trees, and more importantly, the sound of its booming strides, ended.

Reece didn't relax his speed until he was far away from the park. He only slowed the car down when the adrenaline had stopped pumping. Turning to Sid, he said, with exasperation, "It's fucking *Reece*! My name is Reece! And you know what? You really are a fucking idiot!"

16

SID MOPPED HIS MIGHTY BROW. It'd been a hard morning's work helping Jock the Turk make donner kebabs in preparation for the Middlesbrough/Newcastle friendly later in the week. There was always demand when the fat Geordies travelled south. He'd earned thirty notes and two hundred "El Shish" cigarettes from Turkey.

"See you later, Jock. I hope you don't have too much trouble from them Geordie bastards!" called Sid from the door of the butchery. He lit up his first Turk, but not his first cigarette, of the day.

Jock waved back and let out a battle cry, "Ayayayayayayaya! Don't you worry about me, Mr. Sid. You watch out for them Benefit Bastards, too, my friend. Here, take this!" Jock threw the big man a full carrier bag, which he caught with a squelch. "Miscellaneous meat! Enjoy, my friend!"

Sid left the butchery. He'd often been given miscellaneous meats from Jock the Turk, and he'd never once opened the bag. Some things weren't worth it.

Sid walked from the back of the butchers to the main street. It was a warm, beautiful summer's morning, and the pubs were open. He threw his leather jacket over his shoulder and strutted along, very casual, very Arthur Fonzarelli. It was a good day and he was proper flush. Five hundred notes last night, thirty quid this morning, and tabs for the next few days. He lit up a second Turk. "Not bad, not bad at all."

It was a funny evening, last night. That thing, whatever it was, was damn strong. Sid doubted whether Daly Thompson could throw trees that far. It was as quick as Brian over thirty yards, too, and anything with Daly Thompson's power and Brian Garforth's thirty-yard dash was going to be a handful in a brawl.

That Rich fella had acted a bit weird. The guy was normally a gobshite, an absolute gobshite. However, after they legged it from the big bastard, he'd hardly said a word. When they'd pulled up to The Miner's Arms, it was too late, even for a lock-in sent from heaven.

Rich was as white as a sheet. "I don't know what that was; it had to be a vampire. It had to be. It was enormous. It had bitten a man's head clean off. It was more animal than humanoid. It was all muscle and teeth. First you, now this. It can't be what I think it is..." He'd shaken his head and then said, "I'll be in touch." And that was that. Five hundred quid and no chance of being caught by the Benefit Bastards.

The welcoming stench of cigarettes, alcohol, and the undertone of vomit, greeted Sid when he opened The Miner's door. The lads were all watching a repeat of Tarrant on the old set. Kevin Ackroyd tended the bar, engaging the one and only Arthur Peasley in conversation.

"Gentlemen, what can I get you to drink?" cried the flushest man on Teesside.

Kevin looked at Arthur, who returned the same look. It was a look that a man would give if he witnessed a pig flying or a fifth wedding anniversary in Middlesbrough.

"I take it you went out with that weird vampire fella last night, then?" enquired Kev.

"Five hundred quid says I did!"

Kevin waited to see the colour of Sid's money before pouring out three pints of Bolton. He handed the two beers to his patrons and then took a sip of the beer bought for him.

"Good health," toasted Sid.

They all took a long, enjoyable draught of the fine beer. The three connoisseurs savoured the goodness of ale. Arthur was the first to come out of his ale-induced trance. "What did you get up to last night? We were surprised you weren't in here, to tell you the truth."

"Well, it happened to be the easiest five hundred quid I've ever earned. We went out looking for some more vampires, but ended up going to some park and I fell asleep."

He wasn't technically lying; part of his Gay Defence System involved his brain re-writing past encounters. Sid, even under regressive hypnotherapy, would never remember looking eye-to-eye with the dogger's body part. "Next thing you know, we're speeding away and this 'thing' is chasing us."

He took a large, final swig of ale and pointed to his glass. Kevin obliged.

"You mean one of them vampires?" asked Kevin sliding over Sid's second pint.

"Well, I didn't actually see it. By the time I'd come to me senses, we were getting the fook out of Dodge." He lit up another Turk and, amazingly, offered them round. The two gents turned down the cigarettes that contained thirteen per cent powdered cancer. "That Rich fella proper shat himself, like. He said the thing was proper massive and had bitten the head off one of them dirty bastards who goes into them woods for a shaggin'."

"That's pretty scary, like," said Kevin. "Them other vampires sounded like nasty buggers, but at least they were normal size."

Arthur nodded in agreement. "You're right. I'm gonna increase my karate training." He threw a few devastating punches in mid-air.

The air felt pain.

SHEILA FISHMAN SHUFFLED THE PAPERS IN FRONT OF HER. It'd been a long day and it was only eleven a.m. She loved and loathed her job with equal passion. She loved the feeling of taking the illegally acquired money from lying, lazy, worthless scum, but she loathed having to speak politely to the losers who contributed nothing to the world; parasites in the lower bowel of society. If she had her way, she'd castrate the non-working class so they couldn't produce any more Hellspawn, which they did at an alarming rate.

The job was everything to Sheila, but her beloved cats came a close second. She loved her cats and they loved her, but this wasn't the time to be thinking about her cats. This was work time, and she was wasting taxpayer's money by thinking non-work cat thoughts.

Back to business: Sid Tillsley.

She'd circled the date in her calendar a month ago, after being assigned the lowest of all the lowlifes in this disease-ridden pox of a town. She'd seen him in here before, being interviewed by that cretin, Wally Harwood. She hated Harwood. She knew he was a crook, but she couldn't prove it. If she could, she'd have him sacked in a heartbeat.

That would be something, to take a cheating man down at sixty-four, just before he claimed his pension. Too many people were paid too much for doing a bad job. There were no decent people left in the world. Sid Tillsley, the fat, smelly excuse for a man, was now in her hands, and by God, he was going to pay. She'd force him into a job and make him pay back every penny he'd taken from the government illegally.

IT WAS ONE-THIRTY. Sid had enjoyed about six pints of Bolton with his friend Arthur. Debates were volleyed back and forth, and it had been an enjoyable time for Sid who had completely forgotten about his forthcoming benefit interview.

"Well, Sid, I thank you for the drinks that you've bought me on this fine day, but I have some jobs to attend to, so I best be on my way, baby."

"See ya, mate."

Arthur gave Sid a friendly pat on the back, which the big fella couldn't even think of taking the wrong way, and Arthur Peasley left the building. Kevin joined Sid after he'd finished cleaning some glasses.

"So, what you got planned for the rest of the day?" asked the landlord, eyeing the wad of cash protruding from Sid's ultra-tight jeans.

Sid scratched his head. "Don't know, but I swear I've got to do something this afternoon, and I think it's something which isn't enjoyable, either."

"What about washing? I doubt you enjoy that, and you reek. What have ya been doing this morning, like?" asked the nasally assaulted barman.

"Been graftin,' mate. I was helping Jock the Turk make kebabs, like."

Kev pulled a face. "That's a filthy job, mon. Them donners are horrible things. Big, dirty, elephant legs, and I'm sure that Jock's are far worse than your everyday kebab. He's a reet dirty bastard, he is."

"He's a good lad," defended Sid, who liked anyone who paid him illegally. "His donner kebabs are just a little more continental than most. 'Extravagant animals' is what he calls them."

"Extravagant? What? Bloody German shepherds?" joked Kevin.

"Nah, mon, but I didn't know you could get a whole hedgehog in a mincer."

Kevin giggled but didn't say anything.

"Shit the bed!" exclaimed Sid, suddenly.

"Ah man, not again! Get in that bathroom and sort yourself out, ya dirty bastard! It ain't bloody right for a man of your age to have so many bloody accidents!"

"What?" asked Sid confused. "Oh no, not that, well...I don't think I have, like. I've just remembered, I've got another fooking Benefit Bastard interview—and it ain't with Wally Harwood!"

Kev rushed the big man into action. "Hurry up, mon. You need a change of clothing at the very least. You stink!"

Sid scrambled out of the door at a slightly quicker pace than normal.

SHEILA LOOKED AT HER WATCH. It was two o'clock, and it was time. She'd arranged the office in the most intimidating fashion. Grey walls were scientifically proven to be the most depressing. It looked like an interrogation room. She'd even hung a massive mirror which the scumbags might think is a two-way one, like in the movies. Her desk was massively oversized, as was her executive chair. The interviewee's chair was a tiny stool, designed to make the suspect as uncomfortable as possible.

It was two o'clock, and he was late. She wouldn't show leniency. She wouldn't show mercy. Sid Tillsley was about to meet his maker. "Mr. Sid Tillsley?" she yelled. "Mr. Sid Tillsley!"

SID AMBLED UP TO THE FRONT ENTRANCE OF THE JOB CENTRE. He'd managed to change into another pair of jeans, a *Police Academy 4: Citizens on Patrol* T-shirt, and his killer-look leather jacket. A whole can of deodorant from Wilkos had done a poor job of hiding the smell of rotten hedgehog meat, but this was probably because Sid, in his mad rush, had bought hairspray. His forest of armpit hair wouldn't be moving for the next two months.

He burst through the front door. The quick amble had built up a lot of sweat, which was competing with the smell of hedgehog.

"MR. SID TILLSLEY!"

The roar ripping through the building caused children to cry into their mother's laps. He followed the voice until he found Sheila Fishman's office. A second bellow of "TILLSLEY!" informed him that he'd found the right room. Sid stubbed out a Turk and put it in his pocket for later consumption. Regaining his composure, he knocked and entered.

Moments later, his ample frame perched comically on the stool, as he weighed up his adversary. She wasn't bad looking, if he squinted a bit. A bit rough around the face, and the lenses of her glasses made her eyes appear to be the size of swan's eggs, but nevertheless, if she did a sexy strip like a secretary...yeah! The wrinkles didn't matter, and at least she nearly had a full head of hair. She wore frumpy clothes, but they didn't hide the considerable pair hiding under the stripy jumper.

When all was said and done, she'd look cracking when he was pissed.

"I'm Sheila Fishman, Mr. Tillsley. I'm your new case worker."

"Call me Sid," he said, acting cool.

"Down to business, Mr. Tillsley. I believe you're well aware of the drill by now. You've been through it more times than anyone else in the UK. However, Mr. Tillsley, you've not gone through this drill with me," she said, with a glint in her eye.

"I'm looking forward to it already, Sheila," said Sid, misreading the glint.

"That's Miss Fishman to you, Mr. Tillsley. Do not use my first name."

Sid's eyes twinkled. "So there's no Mr. Fishman, I presume?"

"Presume nothing. That is of no importance to you. I remind you to keep your simple mind on the business at hand. Previous work experience, Mr. Tillsley?"

"Now, Sheila..."

"Miss Fishman," corrected Miss Fishman.

"Sheila, we have these interviews regular, like. I think you'll find all the details in me file, pet." He winked at her. She'd like that.

SHEILA'S COMPLETE DISDAIN FOR SID TURNED RAPIDLY INTO HATRED. *Pet!* Not only was he a lying, cheating, thieving benefit fraudster, he was also a sexist pig. "How many jobs have you had in the past five years?"

Sid scratched his chins. "Well, first there was..."

Sheila's eyes opened wide for a moment. Was he really going to slip and confess to having worked? It couldn't be this easy, surely.

"...me angina. That played up for a while."

Sheila tried not to look crestfallen.

"It's been a proper hard five years, like. Me back has given me a world of discomfort over the last three, that's for sure. There was a brief spell where I...hang on. You said five years, didn't ya?"

"Yes, I did."

"Reet, I have actively been seeking employment for the past five years," he said officially.

She knew he hadn't worked, but it still made her feel sick hearing the words come out of his despicable mouth. "How many interviews have you had in the last five years, Mr. Tillsley?"

"Well, there's been a few interviews, like."

Sheila shuffled through Sid's rather extensive file. "Let's see, shall we? You had an interview for a position for 'Meet and Greet' at Asda supermarket. Apparently, your previous employment officer thought you'd be suitable for the job because of your familiarity with the local neighbourhood. You weren't offered the job. Why?"

"Oh, aye, I remember that." He gave a nervous laugh. "I didn't quite get to the interview on that one."

"Really?" said Sheila with a hint of excitement. Was this a chink in his armour? If he was in a fit state of health and failed to attend an interview, then he might be liable for paying some of the money back. "So, you didn't attend?"

"Well, I did kinda, like. I was walking to the manager's office at the back of the store when fate played a cruel trick on young Tillsley. There was a tasting stand for that new white-and-brown creamy-booze shite that had hit the shops. You know, the one with the fancy bottle that you lasses drink?"

"What has that got to do with anything?" asked Sheila impatiently, chewing the inside of her mouth to ribbons.

"Well, I tried a few, like."

"So?"

"The lady on the counter said that it was the most sick that she'd ever seen come out of one person," said Sid, beaming with pride.

"OK, OK, OK!" Sheila put her head in her hands. "Let's just ignore the past five years. Let's pretend that you want to find a job." Sid attempted to interrupt. "No, Mr. Tillsley, please. Let's just pretend. What skills or characteristics do you possess that could help you to find a job, any job?"

Sid took a deep breath. "Well, I'm quite good at darts, I suppose."

Sheila gave him a blank look. "I'm sorry, I think I misheard you. Did you say darts?"

"Aye, pet. Had a 137 finish, last year."

Sheila let the "pet" go because this was another chance for her to get the scumbag. If he'd won money playing in darts tournaments, then he may have earned enough so that he was claiming benefit illegally. "Are you a successful darts player?"

"Aye, pet."

Yes! Sheila picked up a biro and prepared to take notes. "How well have you done in the last year, Mr. Tillsley?"

"Been me best year. Came fifth in The Miner's Open," he said proudly.

"How much did you win in this tournament?"

Sid gave a triumphant smile. "Quite a prize actually, Sheila. Twenty-four beef burgers, two pounds of pork sausages, and mince— both beef and turkey." He gave her a knowing nod.

"And that's...it?" she asked, all hope vanishing.

He looked around to make sure no one was listening. "No, there was also a big bit of frying steak in there." He gave her a wink, leant back, and rubbed his belly.

"Take a five-minute break, Mr. Tillsley. I need to speak to my superiors."

As soon as he was out of earshot, Sheila took a stress-ball from her desk and squeezed it, desperately trying to relieve some of the tension of being in a room with twenty stone of scum. The stress-ball didn't work, so she went up a level by taking out a cuddly teddy bear from the bottom drawer of her desk and violently stabbing it with her biro until there was nothing left but stuffing. She felt better.

Sheila picked up the telephone and asked reception to let the oaf back in. Just the sight of him walking through the office door made her blood boil.

"Mr Tillsley, you're forcing me to be frank. We believe you're claiming benefit while working." She gave him the most serious of looks, one normally reserved for convicted murderers or dog owners.

"How dare you, Miss Fishman? I'm an upstanding member of this town."

Sheila was having none of it. "Everybody in this town knows you, Tillsley. Everyone knows you can be found wasting tax payers' money in that hole, The Miner's Arms. Everybody knows you'll do odd jobs, door work, anything for money, cigarettes or any of the other disgusting habits you've picked up in the last forty-six years of your worthless life!" She got slowly to her feet, her voice rising with her blood pressure. "And the icing on the cake? No one will bear witness to your lying, cheating ways. None of your fellow scumbags will say a word against you."

Tillsley attempted to speak, but there was no chance of that happening. She advanced on him.

"You're all in it together, aren't you? You, that pretty boy Peasley, Rathbone, and that Brian Garforth. I hate Garforth. Everyone knows how he skives maintenance payments for all the little bastards he's released into that overcrowded cesspool!"

Sheila was only inches from Sid's ear when she finally realised her temper had truly run away from her. She was bright pink and sweat poured down her face. A silence filled the office. It was a big silence, but not a long silence. It was big because the silence filled the entire floor of the Job Centre, which had heard Sheila's rant. She smoothed down her skirts and sat down behind her desk.

"I apologise," she said calmly. "I shouldn't have let my temper get the better of me. It was unprofessional and rude. Please accept my sincere apologies. If you wish to make a complaint, I can give you the address of our complaints department." She offered a microsecond smile before awaiting his response.

"Ah, pet. Guess the 'boro are playing at home, like?" Again, he gave a wink.

"I'm sorry, I do not follow."

"'Boro at home, lass. Painters are in. You know, the Woman's Curse!"

Sheila threw the first thing that came into her hand. Sid ducked, and her nameplate smashed through the glass of her office door.

"Shit the bed, pet! Calm yourself down! Don't let the hormones beat ya!"

The sexist pig dodged a flying stapler, but Mr. Croaker, her supervisor, who had opened her office door to investigate the breaking of glass, did not.

Never had Sheila seen a man drop so fast. Not in her wildest dreams of sadism could she have conjured up such an unlikely act of brutality. After going into spasms, he passed out, moments later, a white foam formed at his lips.

Oh, she was in big trouble now.

That big silence turned up again.

"Did that hit him in...?" Tillsley asked, crossing his legs.

"Yes."

"Is his leg stuck to his...?"

"Yes."

"What are the chances of that?"

"Mr. Croaker?" When she realised that nothing else was going to be thrown, a young, blonde girl put her head around the door. She edged herself through slowly. "Sheila, what have you done?"

Sheila took her eyes away from Mr. Croaker's mangled private region to look at her work colleague. "I...I..."

"She went fooking mental and stapled that lad's knackersack!" said Sid.

"I think you better leave, Mr. Tillsley," said the secretary. "We'll contact you later if an inquiry is necessary." The lady ushered Tillsley out. He stepped over Mr. Croaker, shaking his head. "I hope he didn't want kids."

"Thank you, Mr. Tillsley.

Sheila could hear Tillsley all the way down the corridor, telling all and sundry, "She stapled the poor bastard's knackersack!"

17

IT HAD FINALLY ARRIVED: LADIES' NIGHT. But this was not the regular fortnightly ladies' evening with twenty pence off a pint of Bolton Bitter for the fairer sex, oh no. This particular event was saturated with glamour, beauty, and sex appeal. It was so special, so prestigious, that Sid was banned from using the ladies' as a "shit-stop."

Kevin Ackroyd was a very excited man. He didn't often get the opportunity to cast his eye over Middlesbrough's finest maidens who would be crammed in here tonight. Usually, he only got to see Mrs. Ackroyd, and she wasn't speaking to him after he'd stuck *Load in My Ring* in the VHS player. Bloody hell, she'd only just stopped beating him.

However, tonight was a night when ladies, far and wide, came to one place, and that one place was his place. And in typical Northeast tradition, they would turn up wearing, at most, nothing. These red-hot firecrackers were horned up at the best of times, and tonight, when they saw what Kev had lined up for them, they'd explode in a sexual frenzy! If Kev were capable, he would have experienced blood flow. But, he wasn't, so he cleaned the pipes on the Bolton instead.

And why were they going to explode? Because tonight, for three quid a ticket, "Obi-Dong Kenobi and his Pink Lightsabre" were going to transform the ladies into animals as vivacious and sexually terrifying as the audience of a Daniel O'Donnell concert. He'd be the first male stripper to appear on the Smithson Estate. Kev had done his market research, and the results were quite satisfactory: Sid said he wouldn't knock the stripper out. Kev had always considered himself a bit of a trailblazer; he was the first landlord to put a condom machine in the bogs. He still hadn't sold any, but it was trailblazing, nonetheless. Ladies' Night was to begin at seven, and Obi-Dong would do his ten-minute act at about half ten. It was going to be a rip-roarer!

Arthur and Rathbone entered the pub. Arthur was dressed in a black jumpsuit this time, the sequins sparkling almost as brightly as his pearly whites. His thick black hair was styled to perfection as always. He looked a million dollars. Rathbone looked the same as ever, a greasy, little, horrible bastard.

"Gentlemen!" said Kev. "I hope you're excited about this evening's entertainment? How may I serve you on this fine afternoon?"

"You're unusually perky today," said Rathbone. "You're normally a miserable twat." Rathbone was good at taking away people's happy face.

A seething Kev pulled two pints of Bolton. "Four pounds."

"How fooking much?" said an outraged Rathbone.

"That ain't on, man!" backed up Arthur.

Kev's smile returned. His two favourite past-times: annoying people and making money. "Relax, gentleman. It's only for tonight, and we have an official late license. An extra two measly pence on a pint of ale doesn't really come close to the price of pulling a beautiful lady, does it? Believe me. Tickets have sold like hot cakes."

"How many, man?" asked Arthur.

Kev gave a nod and a wink. "Let's just say about fifteen."

Arthur's perfect eyebrows hit the ceiling.

Rathbone said, "S'all right I s'pose." But, Kev could see the glint in his greasy eyeball.

"It won't disappoint, lads," assured the pimp-daddy.

"KEVIN! SOMEONE'S ON THE PHONE!" The yell filled the bar and carried out onto the street, shattering a car window. Kev cowered. There was a reason he was so miserable.

"Coming, dear!" he tried to yell sweetly. He pointed at the two punters. "You bastards better not steal anything," he growled, before running up the stairs to grab the telephone.

"Miner's Arms?" he answered.

"Ackroyd. It's Terry Fenton 'ere," replied a gruff Geordie accent.

"Who?"

"Terry Fenton. You know, Obi-Dong Kenobi."

Recognition dawned on Kev. "How are ya, big fella? You ready to unleash the beast?" The barman let out an excited chuckle.

"Sorry, boss, hate to do this to ya, like, but I gotta cancel. The Pink Lightsabre will be out of action for a while."

"What do you mean?" A cold sweat washed over the panicked landlord.

"How do I put it?...I've got nobrot," replied the unsubtle, wounded Jedi.

"But...but...you can still perform, can't ya? You must be able to perform?" asked a desperate party organiser.

"I'm pissing puss, mon! I can hardly swing it around now, can I? If I drop it in a lasses' sherry, it's gonna look like Baileys by time I pull it out!"

Kev was well and truly up shit creek. There was going to be at least fifteen of Middlesbrough's muckiest, all baying for the mightiest cock the North of England had to offer.

"HOPE IT FALLS OFF, YA BASTARD!" yelled Kev before slamming the phone down. This was trouble. Big trouble. He'd just six hours until Ladies' Night, and the entertainment had gone down the shitter (or rather down the clap-clinic). Fifteen birds at three quid a pop meant there was no way a refund was on the cards, and they'd be demanding a donkey-dick at ten-thirty. Alternative entertainment was the only choice.

Six hours...

SHEILA FISHMAN FED ALFRED HIS FRESH TUNA STEAK, sourced from the local fishmonger. She'd cut the skin off because Alfred preferred his tuna steaks without the skin. She'd prepared the other nine cats' meals just as meticulously. It took her an hour to prepare their evening dinner, and it had to be served just the way they liked it.

Sheila Fishman lived in a two-bedroom terrace on the outskirts of the Smithson Estate with her ten male cats: Alfred, Bartholomew, Edward, Graham, Marcus, Perseus, Quentin, Reginald, Ulysses, and Wilson. The house was extraordinarily clean considering it housed ten animals, although Sheila Fishman would castrate any man who dared call them "animals." To Sheila, they were little furry people.

The cats' food was served on the dinner table, which Sheila headed. When the cats had finished eating, they left the table accordingly, but Sheila didn't care about their lack of table manners. Her darlings could do anything they wanted, bless them. She finished her dinner and gathered the plates, taking them into the kitchen for washing up. It was like any other day, except Sid Tillsley had ruined this day.

Sid Tillsley was everything that a cat was not. Sid Tillsley was the reason she might lose her job. Sid Tillsley was the reason Mr. Croaker had his testes stapled to his leg and was awaiting surgery. Sid Tillsley was the reason that Alfred may soon be eating tinned tuna instead of tuna steaks. Sid Tillsley was a sexist, arrogant pig of a man.

Tonight, at The Miner's Arms, she'd have her revenge. Tonight, she'd find out where Tillsley was working.

HE CIRCLED THE FAT OAF. How a human could let itself fall into that condition still amazed him. Gabriel leapt, and he disintegrated into ash through the fat man's fist. Gunnar's world collapsed. He ran.

Gunnar awoke. He lived that moment every second of the day, whether asleep or awake. It was about three o'clock in the afternoon, six hours until nightfall. Tillsley was revealed to him at last. At least the Lamian Consilium had given him something of use—a name.

Tonight, Tillsley would begin his slow journey into the afterlife.

SID TILLSLEY LOOKED IN THE MIRROR AND LIKED WHAT HE SAW. He was looking good, extremely good, in fact. The leather jacket shone in the neon-lit toilet of The Miner's Arms. His Esso Tiger Token T-shirt gleamed. He'd even managed to get the curry stain out. Ladies' Night was going to get much more than it was bargaining for.

BRIAN GARFORTH LOOKED IN THE MIRROR AND LIKED WHAT HE SAW. He was looking good, extremely good, in fact. His red tailored suit contained a packet of little blue pills, hidden carefully, like a concealed pistol. Brian Garforth was ready for war.

ARTHUR PEASLEY LOOKED IN THE MIRROR AND LIKED WHAT HE SAW. He was looking good, extremely good, in fact. He was indeed a beautiful, beautiful man. Sideburns cultivated to perfection, black, thick hair swept back with lazy grace. He'd been blessed with his Daddy's good looks, not to mention his singing voice. Arthur was dressed to impress. A white jumpsuit, tight in all the right areas, gave an insight into his religion and his lady-killing abilities. He was gargantuan. At least fifteen chicks were out there tonight. If he didn't leave with at least three of them, it'd be a disappointment. He threw a few karate punches to warm up, checked out perfection one last time, and left the building.

PETER RATHBONE LOOKED IN THE MIRROR. He was looking like a greasy, horrible, little bastard. An extremely greasy, horrible, little bastard, in fact. His disgustingly thin hair fell limply over his pitted, oily skin. His poorly fitting clothes were stained, ripped, and stinking. He hated everyone and everyone hated him. He'd no chance of pulling a woman or making any new friends. Should be a good night.

FRANCO STOLONI had been given what would normally have been the mundane task of tracking a human. It would've been his worst job for years if it wasn't for the exceptional circumstances. A man that could kill vampires was unheard of. He hadn't heard the story of Sparle and Remo Elscachius before. That was kept quiet outside the Lamian Consilium for reasons he didn't know. Ironically, for a spy, he hated secrets.

Out of all the vampires walking the earth, he looked more like a human than any other. Short, and of slight frame for a vampire, but still large for a man. He wasn't as fair as his brethren, but he'd still be considered a model by human standards. His eyes, for some reason, lacked luminescence, which was the most startling feature of an immortal. If war broke out between the races, Franco Stoloni would be a deadly weapon.

He was given strict orders from Michael, whom he'd never seen so agitated. He was terrified of Michael, and only a fool would be afraid to admit it. A cold shiver ran up his spine as he considered the consequences of failing the mission. Blending in wouldn't help him if Michael wanted him dead.

"Follow him closely for one night and do not arouse suspicion," Michael had instructed. "We've reason to believe Reece Chambers has contacted him. Chambers is pathetic, a shadow of his ancestors, but he can get to us through this man. Find out his character, his motives, and his weaknesses. There will be great reward for this, Franco. Failing is something you should not consider."

Franco shuddered. Failing. He knew what would happen if he did. Michael had never threatened him like that before. Tillsley must have him spooked. Tonight, he'd make contact with the target. Franco had watched the man over the last couple of days and was seriously wondering if he justified Michael's cause for concern. The human had spent most of his time inebriated in The Miner's Arms, and on two occasions, he'd had the most disgusting of accidents. Nevertheless, orders were orders, and tonight, he'd discover Sid Tillsley's true character.

Kevin Ackroyd was in desperate trouble. Desperate, desperate trouble. He was without a stripper. In any normal pub, in any normal town, this wouldn't be a problem. However, this was Middlesbrough, and this was The Miner's. You didn't find your average lady in The Miner's. When they wanted cock on show, by God, they wanted cock on show. He had two hours to find a guy brave enough to flop it about on stage in front of some of the toughest tarts of the Northeast. It was going to be difficult...especially because he didn't want to spend a lot of money.

18

IT WAS SEVEN O'CLOCK. It was Ladies' Night. Kevin Ackroyd polished the last of the plastic champagne flutes. Every lady would get a complimentary glass of Yorkshire's finest champagne for the complimentary price of 99p. Though he'd only sold fifteen tickets, he'd polished thirty flutes. He'd found a replacement for Obi-Dong Kenobi, and he was feeling lucky.

The ladies' toilet was fully functional, and Kevin had invested in some potpourri which he'd placed seductively in an ashtray on top of the khazi. He himself was in his finest of fineries: brown corduroys, ironed and clean, and a paisley silk shirt, which billowed with each of his sexy flourishes. His dome had a shine on it akin to Willy Thorne's. He'd never felt so ravishing. The door opened and his heart fluttered. What beauty could this be?

"Maggie! What a fantastic surprise," wooed the barman.

"Fook off, Ackroyd. I'm only here to see how big that stripper is and whether he's worth shaggin'. Pint of Bolton." The Middlesbrough beauty took a seat by the bar, and what a beauty she was. Fitting twenty-eight stone into the skimpiest of outfits would be a feat of engineering, and unfortunately, Maggie wasn't an engineer. "And giv' us a pack of pork scratchings and a Mars bar and a Baileys and a Twix and another pint."

"Someone's flush this month?"

She let out a loud, guttural belch that Kevin could smell from four yards away. "Spat out another couple of sprogs last week, so I'm raking it in this month." She lit up a cigarette.

"Twins? Jackpot! Who's the lucky father?" asked Kevin, bringing her the chocolate, scratchings, and drinks.

"It's either Reg—that lad with the Nova SR—or it might be John—the lad with the fake arm. Thinking about it, it could even be Jimmy who was put in nick for kicking that Kosovan to death. Or possibly Nigel..." she reeled off half the Smithson Estate. Although, it was somewhat disturbing, Kev couldn't help but be impressed that she's gone through Middlesbrough's most virile studs in a week. "...or Mickey and his Magic Raspberry. Get us a half pint of Tía Maria."

The door opened and in walked Arthur Peasley, possibly the sexiest man in the world. Maggie wolf whistled.

Arthur looked nervous, taking on a defensive karate stance.

"If it isn't Arthur Peasley, himself! Fook me, I'm slipping off me chair here I'm so fooking w—"

"A pint of ale?" asked Kev with impeccable timing.

"Yeah, man," said Arthur, edging round Maggie at a safe distance. She looked ready to pounce at any second. When Maggie was out of earshot, he whispered to Kev. "If this is the standard of chicks you've got lined up, then I ain't gonna be a happy man. You dig, baby?"

Kevin did. He was well aware of the deadly karate skills Arthur had learnt from his daddy. Nevertheless, he was not a worried man. Fifteen ladies! The law of averages were in his favour. "Don't you worry. This place is gonna be heaving with fanny by the end of the night."

Maggie gave a dirty laugh. "Me fanny's heaving already, lads."

IT WAS HALF EIGHT, a few hours before the stripper arrived to excite the crowd. Most of the patrons who'd bought tickets were here, soaking up the atmosphere. The complimentary champagne had been a huge success with seven glasses already sold. This was turning into a right little earner. Kev surveyed the crowd. Maggie was near paralytic already. She'd only be able to handle another eight to ten pints at best. Her skirt had rolled up into a belt, and her monstrous gut hung over it giving the impression that she was half-naked. Tarrant had been turned off for the evening, and the lads had to occupy themselves another way, so were trying their luck with Maggie for a quick jump in the gents. Kev smiled; he was like a Northern cupid.

Three ladies surrounded Arthur Peasley and were too tasty to be locals. Garforth was in as well, sleazy little bastard. He had a gaggle from the local hospital with him. All were married, but he'd probably done the lot of them before, the absolute bounder. Kev had seen him with his hand on a few buttocks. He wasn't a hundred per cent sure, but he thought he'd seen him come back from the toilets with one of his harem. She'd bought a pack of extra strong mints from the bar afterwards. Kev had slapped a quid on the price, seeing the desperation in her eyes.

There were a few unexpected guests in the crowd. In particular, an extra group of girls he hadn't expected, all top-notch lasses, but they had one of them there poofter-types with them. Kevin didn't consider himself homophobic. For a Northern man, he was extremely liberal, having once served a male synchronised swimmer a half a lager. What he was concerned about was the imminent arrival of a Mr. Sid Tillsley.

There were also a few others from the estate, which was nice to see.

He felt good about bringing the community together like this. There were a few strangers too. There was an old battleaxe giving the men in the room evils. She'd only bought one small sherry all evening. There was another stranger in The Miner's, a tall fella Kev had never seen before, a good-looking lad, no doubt out for a jump.

All in all, Kev was a happy landlord.

IT WAS NINE-THIRTY. The Miner's Arms was completely packed for even more locals had joined the fray. There were about twenty-five women in there now. All of the newly arrived ladies were friends of Maggie, and unfortunately for the boys, of similar ilk. Maggie was hammered. Her top was now permanently around her belly, revealing breasts that pointed straight to Hell. Three of her mates had already been outside with various gentlemen from the establishment. The alley behind The Miner's often witnessed acts of love; a few more quid to these beauties' pockets was just a by-product of the majesty of the creation of life.

Arthur Peasley was on fire, lined up for a *ménage à quatre*, a mighty feat he'd only pulled off twice in the past year. If there was one man who could obtain a hat trick of lady-foursomes, then Arthur Peasley was that man.

Brian Garforth wasn't sure what he fancied next. He'd already serviced all the ladies from the hospital on previous encounters, and he could fall back on one of them if need be. Maggie's mates were not his style, although the ringing of last orders did strange, strange things to a man's penis.

Sid was on the road to ruination. As normal, he'd sunk a considerable amount of ale in a considerably short amount of time while smoking an incredible amount of tabs. He was smoking a Bangladeshi "Ring of Fire." He'd earned four hundred smokes for helping Dilshan, the owner of the Smithson's only curry house, put a competitor out of business using terrorist tactics: a dirty bomb. Sid Tillsley was that dirty bomb, the detonator: Dilshan's extremely potent Sprout Phaal. Sid had to eat it and then use the competitor's facilities. The plan worked perfectly, except for a couple of early misfires.

"How do, Brian?" asked the big fella. "You got your eyes on 'owt special?"

Brian shook his head. "Nah, mon. There's a lot more lasses than I thought they'd be though, but I'll probably stick to one of the hospital lot. I haven't done the one with the glass eye in a while. How about you then? You seen 'owt?"

Sid smiled. "In fact, I have, mate."

A look of realisation spread across Brian's face. "You ain't gonna do one of Maggie's mates, are ya?" He shook his head. "You'll get nobrot and a bairn for your troubles. It ain't worth—"

Sid cut him off. "Don't be daft. I've got standards you know."

"Aye, I remember the prison guard. I'm sorry I doubted ya," he said sarcastically.

"There's a reet ol' crowd in here tonight, ain't there, Brian? Quite a few people I ain't seen before, like."

Brian looked over the crowd. "Aye, you're reet, Sid. I haven't seen this many in here for donkey's years." The group with the young gay guy were getting closer, a little too close for comfort. Brian didn't consider himself homophobic. For a Northern man, he was extremely liberal, having once sat through *Prescilla Queen of the Desert* without burning down Middlesbrough cinema afterwards. However, he didn't want a "Sid incident" tonight, and the poor gay lad didn't deserve a Sid incident either.

"Look at that fella over there, Brian," said Sid, pointing a giant finger. "He's dressed very flamboyantly, don't you think?"

Brian winced. Flamboyant wasn't the word for skintight white trousers, a Hawaiian blouse, and an excess of orange cover up.

"He's doing reet for himself. Look, he's got three birds on the go!"

"Oh aye, Sid. Bet he's a devil with the ladies, like," said Brian. "I'll buy you a beer, come on."

"Hang about, Brian. He's got a funny walk, too, hasn't he? He really uses his hips to strut his stuff. Guess that tells the lady where the power comes from." Sid demonstrated with some lewd thrusting movements. "He's got very dark eyes as well. I bet the ladies go for that sort of thing, Brian, the mystery man!"

Mascara, thought Brian. It was only a matter of time before all Hell broke loose.

"And who is this big brute of a man, then?" asked a voice which made Dale Winton sound like a 1980s action hero.

Brian groaned. The time all Hell broke loose was now. He called Kev over. "You may want to get an ambulance on standby."

"What are you on about? I've got people to—" Kevin clocked what Brian was talking about. In fact, the whole pub had stopped talking and watched as opposite ends of the spectrum came together: the unstoppable force and the immovable object, beauty and the beast, homo and hetero, a gay bloke and an idiot.

No one dared intervene. Everyone knew it'd make no difference if they did. There was nothing anyone could do now. Nature had to take its course. Nature was so cruel.

"I must say, that is an *adorable* T-shirt, you big, big bear, you!" He rubbed Sid's belly, the Esso Tiger stared back, demanding blood and for the wearer to buy more four-star.

Sid giggled. "I like your funny voice!"

The gay guy put his head under Sid T-shirt and blew a massive raspberry.

Sid looked confused, concerned...violated? No. Sid let out an almighty roar of laughter, giggling and clapping his hands.

The pub breathed a sigh of relief.

"Your shirt is pretty flowery," said Sid, "and I've never seen a tighter pair of trousers! Is that what the hip kids are wearing these days, like?"

"I like to think so. Some people are quite stiff and don't like the shirts I wear. How about you, mister? How *stiff* are you?"

A few of the knowing locals entered the foetal position.

"Me? I think I'm pretty hip with the kids, like. I may get myself a shirt like that. Reckon it'll suit me?" asked Sid hopefully.

The lad grabbed Sid's lapels. "I think anything would suit you, you big, sexy bear!" He picked up his Bacardi Breezer and took a long provocative swig from the bottle, licking the end of the bottle.

A big gasp went up from The Miner's Arms regulars.

"Don't want to miss a drop, eh?" asked Sid, pointing to the end of the bottle.

"I never waste a single drop." The lad winked before turning to dance with his girlfriends.

Sid laughed heartily. Every local in the pub breathed again. Brian took a big gulp of his Bolton Bitter.

"What a nice young fellow, Brian. I bet he doesn't stop shagging."

"Sid, I reckon you're right. Kev, two pints of Bolton, over here."

Kevin poured three pints and downed one in a single gulp before giving the patrons their refreshments. "On the house," he said to Brian, before whispering. "What happened there? Didn't Sid knock someone out for eating Prawn Cocktail crisps 'cos they had a pink packet?"

"Aye, but you know what he's like."

Kev counted his lucky stars and went off to serve another thirsty patron.

"Brian," said Sid, "you remember me telling you about that lass from the Benefit Bastards?" asked Sid.

Brian shuddered at the thought. Even though that Croaker was a Benefit Bastard, he didn't deserve a stapled sack. "Aye."

"She's here, like, and she's all dolled up and everything. I haven't dared say anything to her, yet. I'm just getting some Dutch courage down me first," he said, draining his twelfth pint of Dutch courage.

"Easy, big man! You need to stay a little sober so Little Sid is up to the task."

A smile slowly cracked Sid's face, and he gave Brian a slap on the back, which took the wind out of the much smaller man's sails.

Gathering his breath back, Brian asked, "Where is she?"

"Over there," said Sid, nodding, with surprising subtlety, towards Sheila Fishman.

Brian spat his beer out and was lucky the contents of his stomach didn't follow. She was more hideous than the nipple-cigarette-extinguishing monstrosity Sid dated a couple of years ago. She stood next to the broken jukebox scowling at anyone who ventured near. Her small sherry was untouched. She looked about fifty, but was probably younger and had just aged badly. She wore big, frumpy clothes and a short, balding, ultra-lesbian haircut. Nevertheless, Sid liked her, and he needed a jump more than any man on Teesside.

"She seems...nice, Sid. Why don't you go and talk to her?"

"I'm too shy, mon."

"Don't be daft. Buy a sherry and take it over. Ask her if she's enjoying the evening or if she likes animals or some shite like that. What harm can it do?"

Sid nodded. "You're reet, mon. You're absolutely reet. Kev, a pint of Bolton and a glass of your smallest sherry."

Kevin knew what he meant.

Sid Tillsley was on the prowl.

THIS WAS HELL. Franco Stoloni had been here for an hour now, and for an hour he'd wanted to rip out every throat in the room. He didn't fit in with this crowd at all. They were all hideous, except for a man with immaculate hair who reminded him of someone, and the three attractive women that were desperate for his loins. So far, he'd been groped dozens of times by a disgusting group of teenage girls. They all stank of sweat, semen, alcohol, and baby faeces. Three drinks had been spilt on him, and he'd passively inhaled about a thousand cigarettes.

He'd watched Tillsley drink himself into an inebriated state. The man was a machine and must have been on his seventeenth pint. First impressions were that he was an overweight, drunken idiot. After being in his presence for an hour, Franco came to the conclusion that Sid *was* an overweight, drunken idiot.

Franco could smell the cholesterol in Tillsley's blood. However, his heart pumped slow, strong, and steady like a bull elephant's. He was extremely overweight, but muscle bulged underneath the fat, hairy flesh. He was certainly a handful for a human, but to a vampire?

From overhearing conversations between patrons, he'd discovered that Tillsley claimed jobseeker's and disabled benefit because of various fabricated ailments. Franco could sense nothing wrong with Tillsley's heart, whatsoever. The man was an obvious liar, and a lazy liar at that. This was the weirdest assignment Franco had ever been given, but Michael was involved, so he'd report his findings, to the letter.

The oaf got up, looking very nervous for once. He was talking to the weasley man in the disgusting suit and greasy beard that reeked of sex. Both of them kept looking over at one of the most disgusting-looking creatures Franco had seen in his four hundred years.

This was a repugnant town at the best of times, and for someone to stand out in this way was impressive. The reason for Tillsley's nervousness became apparent when he attempted to make conversation with the woman. He was nervous because he was attracted to her, genuinely attracted! Franco shook his head. Four hundred years and humans could still shock him. Another weak link Tillsley possessed. This was all too easy.

TILLSLEY SNUBBED OUT A CIGARETTE. Sheila had called the police immediately when she'd discovered there was smoking on the premises. When she'd told the operator the address, he'd hung up the phone. Cowards! Tillsley picked up a glass of sherry in his massive hand and walked over towards her. Contact was inevitable but she couldn't help but scowl.

"I knew you'd be here, Tillsley. I knew this was your kind of disgusting entertainment." She spat each word with pure hatred. She was here to gain his confidence, but she couldn't hold back the rage.

"Howay, flower, I've bought you a drink. I'm here to make amends for what happened the other day at the office. How is the poor fella and his knackersack?"

"Stop saying knackersack!" Sheila knocked back the sherry from her own glass and then snatched the sherry from Sid. She wasn't a drinker, but these were unusual and distressing circumstances. "He'll be fine, as if you care. I could lose my job because of you."

Sid rubbed the rolls on the back of his head, awkwardly. "Come on, love, it wasna me who stapled his knackers together. I don't know why you hate me so much. I'll get you another sherry, pet."

She drank the other small sherry at the mention of stapled knackers. Before she could tell him where to stick his sherry, he'd ambled off to the bar.

He returned seconds later to give her the refill. "Look, if you get to know me, I ain't so bad. None of us are, really."

Maggie, the serial child bearer, took the opportunity to ask if anyone had ever seen a starfish wink.

"Well, most of us are decent folk, like," he smiled awkwardly, trying to cover up the horrific situation.

"Burdens on s-s-society, all of you!" Sheila finished the sherry. It was going straight to her head.

Tillsley disappeared and instantly reappeared with a large sherry. "Have a drink, love," he said. "When I saw you in that office the other day, it put a smile on my face. I said to meself, 'Sid, there's a lass who takes pride in her job.' I tell a lie. I actually said, 'Sid, there's a *beautiful* lass who takes pride in her job,'" he beamed at her.

"R...really?" she said, letting a small amount of rage drift away.

"Oh, aye. I really admire you, Miss Fishman. I'd love to do a job like yours, it's just that...I canna. I'm not the smartest of men. I ain't the brightest penny in the pile, not by a long way. All I can use, Miss Fishman, is me hands...and when you're crippled with a back like mine, then, Miss Fishman, the world is not your oyster." Maybe it was the booze talking, but he seemed genuine.

"I...didn't realise that you f-f-felt like that, Mishter Tillsley," she slurred, "I didn't realise at all. I thought...I thought you were scamming the government out of thousands." The corner of her heavily wrinkled mouth turned almost to a—a smile? She wasn't sure, she'd never done one before.

Sid casually reached down and tweaked her breast. "Howay the lads, mon!"

The glass in Sheila Fishman's hand shattered. The colour drained from her face, and ever so slightly, she began to shake.

"You all right, pet?"

The rate and the magnitude of the shaking increased. Her lips peeled back to reveal gritted, yellow teeth. Her veins visibly pumped blood up her neck, and colour returned to her face. Her eyes bulged with the increased pressure, and her face reddened to the same hue as Sid's.

He scratched his head. "Was I a little forward?

Her teeth started chattering as her shaking body accelerated to an unnatural frequency. "T...T...T..." she stuttered with each breath.

"I better be going, petal." Sid made a quick beeline for the gents.

"T...T...TILLSLEY!...YYYYOOOUUUUU CCCCCUUUUUN—"

19

"LADIES AND GENTLEMAN, IT IS TIME!" Kev roared the announcement from behind the bar, drowning out the obscenity echoing round the pub. There was rapturous applause and shouts from the women (and one man). Groans came from all the men not big into musical theatre. There was a general migration of the men towards the bar where they stood with their backs to the stage, which consisted of a cleared space near the broken jukebox, while the women fought to get to the front.

"Tonight, we have a replacement for the advertised Obi-Dong Kenobi..." He was interrupted with jeers and boos from the incensed women. He held up his hands. "Don't fear, ladies, we have a replacement and he is—MR. NEWCASTLE!"

Screams erupted from twenty-five women and one flowery shirt-wearing gentleman.

"Two Tribes" by Frankie Goes to Hollywood blared out at full volume from a stereo Kev had borrowed from a mate. A man about twenty-five years old jumped out from behind the bar dressed as a fireman. The women went wild. He jigged his way to the makeshift stage, while being groped and probed as he passed. To the music, he took off his hat to reveal an extremely good-looking young man. Kev beamed with pride as the ladies from the Smithson Estate roared in appreciation.

Maggie threw her knickers, and Mr. Newcastle skilfully dodged to one side. The knickers stuck to the wall behind him with a stomach-churning squelch.

Off came his overalls to leave a pair of tight, white trousers, rippling abs, and a beautifully sculpted torso. The baying women loved it. He danced around and the ladies pawed and molested him. After a few minutes of prancing, he ripped off his trousers in a magnificent finale. All that remained was an impressively filled thong above well-muscled legs. The women went wild. They cheered, they roared, and they screamed vulgarities against nature itself. The atmosphere was absolutely terrifying and the men rubbed their hands in glee. These ladies were going to be red hot after this.

The music ended in perfect time with his routine. Mr. Newcastle took a bow and started to pick up his equipment.

"Oi, ya bastard!" yelled a drunken harpy. "Where the fook do ya think you're going?"

"You arsehole! Get that thong off! We paid good fooking money to see cock!" screamed one of Maggie's drunken gaggle.

Poor Mr. Newcastle. He'd never worked a venue like The Miner's before.

"Sorry, I only strip down to the pants, like."

This incensed the women further.

"Kev!" called the stripper, desperately, "Kev, you knew the deal!"

Kevin Ackroyd looked on. He'd sold his soul to the Devil that night. He knew the score, all right. He'd thrown the poor lad to the wolves and was willing to face judgement for it before going to Hell. Kev slowly put out his hand in a fist. There was no emotion. He'd made peace with his own demons. Looking Mr. Newcastle straight in the eye, like a Roman Emperor, Kev turned his thumb down.

"COME 'ERE, YA BASTARD!"

One of Maggie's clan reached out and grabbed at Mr. Newcastle's thong. He recoiled too late, and as his pants were pulled away, a pair of socks fell out and rolled across the floor before coming to rest at Maggie's feet.

Silence fell upon the pub.

The gents who had their backs turned for the past five minutes had regained interest after hearing the fracas caused by the angry women. They knew what was coming.

Some say that the anticipation of pain is worse than pain itself.

That's bollocks.

Four of them attacked Mr. Newcastle. All grabbed for the G-string. There were screams of rage from the women and screams of fear from Mr. Newcastle. There was an almighty *twang!* as the G-string snapped under the ferocious tug of the 'boro ladies. Karma had come to Kevin Ackroyd, and it had come with vengeance.

"WHAT THE FOOK IS THAT!"

"THAT'S A FOOKIN' MAGGOT!"

"THAT'S A BABY-COCK!"

"THREE QUID TO SEE THAT WORM!"

Mr. Newcastle stood frozen. Perhaps it was smaller than average, but the fear that consumed him had materialised as an "inny," an "egg in the nest," translation: a tiny, tiny pecker. He stood transfixed by his attackers until the barstool hit him between the eyes.

The men roared with laughter and the women roared with sexual frustration. Chairs filled the air. Many were aimed at Ackroyd, many were aimed at the laughing men, and many were just thrown randomly in rage. Kev pulled down the shutter of the bar. He knew when the ship was going to sink and that time had come. All he could do now was watch the mob destroy his beloved pub. This would require rubber bullets, tear gas, and half of Middlesbrough's police force to calm it down. Glass shattered through the shutters, and Kev left for higher ground, hoping that this time they wouldn't set the place on fire.

GUNNAR IVANSEY APPROACHED THE MINER'S. He doubted whether this night would quell his sadness, but it didn't matter. As long as Tillsley died by his hand, he'd have revenge. Fifty yards from The Miner's, a figure approached from the opposite direction. He recognised the scent and couldn't help but laugh. He'd the pleasure of meeting this human once before. They arrived at the pub at the same time.

"Hello, Chambers." The human almost jumped out of his skin. So much for his ninja-like abilities.

"Who's that?" Chambers said. He looked closer and answered his own question. "Ivansey!"

Gunnar smiled. "Yes, the very same. Have you missed me?" Chambers didn't respond to Gunnar's taunt. "Tell me, Chambers, how many have you killed since the night I let you live?"

"Sixteen. Sixteen bastards I've sent back to Hell," he spat.

Gunnar laughed mockingly. "Sixteen! Fifteen years and you've managed to kill sixteen of my brothers and sisters. Chambers, you amaze me. How someone can disgrace an already pitiful line is beyond me. You're better than your father, though, if that's any consolation."

Chambers snarled, "What are you doing here?"

"The complete opposite of you, I should imagine. I'm here to kill Sid Tillsley in a slower and more excruciating way than I killed your father. Would you like to watch this time, as well?"

Gunnar grinned. The vampire hunter was fighting desperately to hold back tears of frustration. The helplessness of the human race was pathetic.

"What makes you think that you can manage the job?" Chambers managed. "Gabriel died with a single p—"

Gunnar choked the words out of him, lifting him a foot off the ground. His fangs had descended. He felt fear saturate the human's heart. His voice was as a guttural growl. "You're not worthy enough to mention his name. How that thing came to kill him, I do not know. How or why, I do not care. I will avenge my brother, tonight!"

He threw the pathetic hunter against the wall, leaving him a wheezing wreck on the ground. As Gunnar turned towards The Miner's, a window exploded out into the street.

"FOOKING SMALL-COCKED BASTARD!"

A barstool followed shortly after and struck him hard in the windpipe, crushing it. He fell to the ground and clutched at his neck.

Another stool smashed through the window of a car parked behind him. A dozen or so men herded out of the door and watched the carnage within. Through the crowd, Gunnar could see overweight, drunken, tattoo-covered, jewellery laden, behemoth-women rampaging uncontrollably.

Outside, he recognised Franco Stoloni. The Coalition were already on to Tillsley. Another two definitely weren't locals and were most certainly agents from the Hominum Order. And there...

Tillsley!

He was just yards away, a pint of beer in each hand. He was inebriated, terribly so, but it didn't matter, he'd feel pain no matter how much alcohol he consumed. Gunnar's throat had almost healed.

Chambers had managed to get to his feet, wheezing, struggling to stand tall. "Sid...S-Sid!"

"Eh!" Tillsley turned round. "Ah fook me, mon! Canna you leave me alone for one good piss-up? It's just started to get going in there, and I'm definitely on for a jump, like."

"There's...there's a vampire here to kill you!" Chambers spurted out in a single breath.

That got the local's attention. One horrendous individual with a greasy goatee and a vile red suit picked a bottle up from the ground, while another human, possibly the fairest human Gunnar had ever laid eyes upon, began an utterly ridiculous karate kata. Both took up their position behind Tillsley.

Gunnar rose to his feet. His throat had completely regenerated.

"Sid Tillsley!" he shouted in a booming tone. Everyone in the street turned round, while the women inside the pub continued to rampage. "Do you know what I am?"

"A tosser!" was shouted from the crowd, followed by giggling.

"No idea, mon." Sid scratched his head, and then his behind. "Actually, don't you play darts for The Tap and Spile?"

"He's a vampire, Sid," said Chambers.

"Really? All them years and I never knew. To be honest, I should have realised. He's a pale fella, and I only ever see him at night, and he's good at counting too."

"Aye, they love to count, our Sid," said the one in the red suit.

Gunnar ignored their drunken blabber. "I am Gunnar Ivansey."

"I thought your name was Stan."

"I'm here to kill you."

"I've been calling you Stan all these years. It's embarrassing when that happens."

"You killed my brother, Gabriel. I'm here to repay the debt...and to add to it!"

Tillsley looked at the weasel in the suit. "I thought Stan's brother was humped to death by that horny bull in Stockton-on-Tees?"

Enough, thought Gunnar. While Tillsley's head was turned, Gunnar charged in, firing four punches, the power of which was inconceivable to the human race.

Gunnar's eyes widened. He'd unleashed all he had...and the man had only stepped backwards. He still held on to his two beers.

Gasps filled the air.

"Did Sid just take a step back!" said someone in the crowd.

"Surely he stumbled," said another.

More murmurings from the crowd, "These vampires must be pretty handy if they can move Sid."

Tillsley gave his chin a wiggle and then wiped the trickle of blood from his lip with his sleeve. His eyes darkened. "Now then, lad, I nearly spilt me beer there." He looked down. "You're lucky the ground's dry, pal. Now then..." He finished both pints in single slugs and placed the glasses on the floor. "That's me warm up done. Now it's scrapping time."

Gunnar held up a guard. Tillsley was still standing, but how? Tillsley fired off a left jab and Gunnar's nose broke. His knees buckled, but he managed to keep his feet. In his heart, fear began to overtake hatred because his nose wasn't healing. It must be badly broken. Gunnar threw a couple of quick punches, but Tillsley dodged both with expert timing.

"Now, I'm gonna go easy on you, lad, 'cos you're upset about your brother and all. I'd be upset, too, if my brother was crushed to death by a giant set of bollocks. I'll wait 'til you get ye senses back, and we can call this a day."

The next jab Gunnar didn't even see. Blood poured into his right eye. Tillsley was so fast, there was nothing Gunnar could do. He spat the blood out that had gone up his nose and down the back of his throat. "If I can't kill you now, then I'll kill all the people you care for, you bastard!" Gunnar screamed the words in desperation.

"Reet, now you're playing silly buggers."

For Gunnar, the world went into slow motion. Tillsley stepped forward. The look on his face caused Gunnar to flinch. This was going to hurt.

Tillsley's left foot came down and he stepped in with the right. However, as he threw it, he slipped sideways.

Gunnar looked down. Tillsley had slipped on a pair of knickers, the contents of which caused Gunnar to wretch. But the punch was thrown and there was no calling it back. It sailed wild to Gunnar's right and landed square on the jaw of a spectator—Franco Stoloni!—who instantly exploded into a cloud of dust.

Gunnar stared into the space where Stoloni had once stood. He'd suffered the same fate as Gabriel. It was no fluke. Tillsley was scratching his head, looking slightly embarrassed. Gunnar had hit him with four punches that would've felled an oak, but he only stepped backwards. His jabs were more powerful than the impact of a car. There was no other choice.

Gunnar fled.

SID LOOKED PRETTY AWKWARD ROUND ABOUT NOW. Out of the spectators, he knew everyone apart from a couple of young lads. "I didn't mean to kill him, like." He rubbed the back of his neck awkwardly. "I tried to give that other wanker a proper smack, 'cos he deserved it."

Brian squatted over the remains of the vampire. He picked up a bit of ash and rubbed it between his thumb and forefinger. "Is this what happened after you hit them other vampires, Sid?"

Sid nodded. "Aye, mon, but them bastards deserved it. This poor fella was only down here for a few jars at Ladies' Night. He didna deserve this! He just wanted a jump!"

"Casualties of war, man," commiserated Arthur. "The undead want to start throwing their fists around, then someone's gonna get their ass kicked. He was one of them."

"Aye," said Rathbone. "I kicked fook out of three of the bastards, earlier in the gents. Caught 'em looking at me tackle."

"Shut up, Rathbone!" said numerous voices in the group.

Rich stepped forward. "Sid, he wasn't here for Ladies' Night. He was here to spy on you, possibly kill you. Just like the two agents, here, Rickson and Pervis."

One of them stood, stony-faced, whereas the ginger, geeky one looked as if he was about to burst into tears. Probably a student.

"Tell the gentlemen where you come from," commanded Rich.

The geeky one wilted immediately. "We're from the—"

"Shut up. Pervis!" said the stone-faced one. He pointed at Sid. "It doesn't matter who we are. What is important is *what you are*."

He was interrupted mid-flow by the sounds of police sirens. The riot inside the pub was escalating and Mr. Newcastle was in serious need of medical treatment and, unknown to him, an STD test. As in every corner of Middlesbrough, when sirens were heard, everyone legged it.

20

GUNNAR AWOKE FROM HIS TROUBLED SLEEP AND WINCED. His broken nose still hadn't healed. The human's power was immense. He was stronger than anyone Gunnar had ever fought. Stoloni—the poor worthless bastard. He wasn't a great loss to the vampire world. The wretch was born more like a human, but to die by accident...worse luck couldn't happen to an immortal. A month ago, Gunnar would've scorned any vampire killed by a human, but now, things were different.

He left his crypt and followed the stairs up to the grand hallway. It was one in the morning. He'd slept hours longer than usual with his body struggling to heal his wounds. He walked up the curving staircase and into his massive shower room, turned the power to full and the heat to high, and allowed the water to massage his body.

There was only one thing that mattered now: destroying Tillsley. He wouldn't rest until he'd ruined him completely. He needed to move fast because the oaf could die from ill health at any moment. The dilemma was: how?

He couldn't beat him in unarmed combat. The man was drunk and still could take blows that would knock out a bull elephant. Gunnar would be damned if he'd take a weapon to the man; his honour held him firm to that. But how could he hurt him? How could he hurt him so badly that he yearned for death? Gunnar recalled the fight. Chambers witnessed the ordeal, but he'd prove tricky to find. Chambers had eluded better than he for over a decade now. There were many people present who were obviously local, but there were definitely two from the Hominum Order.

They thought they'd blended in so perfectly, but Gunnar could've spotted them with his eyes closed. The stench of fear that'd emanated from the bespectacled ginger agent had given him away and his counterpart. The coward would scream everything that Gunnar needed to know. However, the fun Gunnar could have with his cool accomplice... The hard exterior would soon disappear.

Gunnar cut his shower short. There was work to be done. He dried off quickly and got dressed. He needed the names of the humans, and he knew exactly the vampire who would give him the answers he sought.

GUNNAR SPED ALONG TO RICKSON FLATLEY'S RESIDENCE, the human whom he desperately needed to...*interview*. He hadn't enjoyed what he'd just done, not in the slightest. The name he wanted came from Augustus, member of the Human-Vampire Coalition. They were once good friends, and if Sid Tillsley didn't walk on this earth, they still would be. Augustus would live, but Gunnar didn't enjoy extracting the information he needed. Torturing Flatley would make up it.

Gunnar was lucky Flatley lived locally for the sun would soon rise. He was sure Flatley would offer him his hospitality. There was no wife or kids to deal with, just the possibility of a boyfriend. Gunnar didn't care what waited or what mess he'd leave for Sanderson and his team. Honouring Gabriel was all that mattered now. He feared no other vampire, and only Michael could defeat him in combat. Would Michael remind the world of what he was capable? Gunnar was almost there, and his questions would soon be answered. His impatience led him to drive faster into the suburbs.

RICKSON AWOKE WITH A START. Had he heard something? Probably not. He was suspicious at the best of times and was the first to admit it bordered on paranoia. Nevertheless, that's why he was in the Hominum Order. He glanced over at the bedside clock: 3.30 a.m., five hours until he briefed his superiors on the week's remarkable events.

What a week! It was painful being in Pervis's pitiful company. Tracking the movements of Tillsley had been just as bad, but it finished with the most amazing sight: the slaying of a vampire. Was this a chance to wipe them from the face of the planet?

Rickson jumped out of bed. That was definitely a noise! He reached into his bedside cabinet and pulled out his handgun. One good thing about working for the Order was that he could put a magazine through the bastard and have it all taken care of.

He walked through the house holding the gun, with both hands, in his line of sight. The noise had come from below, in the lounge. He crept down the stairs without making a sound, years of military training ingrained in his every action. It could only be a burglar. Lee was the only one with a key, and he was away until tomorrow.

He peered slowly around the doorway of the lounge. *There you are.* The burglar stood in the middle of the room, obscured by the darkness. How had he bypassed the security system? No matter. Rickson fired a double tap into the burglar's central line. The burglar spun, falling backwards into an armchair. One more double tap left the burglar lifeless.

"Boooyaahh!" Rickson blew the smoke from his pistol.

"Aren't you meant to shout a warning first?" said the corpse.

Rickson stepped back, startled. *A vampire!* The thought had never entered his mind. "I'm with the Hominum Order. You can't touch me!"

The vampire rose from the armchair, steeped in shadow, and walked casually over. He lifted his finger, which was illuminated by the moonlight shining through the window. He tapped Rickson on the forehead. "Guess what I just did?"

"Get out of my house!" yelled Rickson

"That's not very nice," said the vampire, condescendingly. He pushed his head forward into the moonlight. "You know I'm sensitive."

Rickson needed all his strength not to buckle at the knees. A living nightmare stood before him. This was it. This was the end. He swallowed. Got to go out like a man. "I know who you are, Ivansey," he said, managing to hold his voice steady. "More importantly, I know exactly *what* you are."

Gunnar smirked. "I've never seen such courage. Maybe I'll finish you quickly after all, but first, pray tell, what exactly am I?"

"You're evil, Ivansey, evil..." spat Rickson.

Gunnar waved his hand dismissively, as if he'd had just been given a compliment.

"You're worse than a murderer, worse than a rapist, worse than a fucking paedophile."

"Enough of this flattery." Gunnar pulled back his shirt to reveal unbroken skin where Rickson had shot him. "Now, we can get down to business. Take a seat; I've a couple of questions, and then, I'll be on my way." He walked over to the window and looked at the sky. "That is, unless the day comes and I have to stay the night." He gave Rickson an evil smile. "How would you explain that to your boyfriend?"

Rickson's face contorted into rage. "You leave him out of this you fuc—" his words curtailed into an agonising scream and he collapsed in a heap on the chair behind him.

"There's a good chap," comforted Gunnar, who had leapt across the room and stamped through Rickson's knee, snapping his leg to an impossible angle. Rickson looked at his leg. The pain...Oh God, the pain. Mercifully, he passed out.

Mercy was not a word in Gunnar's vocabulary. He massaged part of Rickson's neck, influencing the blood flow back to his brain, throwing the agent back into consciousness and agony.

"I believe I have your full attention," said Gunnar. "Now, that may be your only injury. You can walk away—well, limp away—a relatively unscathed man. Let's be honest, Rickson, if you really know *what* I am, you'll know your wound is equivalent to a paper cut."

"What do you want to know?" he finally conceded.

Gunnar delighted in breaking humans. He'd never get tired of that look of helplessness and desperation. "The human I fought in Middlesbrough, what do you know of him?"

"His name is Sid Tillsley. Pervis and I were assigned to...to...gather information." Rickson struggled to talk through the pain.

"So, you monkeys know he can kill vampires? Do you know he killed Gabriel?" After Ricard, this was the first soul he'd spoken to about Gabriel's demise. His shame for his friend's death had passed since his confrontation with Tillsley. The man possessed a power; the death of Franco Stoloni had proven that.

There, Gunnar saw it, a slight smile. Only slight, but it was there...Red mist descended. Gunnar drove his foot through Rickson's shin, snapping his leg like a twig. Bones ripped through flesh. The monkey screamed in pain, but most of all because he knew that a far worse fate waited.

"Smile again, I beg you."

"We knew Gabriel was dead." He quickly tried to give what information he had. He couldn't spit it out fast enough. "We know he's killed four other vampires. The Lamian Consilium sent us the report filed by Richmond—"

"Four more?" Gunnar interrupted him. "Tell me all you know."

Once Rickson had finished telling the vampire of Richmond's report, Gunnar took a moment to think of all that had befallen. Tillsley was extraordinary. Had there been others like him before? Gunnar's history on his own kind was poor. He'd have to consult Ricard once more. Nevertheless, one thing was certain, Tillsley couldn't be beaten in unarmed combat.

"Tell me all that you know of Tillsley."

"He's nothing more than a drunken bum. He spends all of his time in a small, rundown pub, which was all but demolished in the riot that ensued during your...encounter."

"I bet you loved watching last night, didn't you?"

The monkey did his best to keep his face blank, saying nothing, looking past Gunnar with a distant stare. It was the one response that would leave Rickson Flatley arms hanging from his shoulders. "Please, continue," said the amused vampire.

"He's been claiming jobseeker's benefit for thirty years. He has also claimed numerous fraudulent sickness benefits for his heart and bad back." He winced, the pain in his legs was almost impossible for him to bear. "We were going to consult the Job Centre tomorrow to find out more. He would've run up a considerable sum in illegally claimed benefit monies."

Was this Gunnar's way to destroy the man? He couldn't beat him in unarmed combat, and he'd accepted it, although it cut him deep. Nevertheless, destroying the man's wellbeing could hurt him more than death could.

"What else do you know about his benefit fraud?"

"When you fought Tillsley, did you see the woman who was outside? She was the only woman outside of the pub, hideously ugly?"

"All of you monkeys are hideous to me," said Gunnar, spitting into Rickson's face. "But yes, I do remember her, why?"

"Sheila Fishman. She works at the benefit office. She's declared it her life's work to bring Tillsley to justice."

This could be Gunnar's best chance. He'd have to contact Sheila Fishman and find out everything he needed to know to put Tillsley behind bars. It'd be worth it, even if he'd be working with a human. "Is there anything else you can tell me?"

"No. I was going back to Middlesbrough after I'd reported everything to the Order." The human couldn't hide the anxiety in his face. He'd given all he had and knew he was worthless now. He wasn't looking forward to the rest of his life.

Gunnar knelt down in front of the man and reached out slowly towards his right eye. The cripple tried to pull his head back, but Gunnar grabbed his eyelid between his thumb and forefinger. "Are you telling me everything?" He pulled gently to let him know what was going to happen next.

"Yes! Yes, I swear to you! I fucking swear it!" he screamed, desperation and panic filling him until pain took over. Blood poured into his eye, half blinding him. He grabbed at it and wept.

Gunnar dangled the eyelid in front of the despairing human, wiggling it. He dropped it and grabbed the left eyelid. "Are you sure?"

This time, Rickson didn't even answer.

"Kill me!" he screamed. "Fucking kill me!"

Gunnar laughed to himself. He'd said he'd make the death quick. No death was quick if he had the opportunity to play. Sanderson's team would know who'd done this. All that was important to Gunnar was taking Tillsley's livelihood away. He'd claim benefit no more!

There was a click at the front door as a key turned in the latch. A male voice called through the house. "I'm back early, babe!"

Gunnar put his hand over Rickson's mouth before he could yell to his boyfriend to run. This was priceless. Gunnar leaned down and whispered gently into Rickson's ear, "Do you know what? You may survive this night after all."

21

IT WAS ABOUT HALF PAST ELEVEN ON SATURDAY NIGHT and Sheila Fishman was hungover. It was her first hangover and the reason she was in a terrifyingly bad mood rather than an extremely bad mood. She should be fast asleep but couldn't risk the nightmares after what'd transpired the previous night. She'd never forget the horror for as long as she lived.

Tillsley.

The name made her sick to the stomach. She'd gone to the pub to mine information, to bring him to justice. Everything after that was blurry...except the grab. To think, she'd accepted drinks off the man, drinks bought with illegally acquired money! Her own hypocrisy burnt her like a hot iron.

"Tillsley!" she yelled at the top of her voice with fists raised to the heavens. She'd let her guard down. Up until he arrived, she'd only had one sherry, and that was to fit in with the scum. She would've had a glass of mineral water, or something else equally respectable, but every other woman in the place was drunk and out of control. She recognised ninety per cent of them from the office. She was convinced that Middlesbrough women had actually evolved so that their gestation period was shorter, allowing them to obtain more benefit money over their lifetimes. Her rage was getting sidetracked.

Tillsley.

She remembered the horror of smiling sweetly at his hideous face and the horror of listening to his horrible language. But, as she found herself at the bottom of her third glass of sherry, she found the worst moment of all, the moment that'd haunt her for her natural life. For a second, just a second, she'd thought that maybe, just maybe, he wasn't so bad...

Sheila spat. A large, oyster-sized piece of saliva landed on her impeccably clean floor with an almighty squelch. Feeling anything but disdain for the man filled her with a shame so great, nothing could cleanse her soul. She gave the spitball on the floor a bigger, slimier twin brother.

The grab.

She'd washed her right breast thirty-six times that morning. The pervert! Sid *Fucking* Tillsley. Alfred the cat walked up to her feet, purring because he wanted feeding...again.

"Fucking cat!" she let lose a toe-punt that sent Alfred fleeing for one of his nine lives.

"Fucking Tillsley!" It was the third time she'd sworn in nigh on forty-five years, and it was all because of him. He had more to answer for than any other man did, including Hitler and Richard Madeley.

She was off to visit Mr. Croaker tomorrow. He was recovering in Middlesbrough Hospital. She hadn't seen him since the stapler incident.

"Tillsley," she growled through gritted teeth.

If it wasn't for Tillsley, Mr. Croaker would still have the ability to achieve an erection. The word "erection" made her shudder. Croaker was a worm of a man, not the supervisor the benefit office needed. The benefit office needed an iron fist to crush all who do not follow the rules, no matter what. She had to visit Croaker and keep him sweet so she'd keep her job.

She walked into the kitchen to finish a cup of tea and, in a reflexive move, unleashed a mighty toe-punt into the groin of the man that suddenly appeared before her. She felt the stern leather of her pointed shoes puncture both testicles with a satisfactory pop.

"Have it, you bastard!" she screamed.

GUNNAR DROPPED LIKE A SACK OF CONCRETE. Usually, he'd heal instantly, but two split gonads were complicated pieces of machinery to put back together, and the pain was immense. He took the foetal position and hoped things would—

Boiling water poured into his eyes.

"Have it, you bastard!" yelled Fishman after pouring a kettle's worth of water into his face. "Try and burgle a defenceless lady? You're gonna pay! I'm going to get the blowtorch and stick it up your arse, just like I did to your accomplice, last week!" She ran out of the kitchen to get the tool of unthinkable torture.

Gunnar raised a hand. "Stop! I'm not a burglar!" He needed to get to his feet. Vampire or not, he didn't need to feel what a blowtorch in the rectum felt like. His testicles were healing, but it'd be a minute before he could see. He rose to his knees as he heard the strike of a match. "I want to get even with Tillsley!" he yelled.

"Why didn't you say so?" Sheila Fishman blew out the crusty blowtorch.

GUNNAR SIPPED HIS TEA FROM A BONE CHINA MUG. Cats purred around him and rubbed themselves against his leg. He hated cats. The past five minutes had been some of the strangest of his life. It was the second time in a weekend a human had him at their mercy. Tillsley was not a normal human, but this hideous woman was nothing out of the ordinary, except for her revoltingness.

There was nothing he could've done after the attack. Her kick to the groin would've been fatal to a human. It was as if her shoes were designed to puncture a man's genitals. A blowtorch in the anus? This woman shared his sadistic streak. Working with her might not be as bad as he'd imagined.

"I want to ruin Tillsley's life," Gunnar said, "I've heard you want to do the same."

Sheila put down her cup of tea. "I hate that man more than anything. I hate him more than disease, more than cancer, more than war. I'd go through Hell and back to bring him down."

Her aggression and hatred were satisfying. "Then I guess we're not as different as I once thought. I want to bring this man to his knees, but physically, I am not able to out-power him."

"You want me to run him over in my car?"

"No. If I cannot beat him in unarmed combat, then the route of violence I will not take. I thought of killing his loved ones, but he has no one except the people he drinks with, and drinkers never have proper friends. The best way to get to this man is to take away his livelihood. Sheila, this is why I've contacted you. I understand you're trying to take away his illegally acquired income?"

Sheila nodded with vigour. "I'm gonna catch him working and bring him to justice." She paused. "But..."

"But what? Name the problem and it will be dealt with."

"What can you do?"

He smiled. "I'm sorry, my dear, for I've not introduced myself. I'm Gunnar Ivansey. I was born centuries ago in the forests of Germany. I'm not human. I am a vampire."

"Well, you still went down with a kick to the stones, didn't you? Look, I don't care if you're a vampire or a duck-billed platypus. If you help me get even with Tillsley, you're all right by me."

She didn't believe him. It mattered not. She'd believe soon enough. "Tell me your problem."

"Very well, but if you don't sort it out, you're on your own."

Sheila told Gunnar about Mr. Croaker, and of how he'd lost the use of his genitalia in one of the nastiest desktop stapler accidents ever seen by the A&E team at Middlesbrough General Hospital. She told him if she lost her job, she wouldn't have the powers to bring Tillsley down, and the only chance of her losing her job was if Croaker complained.

"Where exactly is he staying?"

"C-Wing, Ward Four."

"I'll be back once the problem is sorted." He got up to leave.

"When you coming back?"

"Soon."

IT WAS ONE O'CLOCK IN THE MORNING and Sheila still couldn't sleep. She was excited about having a partner. No one at the benefit office shared her passion for the job. They were only there for the money.

"Bastards."

She couldn't stop swearing, but she didn't care as it enhanced her rage and focused her on the battle ahead.

She now had an ally in her fight against benefit fraud and the bastard Tillsley. It didn't matter that Gunnar was a loon, thinking he was a vampire. What mattered was that she had someone willing to fight by her side, for nothing else than revenge.

There was no way she'd sleep tonight. She was far too excited. Maybe a warm cup of cocoa would settle her. She kicked back the covers and Ulysses the cat flew across the room, hitting the wall before scurrying for cover. She swung out her legs and landed with both feet on Alfred, who screeched before fleeing to join his friend in hiding.

She put her large, repugnant feet into her shoes, the nearest footwear to the bed. Her cats used to be one of the most important things in her life, but now, she'd skin every one of them alive to bring down Tillsley. She walked through to the kitchen to put the kettle on and swung a lightning toe-punt into the groin of the man standing in front of her.

GUNNAR HIT THE FLOOR LIKE A SACK OF CONCRETE. Both gonads destroyed for the second time in the evening.

"I'm sorry!" she yelled before he'd reached the floor. "You shouldn't sneak in like that! I thought you were a burglar!"

Gunnar didn't respond. He breathed deeply to allow the healing to take place.

"You all right? Do you want a cup of tea?"

Gunnar got to his feet slowly and took a seat at the breakfast table. "Yes, please...Where do you get those shoes of yours?" he asked through gritted teeth.

She looked down. "I make them myself. I call them my 'nutcrackers.' A lady cannot be too careful in this day and age."

He rubbed his swollen scrotum. "Your problem is now sorted. Croaker won't launch a complaint, and you're likely to get a raise for all your hard work."

She nodded. "Good. We can press on then."

"There is one problem with our mission. Daylight will kill me. If we're to go out together in the day, I must be enclosed by complete darkness."

"How are we going to work around that then?"

"I'll sort something." He already had a van that was suitable. He just needed the surveillance equipment.

Sheila gave a wicked, hideous grin. "When do we start?"

"Soon. Very soon."

22

CAROLINE WAS ENJOYING A LONG, HOT BATH in her extensive Kensington flat. This was her time. This was when she tried to let all the troubles in the world and all the blood on her hands wash away. This was when she tried to forget about the hundreds and hundreds of children who were dead because of the decisions she made. They'd haunt her forever.

Bach played softly in the background and candles burned aromatic fragrances. She was finding it harder than usual to forget the troubles of the week, but it wasn't a surprise. Could the Firmamentum be here? Were the murders in the Northeast caused by a vampire born stronger, faster, and more bloodthirsty than the most powerful vampires of the old age, something even more terrifying than Michael? Could this Sid Tillsley be the answer? She hoped not. She had *other* plans that required her attention.

"Sweetness?" called Caroline's husband through the closed door. He knew she didn't like being disturbed during this personal time.

"Please, Jeffrey, give me an hour," she called back, annoyed.

"It's the office. They say it's important. I told them you'd phone them back, but they're adamant."

The office knew not to call her now. It must be urgent indeed. "Bring me the phone."

Her husband opened the door and handed her the cordless telephone. He left promptly, not wanting to hear the conversation. Two minutes later, she was out of the bath and rushing clothes on in order to get to the local hospital.

CAROLINE ARRIVED TO FIND THE ORDER WAITING outside Rickson Flatley's hospital room. The mood outside was extremely grave.

"How is he?" she asked as she approached the group.

Charles shook his head. "He'll survive, but I don't think he'll want to."

"What do you mean? What do we know?"

Caroline didn't like to mince words, and Charles, thankfully, got to the point. He looked around to check no one was near. "It looks like a vampire has tortured him and his now-deceased boyfriend."

"How do you know it was a vampire?" she asked quickly.

"His wounds are unbelievably severe. Only a vampire could commit such atrocities and not kill. He—" Charles swallowed to fortify himself. "His eyes, his ears...most of his appendages have been removed. His body has been *decorated* with a knife. All of his limbs and ribs are broken. The boyfriend had similar injuries, except some of his veins were opened."

Pervis ran over to a waste paper bin and emptied his stomach. Tears streamed down his face that were not caused by the sickness.

Caroline looked on, her face stone, but inside her mind raced. A vampire wouldn't attack a member of the Order, surely?

"When can we speak to him?"

"The doctor said he'd be awake in about an hour," replied Charles.

"OK, Pervis, we need a full report."

With a few words to one of the nursing staff, a meeting room was set up. Members of the Order carried the sort of papers that meant things were done for them, instantly. It gave them authority over police, paramedics, and the fire service. They were extremely powerful yet unknown politicians. Once the room had been scanned for bugs, the impromptu meeting began. Jeremy Pervis gave an accurate account of all that had happened at Ladies' Night at The Miner's Arms. He told the group of the riot that had ensued, the emergence of Reece Chambers, and the amazing fight between Tillsley and Ivansey. When he'd finished, the group sat quiet.

Sanderson was the first to speak. "This is fantastic news. We have a real vampire hunter. A real warrior that can kill these bastards!"

"We know your views, Sanderson, and they're not those of the Order. We do not want a war," Charles said sternly.

"War? I see war every day! When you say 'war,' what you mean is the vampires may take some casualties," Sanderson retorted.

"If Franco Stoloni is dead, the vampires won't know any of this. We must inform them," said Charles.

Sanderson almost choked. "Are you crazy? We have a weapon they don't know about!"

"Charles is right," said Caroline. Her calmness contrasted Sanderson's manner. "They will find out eventually. Both sides have their spies and there's no point holding back information. Both sides will need this man if he's the answer to the vampire Firmamentum. It's too much of a coincidence that this man is discovered as the bloodshed in the Northeast come to light."

"If the Firmamentum is here," said Pervis, "it's not the only beast on the loose. Ivansey is the most likely culprit for Rickson's torture. If he'll do this to a member of the Order, what else will he do?"

"Another reason the Lamian Consilium must be told," said Caroline. "I promise you, Michael will come down on Ivansey like a tonne of bricks. He won't have the Agreement broken, not by anyone."

"Can we be sure?" asked Sanderson. "Everyone knows what those animals did together."

"The Agreement is the only thing Michael cares for. Trust me, he'll—" A knock on the door cut her off. "Come in."

A nurse popped her head round the door. "The doctor says you can see him now. He's conscious, although it's a miracle he's alive."

"Thank you," said Caroline, before following the nurse with the other councillors.

Rickson was a mishmash of bandages. Only his jaw-line was left unscathed.

"Rickson?" asked Caroline gently.

"What's left of him," replied the wounded operative.

"What happened?"

"Ivansey left me alive so I could tell you what he did, and why." Rickson managed to talk between wheezed breaths. He was barely audible because of his broken ribs. "He tortured me for hours. He made me carve...he made me kill Lee. If I didn't do it, he said he'd leave him alive...in a worse state than me. I...I had to. He said he'd do anything to get to Tillsley, that he'd avenge Gabriel's death at any price. The only reason he didn't kill me was so I could tell you."

"What else did he do, Rickson?" asked Charles.

Rickson ignored his question. "If there's any decency in you, Caroline, I will be dead within the hour."

"You have my word," she replied. As ever, she was stone.

"Thank you."

"Goodbye, Rickson." She left the room and was followed by the rest of the group. There was much to discuss.

"Hello, Ricard."

"Michael! What an unexpected visit." Ricard couldn't hide his shock when he opened the door. He regained his composure in the blink of an eye. "Please, do come in."

It was midnight at Ricard's dwelling in the North Yorkshire Moors. He never had visitors here, especially not visitors like Michael Vitrago. Ricard walked through to the sitting room of the seventeenth century cottage. A fire raged in the hearth.

Michael took off his long black coat and threw it over one of the large armchairs. He wore it to disguise his immense size rather than to stay warm. Underneath the coat he wore a fine-tailored black suit. "How long has it been, Ricard?"

"Fifty-seven years, two months, and a day if my memory serves me well."

Michael offered a brief smile. "I'm sure it does." He took a seat.

Ricard poured two large single whiskies from the drinks cabinet. "Business or pleasure?"

"I think you know," said Michael.

"I'd be lying if I said I couldn't remember the last time we met on a social occasion, but it has been a great number of decades, has it not?"

The huge vampire nodded his head slowly. "Happier, greater days, which I miss dearly."

Ricard raised an eyebrow. "I'm sure that's not your official line on the matter though?"

A mirthless laugh greeted his question. "Very true." Michael looked long into his glass. "Nevertheless, if anyone had to change with the times, it was I. Until I'm ready to leave this world, I'll do what's best for the lamia."

Ricard nodded. "What brings you here?"

"Two things. The first: Gunnar. I must take him," he said plainly.

"The death of Gabriel was more destructive to his vulnerable psyche than I imagined. What has he done?"

"He's broken the Agreement. He tortured a human agent, and as you can probably imagine, he was thorough in his work. He sent a message that he no longer holds any oaths."

Ricard nodded. It was never a question whether Gunnar would go off the rails; it was always a question of when. "I appreciate you telling me. I shall mourn his loss deeply."

"As will I," said Michael.

"Why do you seek my council?"

"When did you last see him?"

Ricard answered without hesitation. "Thirteen nights ago, the night after Gabriel died. He didn't come for advice, he never does. He needed to pour his heart out."

"You never told the Lamian Consilium about Gabriel's death. Why?"

"Gunnar needed time and wasn't ready to face an interrogation. I gave him the chance to seek revenge. It would not have gone well if someone else had intervened." Ricard answered the questions calmly and carefully. This was an interrogation, and Michael would kill him in a second if he jeopardised the Agreement in the slightest.

"Gabriel." Michael paused after the mention of the name and stared into his now-empty glass of scotch. "His blood line has ended now, and I do not see another lamia ever matching his feats. I miss him dearly. How could he fall to the empty hand of a human?"

Ricard paused before answering. "That was one reason why I didn't tell the Lamian Consilium immediately. I wanted to investigate the matter further, because I wanted to know how a lamia could be killed by a man—"

"Which brings me to my second reason for being here," interrupted Michael.

"The Firmamentum," said Ricard softly. "When Gabriel died, I thought it was a freak accident. The Firmamentum didn't cross my mind as there was no balance. A vampire of such might can't hide. How could one stop the world knowing of such a beast? How could one stop the war certain to follow? It was for this reason I didn't suspect Tillsley of being the Bellator."

Ricard pointed to Michael's glass and got a nod in return. Ricard went to the drinks cabinet, returned with a decanter of whisky, and filled both glasses.

"So, the increase in human harvesting has not been a coincidence at all," said Ricard. "There is something out there with an appetite for killing larger than ours, or should I say yours. Nevertheless, the Firmamentum? You saw Sparle. You saw the answer that mankind produced. From all the reports that have been filtered through to me, Tillsley is a drunken bum. He is no Remo Elscachius. The human bloodshed hasn't been that great, and how many would Sparle have killed by now? Tillsley is forty-six!

"My council is this: the Firmamentum may be here, but if it is, then it's a weak strain. You're not going to have to kill the man you did two thousand years ago."

Michael considered Ricard's council as he sipped his whisky. "Why are you living here?"

"I've been here a while. I travel from house to house, and at the moment, this is where I hang my hat," he said, undeterred by the accusing line of questioning. "I cannot deny my interest in what's happened here."

"And what have you discovered?"

"Very little, if truth be told. I've found no vampire answer to Sid Tillsley, even though the brutal killings have been plentiful."

Michael stared deep into the eyes of the scholar. It was a look that went deep into the soul and would scare any living creature on the Earth, but not Ricard. Ricard was one of the oldest of his line, and though he'd never possessed physical power, his mental prowess was second to none. He looked straight back at Michael with equal intensity.

It was Michael who broke the deadlock. "I'm surprised you've not uncovered any clues. It also surprises me that the vampires I assigned to watch the area have found nothing. My respect for you is unquestionable, but I know your power does not lie in your fangs. If there was something to be found in these parts you would've found it. I assigned good lamia to the area, quite capable of tracking whatever is causing the unrest, unless there was someone better to hide it."

Ricard laughed. "If it wasn't you I was talking to, I would assume that was a joke, but everyone knows no mirth lies in your heart. This puts you in a difficult situation, Michael."

"That it does, old friend."

"Taking my life wouldn't be difficult. Ties mean nothing to you. However, these accusations I can guarantee are yours and yours alone. I know the Lamian Consilium wouldn't believe any of this nonsense, and believe me, it is nonsense. I have nothing to do with the blood spilt across these lands."

"I hope so, Ricard. It may surprise you, but it'd pain me to take your life, not for the loss of our greatest source of knowledge, but because you are someone who I am fond. It galled you that you couldn't change Sparle. Up until that point, you'd never failed at anything. Not being able to tame him hurt you. If the opportunity arose again, I don't think you'd turn down the chance to right the wrongs of the past, to succeed where you failed before."

A stern look came over Ricard's face. "You offend me by assuming my pride is greater than my intelligence. I saw what Sparle did. I witnessed it first hand, and it petrified me. If the beast was reborn, I wouldn't let it loose on the world, not for a second. It does not belong anywhere. Nothing that desires murder as he did deserves life."

"I hope you speak the truth." The huge vampire stood up and placed his glass on the side of the table. "Farewell."

MICHAEL ARRIVED BACK IN LONDON WELL BEFORE DAYLIGHT. He threw open the grand double-oak doors of the vampire meeting hall and was greeted by a wall of noise. Conversation was ripe, and it wasn't until Michael had taken his seat that the group settled. They'd waited for hours, wanting to hear about his meeting with Ricard and to discuss what should be done with Sid Tillsley.

Michael began. "I've met with Ricard. I questioned his involvement with the Northeast. He said he has no clue as to what is causing the bloodshed."

"Is he telling the truth?" asked an elder.

Michael cupped his chin in his hands. He'd pondered over the question since he left the old lamia in his cottage. "I don't know. He's too wise to give anything away. Whether I believe him or not comes down to my gut feeling. I think Sid Tillsley will have the answers. The disturbances in the Northeast look like the destruction Sparle caused two thousand years ago. But Tillsley is not Remo Elscachius, the Bellator."

An elder female vampire addressed the floor. "We need to meet Tillsley. Then, we can decide on what he is and whether we can dispose of him."

Michael nodded, as did most of the Consilium. "You're right. Reece Chambers has latched on to him, but reports shared between us and the Hominum Order says that Tillsley is not a man of action. He doesn't pose a direct threat to us. We'll send a greeting party. There's no rush to apprehend him. It's the blood flowing in the Northeast that ails me."

23

SID TILLSLEY HAD A WICKED HANGOVER. Because of The Miner's temporary destruction, he was forced to drink in town. The unusual beer had done him a wrong'n. The hangover was worsened by his guilt. He still felt bad about killing the vampire fella. It really was an accident, the poor bugger. The gobby one, the tall skinhead, was a right arsehole. He needed a pasting. If these vampire bastards were going to start playing silly buggers on regular occasion, then he'd have to start handing out more slaps.

It was nine in the morning and he was on his way to do a bit of construction work for Pervez, Middlesbrough's only Indian docker. He'd get a fair few quid for the day's work and hopefully a few ciggies as well. Bit of hard graft today should set him up with beer tokens for the next week, and The Miner's was opening tomorrow.

Sid lit up another "Chickboyo" Thai cigarette. He'd come into two hundred for helping some Welsh-Thai prostitute get rid of a couple of unwanted gentlemen trying to seek her attention. She'd offered Sid a freebie, and she was red hot, too, but Sid had this job to get to, and he was a professional. He may go back later to see the surprise she said she had waiting for him.

He finally arrived at Pervez's. It had been a tough walk, and it was going to be a tough few hour's work, but it was money in the bank and tabs in the lungs.

SHEILA FISHMAN SAT IN THE DRIVERS' SEAT of Gunnar Ivansey's transit van with a pair of binoculars. The unlikely couple had trailed Sid to the entrance of Pervez's docks. Gunnar was setting up surveillance equipment in the back of the lightproof van. She had no idea where he got it all from.

"I can see the bastard," she growled. Swear words were now a regular part of her vocabulary, every blasphemy fuelling her hatred.

"I've nearly got it set up to record." Gunnar said. The van had cameras looking from all angles. The lenses were camouflaged by the writing on the side of the van.

"Hurry up. I can see him bloody working! I can see him bloody working!" she yelled excitedly. "The bastard just picked up three sacks of concrete! Three sacks of concrete and he reckons he's got a bad back! He's claimed thousands on his fucking bad back!"

"Calm down, otherwise you'll give the game away," Gunnar barked through the intercom.

Sheila suppressed her excitement with difficulty. "I'm sorry, but we've never got this close before."

Gunnar continued tweaking the surveillance equipment. "OK, we're ready. We're rolling."

ARTHUR PEASLEY HUMMED A TUNEFUL TUNE as he strolled along. He occasionally broke into a few words of song, much to the delight of the passersby. Ladies' Night had been successful for Arthur. He'd booked the forthcoming weekend to settle some unfinished business with some of the lovelier ladies of Middlesbrough. Unfortunately, the *ménage à quatre* hadn't come off since everyone had beat it when the cops turned up.

"Hey, little lady!" Arthur stopped off to speak to a beautiful young brunette who was passing his way. Arthur wasn't as dapper as usual, because he was dressed in his plumbing overalls. Still, they were ice white and gave the illusion of a jumpsuit. However, while not looking particularly dapper compared to his normal sleek appearance, he still looked a million dollars compared to most film stars.

The girl stopped to talk to the beautiful man but found herself tongue-tied, intimidated by his lady-killing looks. Arthur was used to this and, as usual, he took care of business.

"How about a drink sometime?" he asked. The question was rhetorical, of course. "Well, here's my card. Just drop me a phone call one evening when you're lonesome that night." He offered her a wink over his shades and went on his way.

It had been the third card he'd dropped off to beautiful women that day, an average day with the chicks. He'd have three messages on his answer phone when he got back home. At this rate, he'd start to get booked up for next week too.

Arthur was on the posher side of town. A top-notch hotel had problems with one of the toilets, and he'd been called in to take care of business. He reached his destination: The Royal York. It was a lovely hotel and very stylish. He'd never done a plumbing job anywhere this swanky, but he'd performed a few jobs on some rich wives and widowers in places similar.

He walked through the marble foyer to the impressive reception where three attractive girls were taking telephone calls and dealing with guests. Arthur walked over to the only free (and most attractive) of the receptionists who was busy looking through the current guest list.

"Miss, I'm here to do the plumbing job," he said professionally.

"You're meant to come via the tradesmen's entran..." She trailed off when she looked up and into the eyes of the beautiful man.

Arthur gave a cheeky wink. "Hey, baby, I don't mind coming in your tradesman's entrance."

Most men would've been slapped, but the receptionist giggled like a schoolgirl with a crush. "I'll get the porter for you, Mr...?"

"Call me Arthur, baby," He gave her one of his infamous calling cards, and she rushed off to get the porter.

"WHERE'S HE GONE? WHERE'S HE GONE?" screamed Sheila. Sid had wandered out of sight of the van. "This is what always happens. He always gets away!"

"Calm down," Gunnar said impatiently, "You didn't have me with you last time."

"I'm sorry, I'm sorry," she said excitedly. "It's just the prospect of putting him behind bars is the only thing that holds my rage at bay. If we can get some shots of him lifting that concrete, we can put an end to him!"

"Why are you so driven to put these people behind bars and take away their money?"

"It's my job, and it's in the rules. Breaking the rules is against the rules," she replied logically.

Gunnar didn't question her any further. What a horrible existence these humans had, working their fingers to the bone performing menial tasks. Then, after working over half their lives, they retire. He'd concluded that retirement meant "waiting to die." They may live longer now, but their existence was as pointless as it was five hundred years ago.

"I can see him over by the forklift truck! Have you got him?" she screamed.

"I won't if you keep jumping around, calm down."

Gunnar took control of the appropriate camera. He'd not known where to buy the equipment and had wandered into a high street electrical store. He was trying to put the experience behind him. The staff were abhorrent, spotty, greasy, and reeking of puberty. He had to be inconspicuous, but he'd yearned to murder them all. They'd refused to sell him anything without a five-year warranty, and they'd forced him to purchase the store's own gold-plated cables that seemed ridiculously overpriced. Then, when he'd got everything back to his house, nothing had worked and the shop had refused to deal with him, forcing him to phone customer services...

When this was all over, he *was* going to kill them all. He was going to hunt down every member of the high street chain, and their support staff in Bangalore, and murder them. Especially, Ralph. Ralph had put him on hold for an hour and hung up on him twice. Gunnar was going to desecrate Ralph's corpse.

Gunnar still wondered whether Ralph was his real name.

"I have him." He zoomed in on the fat oaf who, unsurprisingly, was taking a break. He was smoking his life away and occasionally lifting a buttock to pollute the atmosphere.

"The bastard!" said Sheila through gritted teeth. "Not only is he getting paid benefit money by us, he's also getting paid to do a manual-labour job. The ultimate insult is that he's not even working. The lazy bastard is taking a break!"

The vampire ignored her. Sid finished his cigarette and then instantly lit another, and then another. He surely couldn't see many more years if he carried on this way.

Sid got up from his seat on the front of the forklift truck and walked behind some crates. He was still visible to the camera.

"This is it!" said an excited Sheila, through the intercom.

"I have him on the video."

Sid bent down, out of view.

"He's picking something up. This is it!"

"THERE YOU ARE, MY GOOD FELLOW. This is the toilet. Apparently, the flushing mechanism won't flush." The porter was an extremely well-spoken, middle-aged gentleman. His rotund torso strained against the waistcoat of his uniform. "Is there anything else you require?"

"I'll sort it, baby." Arthur gave the porter a respectful nod and went about his work in a professional manner. The porter nodded and left the hotel room. The room was strange to say the least, but not in its layout, a normal five-star hotel room, or so Arthur should imagine. The peculiar thing was that the room was underground and he'd no idea how far. They'd walked down a staircase in the foyer to a separate lift and travelled down for a considerable length of time.

The lift only had one other stop, the one to this long corridor with rooms either side. Why they were underground, Arthur had no idea. Oh well, to work. You saw some strange sites as a plumber, and Arthur had seen much stranger than this.

Arthur was a good plumber, and this was going to be a simple job. All he needed to do was replace the siphon diaphragm and he'd be on his way. Well, if it was in a residential area, he would be. He was a good man, but this hotel had money coming out of its ears and the rich assholes could afford to pay a few extra quid.

Arthur took the cistern to pieces and laid everything neatly on the floor. He then went into the main bedroom to watch a bit of telly. Making himself comfortable on the bed, trying not to get some of the nastier stains from his overalls on the clean sheets, he flicked through the satellite channels and was disappointed by the lack of porn.

"Man, I may as well get back to work." He got off the bed and headed back to the bathroom, but, through no fault of his own, he walked past the mini-bar. Arthur stopped dead, not being able to walk past the call of the miniature bottles of spirits. He opened the door to see what magic waited inside.

"WE'RE GONNA GET HIM PICKING SOMETHING UP! We're gonna get him!"

After bending to pick something up, Sid emerged clutching a rolled up magazine in his hand.

"Lazy bastard!" Sheila shouted.

The bookworm sauntered back towards the forklift and took a leisurely seat on the side of the vehicle. He opened the magazine and began to read, or rather, he began to look.

"Dirty bastard!" she screamed.

Gunnar shook his head. So far, all that they had was video footage proving that Sid was an avid reader of *Tits*.

"I hate him, Gunnar, I bloody hate him! Wasting the government's money on that, on that filth!"

Through the intercom, Gunnar heard her spit on the floor of his van.

ARTHUR WAS NOT DRUNK. He was definitely *in drink*. By Middlesbrough standards, he was still all right to drive. He was definitely too drunk to replace the siphon diaphragm though, and he'd managed to snap the toilet seat with his mighty karate-grip.

"Ah, man!" There wasn't any more booze in the mini-bar for drowning his sorrows at the unjust misfortune.

The beautiful plumber was, however, a clever man. He was not as clever as the cleverest man on the Smithson Estate, Brian Garforth, but he could certainly think on his feet. The best course of action was to go into one of the other rooms and change the toilet seat over. If they ever noticed, he would've already been paid.

Arthur snuck out of the front door using his karate training. He looked both ways for the porter before darting across the corridor without making a sound. The door on the opposite side of the corridor was locked. "Damn." It was one of the card-activated doors, which meant that Arthur couldn't pick the lock.

A little light bulb lit above the great one's head. He took one of his remaining calling cards from his inside pocket and placed it into the cardkey slot. The light went green and the door unlocked. Apparently, no slot could say no to Middlesbrough's most beautiful man.

Still not making a sound, Arthur edged around the door. He didn't know if there would be anyone in there but was certain he could sweet talk his way out of any situation.

At first, the room appeared identical to the one where Arthur was fixing the toilet, but there were more doors coming off the main chamber and behind one Arthur could hear a voice. He was a confident man, and after a fair amount of alcohol, he was a tremendously confident man.

If he'd heard a man's voice, then he would've simply turned around and tried the next room. However, the voice was female, and it was extremely sexy. He could only hear her speaking, so she must be on the phone.

Arthur snuck up to the door and put his ear to it.

"I agree," he heard her say, "but Sid Tillsley is the key!"

SHEILA CONTINUED HER TORRENT OF ABUSE, and Gunnar turned off the intercom. It didn't make much difference. The reverberations of her language still managed to get through the soundproof wall. He continued to watch Tillsley pour over the naked girls in a lewd study of the female form. Patience was the key to this. Tillsley would have to do some work, eventually.

He turned the intercom back on to tell Sheila to calm down for the umpteenth time.

"—unting motherfu—"

Gunnar turned it back off and continued to watch the object of his hatred. The man's face had reddened considerably. It was now heart-attack purple. He was either dying or was getting himself into a state that would turn Sheila homicidal.

Tillsley looked around quickly and suddenly hid the magazine behind his back. Gunnar turned up the outside microphone and turned the intercom back on so he could speak to Sheila Fishman.

"—at's going on?" she said.

"Keep quiet or we'll never find out," he warned. Thankfully, she heeded his advice.

Sid's employer stormed up to him. The small Asian man with a moustache was pointing his finger aggressively at Sid.

"Mr. Sid! Why are you sitting around?"

The van started bumping up and down due to Sheila's excitement.

"We'll get him if he mentions payment for service..."

"You're a lazy, lazy man, Mr. Sid!" he lectured in an Indian accent. "What have you been doing all morning?"

"I-I..." stuttered Sid.

"What're you hiding behind your back, Mr. Sid?" he asked after seeing Sid struggle to hide his magazine.

"N'owt, mon!"

"What are you hiding? Tell me, or this will all end now! Show me!"

"I got n'owt!" His attempt to hide the magazine failed miserably as it fell onto the ground between them.

Gunnar panned the camera down. The magazine had fallen open on a page with a revealing picture of a middle-aged Asian lady with enormous breasts. He panned back to the face of the Asian man who was shaking with anger.

"It says that she's from 'boro. You know her, like?" asked Sid.

"Mr. Sid...that is my wife!"

ARTHUR LISTENED INTENTLY TO THE SEXY VOICE. His mind had raced since hearing Sid's name. He couldn't tell what the conversation was about. He was worried the woman could be a Benefit Bastard. More importantly, he wanted to find out if she was as pretty as her voice was sexy.

"Vladimir and Sven are making contact tonight at The Miner's Arms."

There was quiet as the person on the other end responded.

"Six at the moment, but we need more vampires to join the hunt."

Arthur gasped. She was a vampire! The female voice cut off mid-sentence. He'd been rumbled!

The door flew open, and the vampire charged with her fangs fully drawn.

Yeah, she's hot, thought Arthur as she bowled into him.

"GET OUT, MR. SID! GET OFF MY PROPERTY!"

"But—"

"Get out!"

"She's—"

"Get out!"

"—got—"

"Get out!"

"—cracking—"

"Get out!"

"—jugs."

"GET OUT! GET OUT! GET OUT!"

"Alreet." Tillsley mooched away from the seething dock owner who charged back into his office building, screaming obscenities in his native tongue.

"Where's Tillsley going!" yelled Sheila.

"I believe he's been sacked."

"Fucking hell!" Sheila screamed. "That was our chance!"

Gunnar put his head in his hands and turned off the intercom for some peace and quiet. He felt the anger through the truck's vibrations as Sheila punched and kicked the van, screaming for all she was worth. The door of the van opened and then slammed shut. He looked through his camera to watch Sheila storm round the site, kicking and punching everything while yelling obscenities. She disappeared behind the crates where Sid had first picked up his magazine. When she reappeared, it was with a gigantic nail gun she could barely lift.

Gunnar shook his head. She was the most psychologically demented human he'd ever met. Screaming, she uncontrollably fired nails at everything in sight. Within moments, nails stuck out of every crate in the dock and the forklift sported two flat tyres and ruined paintwork. Then, she turned the gun on the van...

"You stupid woman!" yelled Gunnar, not unlike the great swordsman René Artois.

Only Gunnar's sudden blood-curdling scream halted the frenzy. She dropped the gun, finally coming to her senses, and hurried back to the van. She buzzed through the intercom.

"Are you all right?"

"Just drive back to base," he muttered.

"But Tills—"

"Fuck Tillsley!" he yelled. "Drive back to base!"

She complied due to the ferocity of his voice.

The van started, the vibrations causing extreme pain. If he'd been hit with the nail, it would've taken a few minutes to heal. However, he'd been hit with the worst thing that a vampire could face: sunlight. The nail had ripped through the van and caused a beam of sunlight to strike Gunnar, like a laser, in the groin. The agony was paralysing, but Tillsley's pain would be worse.

And then so would Sheila fucking Fishman's!

And then fucking Ralph's!

24

IT WAS THE NIGHT OF THE MINER'S ARMS' GRAND REOPENING. It wasn't particularly grand, but it was a reopening nonetheless. Different furniture decorated the pub, although the new furniture was older and tattier than the previous. There were also a record number of people barred from the pub too. All those involved in the riot that were not in the custody of Her Majesty's finest were not allowed to set foot in The Miner's for at least a couple of days.

It was Monday and the bar had been open for two hours. Tarrant was not on television because the television had been smashed in the riot. The lads sat around, brooding, supping their pints, bored out of their minds with nothing to say to one another. Still, it was better than sitting alone wondering where everything went wrong. At least they were in company where things were just as bad for everyone else.

Celebrating the reopening were none other than Sid, Brian, and Rathbone. They propped up the bar, chatting about the usual: Brian's sexual conquests and Sid's lack of.

"Haven't you been knocking off that bird from that deaf charity shop on Mondays, Brian?" asked Sid.

"Aye, but tonight's a special occasion, like. The Miner's refurbishment doesn't happen too often now, does it?" replied the swordsman.

"True, mate, true. Ain't that bird deaf, as well?" asked Sid as he lit up a Japanese cigarette, a "Smokyo." He'd obtained four hundred for helping the Japanese restaurateur Oniccchewa Hagasaki move a dead porpoise from Seal Sands to his restaurant in Hartlepool.

"Sid!" said Brian, rising up, standing on the moral high ground. "They prefer to be called 'audio-impaired,' and yes, she can hear fook all."

"How does that work?" asked Sid.

"Well, it has its ups and downs. I've had to learn a bit of sign language, like." The impressed looks he got encouraged him to demonstrate.

"This." He mimicked drinking tea with his little pinkie up. "Means, 'Make us a cup of tea, pet.'"

"And doing this." He mimicked pulling a chain before putting both hands on his head in dismay. "Means, 'Your shitter's blocked!'"

"And this one you can guess at!" He mimicked something obscene, which was acknowledged with knowing nods from his audience. Sign Language! Brian Garforth was indeed the most educated man on the Smithson Estate. If he hadn't failed all his O-Levels, he'd be known as "The Professor."

"Deaf? Is that all?" said Rathbone. "I once did a lass with no senses at all."

Even the silence was confused.

"Was she dead?" asked Brian.

"'Course not, dickhead," retorted the idiotic Rathbone.

"Coma?" asked Brian.

"Nooo," said the horrible greasy little bastard. "She was...sort of like...a cabbage... but a cabbage with great tits."

"Shut up, Rathbone," said Brian. "You've never been near a woman!" He went back to ignoring him. Kevin brought over three pints, which Brian paid for. "You get any repercussions for killing that vampire fella, Sid?" asked Brian.

Sid shook his head mournfully. "Nah, not as if he left any evidence like. Been feeling pretty bad about that 'cos it was a proper accident. That other twat deserved a smack, tho'."

"Yeah, he was an arse that one, but you shouldna feel bad about the other fella, Sid. If what that Rich says is true, then they ain't a good bunch of lads, are they? All that drinking blood stuff, it's a bit weird if you ask me."

"Aye, you're reet, mon." Sid lit another Japanese.

The pub door opened.

"Aww, bollocks," said Brian. "Not that twat, Rich, again! Do you want me to give him a smack, Sid?"

"Nah, mon. He may know something about that lad I killed."

Brian unclenched his fist and took the keys out of his hand.

Kev breathed a sigh of relief. "At least me pub won't be smashed up on its opening night."

"Sid, I'm glad I've found you. I have much to tell," said the vampire hunter.

"I'm pretty busy at the moment, you know?" Sid looked at his magically empty glass.

"Very well. Take a seat over there." The lads went to sit on the new furniture, but Reece stopped Sid. "I want to speak to you alone."

Sid gave him a grave look. "I'm sorry, Rich, but these fine gents are my advisors and my friends. They look out for me best interests, and they are both very thirsty."

"It's Reece, by the way."

Two empty glasses hovered in front of Reece. He rolled his eyes. "OK, three pints and a mineral water over here please, Kevin...and one for yourself," he added when Kevin's face dropped at the mention of bringing the pints over. The Miner's didn't usually offer a waiter service, but anything was available at the right price.

"I've researched everything that might explain the mysteries of the past few weeks: the increase in killings, the monster in the woods, and you being able to kill vampires. I believe I have an answer."

Kevin brought the beers over and took a seat to listen to the gossip.

"This isn't the first time these events have occurred. Over two millennia ago, this same thing happened. A vampire monster was born, so powerful, nothing could stand in its path. In nature, everything has its balance, and there was a counterpart to this beast: a man born with the power to kill a vampire.

"Two thousand years later, and history has repeated itself. There is a monster out there committing hideous acts, except this time, he has help, he has a master. That's why he didn't catch us the other night."

"Aye," said Sid. "You should've seen it, lads. I reckon it was as quick as Brian over thirty yards."

The statement got an impressed whistle from the audience. Reece had forgotten he was dealing with idiots.

"Sid, you're the answer to the monster. You must face it, and you must kill it. If you don't, thousands may die."

"Aw, mon, I've just sat down."

Reece put his head in his hands. "You don't understand what you are? You don't understand why you're here? You are the chosen one!"

"But me back, mon!" Sid grabbed his spine. "Brian, tell him about me back."

"He's got a bad back," confirmed Brian.

"You must come with me. You must fulfil your destiny. You can free mankind. Come with me, Sid. I will pay you anything!"

"Bollocks to it, mon." Sid wagged a sausage-like finger. "I've got a sneaky suspicion that you took me to where *them lot* go."

"London?" asked Rathbone.

"I don't know, but it sounds about right," Sid said to him. "Anyroad, I ain't getting involved with any of that funny business."

"OK. Kevin, another round of beers, please," said Reece, regrouping.

"Certainly," said the landlord, almost jumping to his feet. He saw a big wad coming his way and had no problems with the new waiter service. Kevin saw it as a continental way of enjoying an evening, sophisticated, but better than them shit European café bars where them Eurotwats didn't know how to get proper shitfaced.

"Sid," said Reece. "You have a gift, a gift that hasn't been seen for two millennia."

"Shurrup!"

"Sid, you'll be a wanted man. Both races know what you can do. The men who were present at your battle with Gunnar—"

It was time for Brian to get involved. "'Battle?'" he said, sneering his nose up in a way that suggested faecal matter had been smeared on his moustache. "What do you mean a fooking battle? It was a pub car-park brawl, ya posh twat."

Reece shook his head. "Gunnar Ivansey is a gifted predator. That day will go down in the secret history of this country for as long as records are kept."

A nervous look crossed Sid's face. "Hang on, mon, what do you mean by 'records?' I canna be seen fighting outside pubs with me back the way it is. I'll lose me benefit money! I've got to look after me future."

"For God's sake, there are more important matters than your benefit cheque. The world won't care whether you're claiming benefit if you're ridding the world of vampires!"

"You listen to me, mon, there are people out there who'd love to catch me working or to find me doing something that'd compromise my disability benefit. I don't give a fook about a punch-up I had on a Friday night outside me local pub. In fact, I'm a little bit embarrassed about hitting that other fella."

"You weren't fighting a normal human being. You were fighting a super strong, super fast, immortal fucking vampire!" Reece was practically foaming at the mouth with excitement. "Everyone who is involved in the real world, and I mean the *real world*, where murder takes place every hour, will want a piece of you now. And it has nothing to do with your fucking bad back!"

Brian rolled up his sleeves. "I think it's time for you to leave, ya posh Southern bastard!"

"Shut up, little man. This is beyond you."

Brian rose from his chair but was halted by Kev.

"If one of you raises a fist, you're barred for life. I ain't having this place smashed up twice in a week. Now, sit down!"

Both men sat. Reece regained his composure, but Brian seethed in his seat.

"Sid," continued Reece, "there are going to be humans and vampires coming at you, all with different motives. Some humans will want you to help them, just like me, but some will put a knife in your back and you won't know until it's too late. You're in grave danger, do you understand?"

In walked Arthur Peasley, survivor of a vampire encounter. "Hey fellas, you're never gonna guess what happened to me!"

He didn't wait for the response as everyone knew it would be shagging related. "This morning, I ended up nailing one of those vampire chicks while doing a plumbing job at the Royal York. She was the most beautiful woman I've ever slept with."

Mouths gaped. Eyebrows raised. Sid let go of a little fart. The standard of Arthur's conquests was a thing of legend. For him to say that a lady was his finest would be like Da Vinci picking out his finest painting, Beethoven choosing his greatest symphony, Meat Loaf having his biggest dump.

Brian asked, "Was she was better looking than that lass who used to do the football pools?"

His question was answered with a smiling nod. Brian could only be impressed.

Sid asked, "Was she better looking than that lass you found unconscious outside Poundstretcher?"

His question was answered with a smiling nod. Sid could only be impressed.

Everyone looked at Rathbone, "I did her mum and sister." Everyone looked away from Rathbone.

"You...had *sex* with a vampire?" asked Reece incredulously.

Arthur gave him a double finger point and a wink of a beautiful eye. "Ah, man, sex is such a dirty word for something so magical!"

"You can't have had sex with a vampire! Not without being killed afterwards. It's unheard of! How do you even know she was a vampire?"

"I overheard her talking to someone about Sid. I tried to get closer to hear what she was saying, and she rumbled me. She charged out of the door, catching me by surprise. She was unbelievably quick. If it was a fella, then it would've been different as my karate speed would've taken care of business. She was so beautiful though. For a millisecond, I was stunned, and she'd knocked me off my feet and pinned me to a table."

"What happened next?" asked Brian.

"OK," started Arthur once he'd taken a mouthful of beer which Kev had brought over. "So there I am, and this red-hot lady is on top of me with my arms pinned to the table, and she has these teeth," he points to his canines, "and they ain't like a normal chick's teeth. They're long and pointy and that's when I say to myself, 'Arthur Peasley, this little lady is a vampire and it is your duty to make love to her.' So I gave her my look."

"Your look?" asked Reece.

The beautiful man gave Reece another knowing nod. "The look that no lady can resist. Anyway, she looks into my eyes and the lady knows I ain't no normal man. She pauses before going for, what I assumed was, a bite...so I said, "'Hey, pretty lady.' She was a little breathless because I'd given her my look. So, I say, 'I'm a peacemaker, baby. I've got love for everyone, humans and vampires alike.' That's when I knew I had her. She didn't expect a plumber to know about vampires. I went in for the kiss. Then, it went on from there. Man, it went on and on from there! Rock-a-hula, baby!"

"Who was she?" asked Reece. "How did you escape? What did she say about Sid? Who was she talking to?"

Rathbone had his own question. "Did you do her in the ar—"

"Why didn't she kill you?" Reece interrupted Rathbone with a more relevant question.

"Kill me? Why would she do that? She said in four hundred years she'd never been pleasured that way before. I even took her number."

Now that really surprised the congregation.

"But...but you've never taken a birds' number...ever," said Brian.

"I know, man, I know. It's the first time that I haven't given out a calling card, and it's gonna be the first time I ever phone a chick."

"For the love of God, you idiots!" screamed Reece. "The fact that he hasn't handed his number out is insignificant compared to a female vampire having sexual intercourse with a human and not killing them! If I hadn't met Sid, this would have been the most incredible thing that has happened in centuries. Arthur, did she tell you her name?"

"Yeah, man, but I kinda forgot it?"

"Oh for fuck's sake!" yelled Reece.

Suddenly, the front door opened. All eyes turned to face the two strangers that'd walked in. It was still dusk, so they had to be human, but they were still strangers, and after Sid's recent antics, everyone was suspicious.

The two young men stopped and stared at the group they'd captivated. They were spooked, that was certain. They walked to the bar trying to blend in.

"What do you want?" said Kev gruffly.

"Can I have two bottles of Smirnoff Ice, please?" Blending in wasn't going to be easy now.

A flash of rage crossed Brian's face. He rose, crossed the room, and landed an ungainly but accurate haymaker on the first man's jaw, sending him reeling to the floor.

"I fooking knew it!" he yelled wrathfully. "You're not fooking welcome in these parts. Get the fook out, before I really start losing my fooking temper!" He kicked the man's behind as both turned and fled.

Brian, still fired up, lit a fag with a shaky hand and took a seat at the table.

Reece couldn't hide his astonishment. "How did you know that they are involved in the world of the vampire?"

Brian gave him a funny look. "Eh? Oh nah, thought they might be students, like."

25

THE NIGHT WENT ON, and by ten-thirty, the group, with the exception of Reece, were completely wasted. Many different people had entered the boozer, but all were locals enjoying The Miner's renovation. Reece had used this time to really understand the group's mentality, and he'd realised that his first diagnosis was the correct one.

These men were a bunch of twats.

The weasel, Garforth, was a horrid individual. He'd regaled stories of his past that'd made Reece feel physically sick. He'd had sexual relationships with hundreds and hundreds of women, and whoever said that the Northern man lacked diversity should meet this fellow. He'd put his genitals in, on, and at, dwarfs, midgets, amputees, the deaf, the dumb, the blind, giants, lesbians, and every creed and every colour. Sid described him as "Cock on Legs," and "The Penis That Walks." The scariest thing of all was that the others respected his opinion, like he was some kind of scholar.

Arthur Peasley was an interesting character. Not the smartest of men, but he wasn't a complete idiot. He was an incredibly handsome man, and there was something so familiar about him, yet Reece couldn't quite put his finger on it. The thick black hair, the half sneer half smile, the baby blue eyes...what was it?

Tillsley was the most powerful human to walk the Earth. Yet, he was unwilling to take his rightful role as a hunter and live his life as a God. Why? Because he didn't want to jeopardise the fifty quid a week, or whatever it was, given to him by the government. Nevertheless, Reece was still confident he'd recruit Sid to his cause. Soon, the Coalition, the Lamian Consilium, and the Hominum Order would change Sid's life in a way he couldn't possibly imagine.

And finally, there was Rathbone, the horrible, greasy little bastard.

There was that deathly quiet again. It could only mean one thing: someone new in the pub. A tall figure ducked to get through the door, and was followed by another, just as tall, but broader. Night was here, and so was the vampire.

Reece was armed to the teeth under his black trench coat: grenades, pistol, and a sub-machine gun. He wouldn't be able to kill them unless he managed to get a grenade in one of their mouths.

Nevertheless, he still had the firepower to make them think about their actions.

"Sid...Sid..." he said.

"...and that's why you should never sit sideways on a bog...Eh? What is it, mon?" Sid was extremely drunk. As usual.

The vampires approached the group. They stood side by side, both standing six-foot-six. The table was arranged so that Reece faced them and the door, Sid had his back to them, and the others sat round the sides of the small bar table.

"Sid Tillsley," said the vampire with hair slicked back. They both wore contemporary clothes to fit in with the local style of dress. Not that it was worth it—they stood out a mile. It wasn't just because of their height; it was because of their beautiful features. Only Arthur could compare, but then, he stood out a mile in Middlesbrough.

Sid turned around carefully in his chair, trying not to fall off. "Yesh, gents."

"I'm Vladimir," said the vampire with the slicked-back hair, "and this is Sven." His companion had long, flowing blonde hair that fell gracefully over his face. Both vampires had the most brilliant blue eyes. "I take it you know who we are?"

Sid squinted. "Brian?" he ventured. "Is that you?"

"You twat, Tillsley, I'm 'ere ya...ya—fook it!" Brian was extremely drunk. As usual.

"May we join you, Mr. Tillsley?" asked Vladimir.

Sid sat up straight in his chair at the words "Mr. Tillsley."

With a lack of subtlety, Sid nodded towards the vampires who were looking at him and then mouthed "Benefit Bastards" to Brian. He then addressed the vampires. "You...may. But, first, I must first try and get to the gents." Sid made an awkward attempt at getting to his feet. "Me back! Me back! Why has God cursed me so?" He limped dramatically towards the toilets, stopping every now and then to clutch at his spine and have a glug of the pint he, unhygienically, took with him.

"Gentlemen," started Reece, addressing the 'boro locals. "These two are not what they seem."

"What? They're not pricks?" said a drunken Garforth.

"Be careful, maggot," said Sven, his lips pulling back over his fangs. "We're not here to fight with Tillsley, but we won't hesitate in showing you your beating heart."

"And I won't hesitate in putting the nut on you either, you lanky twat!" Brian stood up, rearing up to all of his five-foot-seven.

"Baby, he's got backup like you wouldn't believe." Arthur jumped up from his seat, which was an impressive feat after twelve pints of

Bolton Bitter, and fired off a rapid succession of demonstration karate punches.

"You'd be making a mistake to mess with the friends of Sid Tillsley, vampires," said Reece.

"Vampires?" said Brian, eyebrows raised. "Ah, reet." He shrugged. "I'll still smack the twats, like."

"Chambers!" said Vladimir. "I thought you might have crawled from under your stone. I look forward to hurting you."

Reece smiled. "I wouldn't be so sure. I have developed quite a relationship with Tillsley. I know his power and I have witnessed it firsthand. Do not cross me."

"He thinks you're an arsehole!" said Brian, destroying the front Reece had tried to build. Both vampires laughed. Garforth, the weasel, joined in.

"Listen, if you wanna impress the boy in there," Brian pointed over to the toilet where the occasional groan could be heard. Judging by the terrible, terrible sounds, Sid was no longer acting and was in the middle of something quite horrific. "Then you wanna get the beers in for the lads. That's the only reason he talked to that tosspot in the first place." He nodded scornfully at Reece.

Vladimir nodded. "Very well. Barkeep!"

"Who are you calling fookin—" Kevin Ackroyd halted mid-sentence when the vampire raised his hand....

COULD IT BE?

Could the prophecy be true? Every eye in the pub was fixed on what Vladimir held in his hand, raised high for all to see.

A fifty-pound note.

Legends of a note worth fifty pounds had been told on the Smithson Estate for years, but one had ever believed it.

"A drink for every man in the pub, and keep them coming," said the vampire.

A mighty cheer went up. "Vampires are fooking *mint*," was heard in the background.

Sid returned, limping, from the gents. He didn't need to put this limp on. Where the group was sitting, there was beer, there was whisky, and there was brandy...

"Sid! Sid!" said an excited Brian. "They ain't Benefit Bastards! They're vampires—and they got the beers in!"

"Howay the lads!"

THE ENTIRE PUB WAS DANGEROUSLY DRUNK. As usual. Kevin was the happiest man on the planet. These were record takings for a Monday night.

"Tell you what, lads...you're alreet. I mean...you're alreet." Sid was the most sober man out of the group, with exception to Reece. Sid had room for two pints, tops, before he lost the use of the right side of his body. That's when he played his best darts.

Arthur had passed out with his head laid on his forearm. His karate skills were unlikely to be called upon if the need arose. Rathbone had thrown up in the toilets and had made his way home. Brian was still awake, although he'd lost the powers of relevant speech. He was taking turns staring at the vampires and then Reece, deciding whose side he was on. He disliked the vampire hunter and the vampires, so decided to stick the boot in whoever went down first. He couldn't be fairer than that.

"Thank you, Sid," said Sven. "That is very kind of you to say so. Tell me, would you be interested in earning a substantial amount of money?"

Sid's eyes were rolling, but he could still talk. "Will the Benefit Bastards find out?"

The vampires had no idea what Sid was talking about. "Erm...no."

"What do you...*hic!*...want me to do?"

"It's easy," said Sven. "Come with Vladimir and I. We'll put you up in a five-star hotel, and tomorrow evening, you'll meet some of the senior members of our group. They'll ask you a few questions, and then, you'll be free to go...with ten thousand pounds in your hand, cash."

"They'll kill you, Sid," Reece warned. This was a dangerous time for him. Without Sid, he was dead. "They'll kill you as soon as you walk outside of the pub. You killed one of them on Friday. They want revenge. A life for a life."

Sid rubbed his face with his hands and then shook his head forlornly. "Lads, I'm sorry about that. It was an accident, like. I was aiming at some other twat who really deserved a good hiding. I slipped and caught your mate, and I'd thrown a good'n." He drained the last of his beer and put it down with noticeable force.

"Barkeep!" called Vladimir. Once the beer was brought over, Vladimir continued. "We understand the death of Franco was a complete mistake. You're pardoned by the vampire factions. We just want to find out how you managed to do it. We want to know about your past and whether you've had any contact with us before. The Benefit Bastards, as you call them, won't find out. Nothing will come of this other than ten thousand pounds in your back pocket."

"Ladsh, you canna say fairer than that."

"Sid," said Reece, "They'll kill you."

Sven interrupted sternly. "Chambers, what can you give this man? You skulk around in the bushes with the worms and the dog shit, in hope of bringing us down. You're pathetic. You're holding this man back. Sid is heading for greatness. The vampires revere him, and we'll learn a lot from his methods of combat."

Sid smiled. "Ladsh, please give me five minutes to relieve meself, and then, I'll accompany you to the hotel." Sid got up slowly, and with considerable difficulty, before heading for the gents.

REECE HAD TO MOVE FAST. If Sid left with the vampires, then it'd be the end of both of them. Reece kept the vampires talking. "I'm surprised your great species has to lie to a drunk. Is this a sign your power's waning?"

Sven laughed. "You shouldn't let it concern you. You won't see tomorrow. Fear not, it will be quick as there isn't time to give you the death you deserve."

Fear contorted Reece's insides, though he tried not to show it. "What do you want from Sid? You won't find him easy prey, even with these knife-in-the-dark tactics."

"Tillsley won't be murdered, as you suspect," said Vladimir. "We need to discover his secret. We need to know where this power comes from."

"He's the answer to the Firmamentum. He's the answer to what resides in the woods of the North Yorkshire Moors," said Reece.

Vladimir and Sven glanced quickly at each other. "Speak of what you know."

"I have seen what resides in the forests. I've seen the monster, and believe me, the word 'monster' is an understatement."

Vladimir tapped his lips with his fingers, deep in contemplation. "Perhaps, Chambers, you will survive the night."

Sid came back from the toilets, staggering from left to right in a drunken stupor. Garforth had joined Arthur, asleep on the table. Sid's backup was out of action. It was all down to Reece.

"Reet, gentlemen, I'm ready to join this meeting of yours. Would you mind if I had a little something for the road? A little livener against the cold night ahead?" asked Sid, trying to milk the vampires for all he could. He propped himself up against the bar.

Sven rolled his eyes. "Barkeep!"

Reece contemplated his next move. There wasn't much time. Sven and Vladimir joined Sid at the bar, one either side of him. Vladimir kept his eye firmly on Reece. Reece had to think on his feet. He walked slowly over to the group. His mind raced as he deciphered a plan. As he approached behind Sid, he bent down to tie his shoelace.

It was a gamble, but he'd no other choice.

Vampires are quick, but Reece didn't have far to go, and once he'd reached his target, no speed could save them from their fate. As he began to tie his shoelace, Reece rolled forward, commando-style. Halfway through the roll, he reached back and reached for the buttock of Sid Tillsley...and gave it a delicate pinch before rolling out of Sid's line of vision.

PINK ALERT! PINK ALERT! PINK ALERT! PINK ALERT!

Homophobocity: Level MAX.

Pink Alert! Pink Alert! Pink Alert! Pink Alert

Sid turned in the direction of the desecration. "You fooking vampires are *them lot*, ain't ya?" roared Sid. "I should've known. With your styled hair and your long words!"

"What?" Sven began. "What are you talking abo—" He exploded into dust around a perfect right cross.

The punch was perfect, but Sid's balance wasn't. He stumbled and fell drunkenly through the table where Arthur and Brian sat. They all got to their feet together, dazed and confused. Sid pushed himself to the forefront.

The remaining *them lot* was staring at the dust, the *fairy dust* floating...no, mincing around the bar. Then, his eyes focused on Sid.

Sid rolled his sleeves up. Beside him stood Brian, two broken bottles in his hands and a small quantity of sick tricking down his chin. To the other side stood Arthur who had adopted an aggressive karate stance and was firing punches at not quite a blistering pace.

"Right yous!" shouted Sid. "I ain't having it any more. I ain't having you *them lot* trying your...*ways*...with me. Have you fooking got it?"

"I...I don't understand." The vampire looked bemused, but Sid knew the truth now.

"Yes, you fooking do, Tarquin. Your fooking acquaintance thought he could try and get me drunk and then get *involved* with me!" shouted Sid, angry, upset, and violated.

"But, a minute ago, you were happy to come with us!" pleaded Vladimir.

"That's before you started with ya wandering hands!" He turned to his allies in battle. "Are you gonna settle this or shall I?"

"What's he done, man?" asked Arthur.

"He..." Sid struggled to mention the most heinous of crimes,

"...grabbed me, like."

"I didn't grab anything!" shouted Vladimir defiantly.

"I think this one's yours, mate," said Brian.

Sid couldn't understand what Brian was grinning about. Nevertheless...

"Reet!"

And with that, the shortest pursuit in history took place. Sid ambled after the vampire who immediately turned and fled the wrath that confronted him. Before Sid reached the space Vladimir had occupied, the vampire was out of the door and fifty yards down the road. Sid got to the door in a sweat, but the vampire was nowhere to be seen.

"Bastards!" Sid went back inside for last orders.

26

Brian Garforth sat in the passenger seat of his pride and joy, his motor. Jet black, not a scratch on it, 15-inch Brooklands wheels, leather Recaro interior. This motor car was the essence of his heterosexuality. This was a 1983 Ford 2.8i Capri.

It was half-eleven at night, and he'd just experienced one of the worst hangovers of his life. Drinking with vampires was pretty heavy. He'd slummed it on the sofa all day, missing yet another day of work, but he was feeling better now and was ready to go somewhere... different, somewhere...alternative.

It was Tuesday night, and he still hadn't got his leg over this week. Perhaps he was losing his sex drive? He'd needed the help of the little blue pill a few times now, but the lasses of late were red hot, and he needed the edge. One of the lasses was a bouncer in town and had to take the weekend off sick after he'd finished with her, and it wasn't because he'd give her a bad dose of the clap, either. Well, he *had* given her a bad dose of the clap, but that wasn't the reason she needed the weekend off.

Losing the edge? Middlesbrough's Finest Swordsman? Never!

Brian had about four lasses on the go at the moment, but since he'd suggested to Sid to give dogging a go, he couldn't help but feel a little curious as to what went on in the seedy underbelly of Middlesbrough's swinging society. Well, dogging...swinging for poor people.

His one-day drought had convinced him to give dogging a go. Did he have anything to lose? Well, yes, he did have something to lose. Brian was proud of his reputation as a lady-killer, a reputation known not only on the Smithson Estate, but also in over half of Teesside. He loved watching insecure blokes put their arms around their girlfriends as he passed. Everyone knew a lass that the great Brian Garforth had nailed. It was a good thing Sid was his best friend, or he'd have the shit kicked out of him on a daily basis.

Yes, his reputation did matter, and going to car parks for sex with strangers where other blokes were watching in the bushes wasn't the work of a "cad," or a "bounder," but of a dirty old pervert. Therefore, he'd err on the side of stealth so that no one would ever know. He had no choice now, anyway. His ten o'clock hard-on was raging and the cure was dogging.

The Capri roared into life with the first turn of the key. What a car! However, all attempts of stealth were blown out of the water as the Capri's engine roared with raw, unrelenting heterosexual energy.

"Easy, baby, easy," soothed Brian, stroking the dashboard. He touched the accelerator gently, but the natural growl of the man's-man's car reverberated around the terrace houses. The harmonic frequency caused women to become aroused, gay men to hide in terror, and heterosexual men to investigate, filled with a sudden obsession with the car's performance and the driver's favourite B-roads.

A window opened and out poked the sleepy face of a middle-aged man. "Garforth, you wanker!" he yelled. "I'm trying to sleep here!"

Brian, being the opinionated fellow that he was, rolled down the window and yelled back, "Go fook yourself!" He accompanied his point of view with a one-finger salute. Stealth wasn't his forte.

"It's gone half-eleven, Garforth," shouted a half-naked man leaning out of another window of another terraced house. "Where you bleedin' going at this time at night? Doggin'?"

Brian stalled the car.

"He bloody is! The pervert's going doggin'!" yelled the half-naked man.

Brian slumped into the comfortable seat of the 2.8i Capri. A few more windows opened and more lights came on.

"EVERYONE! GARFORTH, THE LITTLE PERVERT, IS GOIN' DOGGIN!" The half-naked man was in his element. Brian knew the man, Tommy Jackson; he had a personal vendetta against Brian. Tommy had no proof, but he was suspicious that when he was working offshore...

Brian tried to start the Capri. Only when all the lights in the street were on did he manage to get the car going. He raced down the street, away from the jeering voices of the wronged husbands of Teesside Terrace.

"Bastards!" spat Brian as he drove through the town centre. He knew something like that would happen. If someone was driving a Capri late at night, then there was a 50:50 chance they'd be going dogging.

He tore down the country roads heading to Middlesbrough's Memorial Park. Not even the jeers of the street could suppress his ten o'clock, or seven-pint (whichever came first) hard-on. It was a curse he'd been afflicted with since the age of twelve. Was Brian Garforth addicted to sex? Absolutely. How could anyone not be? The Capri made a few untoward noises from under the bonnet.

"Come on baby, hold together!"

The clanking sounds stopped, and Brian breathed a sigh of relief. If the local bill caught him up there, they'd have a bloody field day. The Capri pulled into the car park. This was where Sid had his first encounter with the undead. Brian hoped there wouldn't be any here tonight, not because he was frightened. Brian Garforth wasn't afraid of anything except evolving sexually transmitted diseases (he'd built up a natural immunity to all known ones). No, he didn't want to get into a scrap as that was the only thing that would quell his ten o'clock affliction. He was here now, so he might as well do some shaggin'.

He did a three-sixty in the car park to check out the other cars, and there was only one: a silver Mercedes. *Ah well*, he thought, *might as well make my intentions clear.* He flashed his headlights, the local sign for: "Swordsman," he presumed.

The silver Mercedes flashed three times saying...Brian didn't have a clue, but he was ready for action. "Reet!" Brian turned off the engine and rubbed his hands. "Howay the lads." He got out of the car and headed towards the Mercedes, which turned its full beams on to take a look at the catch. It caught him giving it a quick rub on the sly, trying to gain an extra inch. The full beams went down.

"Shit."

Brian walked around to the driver's side. He couldn't see anything because of the blacked-out Mercedes windows.

At least there were no vamps about. In for a penny...

He opened the door and immediately regretted his decision.

"Oh, God, no..."

27

SID WAS WORKING THE DOOR OF THE CLAGGY MAT. He'd worked this particular venue in Yarm, North Yorkshire a few times. He didn't do these kinds of jobs in Middlesbrough, too risky. He only worked the doors of shitholes paying cash in hand, where they couldn't afford CCTV.

It was quarter to midnight and was a relatively quiet night. There'd been a few punch-ups so far. Just kids throwing their weight around after a few too many shandies. He'd get fifty quid for tonight's work, plus petrol money and two hundred decent cigarettes. The shift had started at eleven, and he still felt a little hungover after yesterday's drinking marathon and...violation.

"Sid!" shouted the manager, as he ran through the backdoor. Sid refused to work on the front door of clubs and sat out the back, someone giving him a shout if it kicked off. "Scrap!"

"Aye."

He followed Gary the manager through the door of the Claggy Mat and into the heart of the small, cramped dance floor. There were two groups of five lads causing the commotion. All had fuzzy moustaches that would blow away if the wind got up. Their furry lips looked pathetic, but the lads were too proud to shave off their first piece of facial hair.

The dance floor parted, allowing the big man to walk through, and it was only the arguing kids that didn't notice. They began to push each other a little more aggressively, shouting various threats they'd picked up from their favourite gangster films. Neither group wanted to throw the first punch, but they didn't want to back down because girls were watching.

Sid didn't say anything. He picked up the first two lads he came to, one from each of the boisterous groups of teenagers. The lads were held at arms' length by the scruff of their necks, hanging limp like submissive kittens, staring fearfully at the scariest bouncer they'd ever seen, and by far the scariest bouncer they'd ever heard of.

"Right, lads," said Sid loudly above the music. "If I hear of any more silly buggers, there's gonna be trouble. I don't give a fook who started it or what's it about or any bullshit, like. You lot...," he indicated one group of teenagers with his head, "...go play over there, and you lot...," to the other group, "...go play over there. Now then. Is there gonna be any more trouble?"

All ten teenagers shook their heads as if their lives depended on it.

"Lovely stuff," said Sid, dropping the lads and returning to his post. He remembered what he was like when he was a lad and gave a chuckle. He didn't like it if he had to get heavy with a young'n. He only did if they pulled a blade; then, they needed to learn. Sid lit up a Tibetan "El Monko." He'd obtained four hundred after helping Dave the Buddhist hand out some rough karma to some Jehovah's Witnesses who had been messing with his turf.

He looked at the clock. "Not long left, like."

SHEILA FISHMAN AND GUNNAR IVANSEY SAT TOGETHER IN HIS VAN. They'd followed Tillsley all the way to the Claggy Mat and were hunting for footage of him doing something physical, thus proving he was capable of work.

The vampire sat behind the wheel, staring intensely at the door of the club. "If we obtain footage of him throwing someone out of the club, it should be sufficient to prove him work-capable."

"You're right," agreed Sheila. "But we haven't seen the fat bastard since he went in." She drummed her fingers on the dashboard.

"Patience," said Gunnar calmly. "It's early. Most trouble starts towards the end of the night."

After watching the club for over two hours, Sheila was verging closer and closer to death. She was annoying the hell out of Gunnar. Patience was something Gunnar learnt during the weeks he was trapped in a Canadian avalanche, but this woman's company was something else.

"Where the fuck is he?" she screamed suddenly.

He bared his teeth. "If you don't calm down, you'll blow our cover."

"He hasn't shown up for hours! He's probably on to us. One of us needs to get in there and see what he's up to!"

"Very well!" he snapped back. "There's a camcorder in the back of the van. You can go in and try to catch him working if you want."

"Me!" she exclaimed. "Me? In there? I'm a lady. I wouldn't dream of entering such a place."

He'd expected as much. "You went to The Miner's Arms. This is a much classier establishment than that."

Her eyes glazed over. She looked into the distance like a war vet with PTSD. "After The Miner's, I cannot bring myself to...I cannot, Gunnar. I'll do anything to bring that bastard down, but please, do this for me," she begged.

Gunnar was in no mood for games. "Very well. Be ready to start the engine."

He got out, grabbed the camera from the back of the van, and walked into the club, glad to be away from the hideous woman that was plaguing his days. His moment of relief was tainted by the stench of human sweat. He passed the sorry excuse for doormen and grudgingly paid the entrance fee. It amazed him that humans paid to get into places such as these. It was decorated in a heinous fashion: fluorescent lime green and pink walls; the ceiling was probably white originally, but now, it was sickly yellow through nicotine staining.

The clientele suited the club perfectly, a mixture of humans that hadn't yet come of age, and humans who were well past their prime. They danced and cavorted with each other under the influence of alcohol and narcotics. There was an aggressive atmosphere on the small dance floor as groups of adolescent boys tried to impress the females who were more than willing to breed. The bar was relatively empty compared to the rest of the club. It appeared that the penniless clubbers had drunk themselves stupid before coming in search of a fight or a fuck. There was no sign of Tillsley, but there were many nooks and crannies where the fat oaf could hide.

"Oi, mate! Take a picture of these!"

Gunnar turned around to the most vulgar tattoos he'd ever seen. The greasy hair hung down lankly over an amazing quantity of cheap jewellery. The woman had pulled her top up to reveal two heavily tattooed breasts.

Gunnar almost gagged. Had she suckled a herd of elephants? He looked away and went about his business.

"Oi! I said take a picture of these, ya bastard!" The horror stormed after Gunnar and grabbed his arm with a vice-like grip, which surprised him.

"I suggest you let go of me, woman."

"Hey, girls, this fella taking pics for the nightclub's website is fit as fook!" she yelled at her drunken posse. "Feel his bicep!"

"Fooking 'ell, Maggie, he's gorgeous!" shouted a lady of similar ilk. "Hey, mate, we're on a hen night from Middlesbrough. Get a video for the club website."

All of them ran over, and as one, displayed their mighty mammary glands. Gunnar reluctantly picked up the camcorder and filmed the horrific display. These women would certainly have kicked up a fuss if he hadn't yielded to their will.

The hen displayed far more than her breasts to the camera. Gunnar was amazed he felt sorry for the human who'd marry her, but realised that the groom was probably far, far worse. At the sound of a commotion, Gunnar looked up.

"Where the fook are they? Where the fook are they?" Tillsley bounded through the club knocking clubber after clubber out of his way with swings from his mighty arms. Gunnar could sense his heart pumping at a dangerous rate and hid behind the camera as Sid approached. This could be just what he needed.

"HOWAY THE LADS, MON!" yelled Sid as he caught sight of the exposed breasts and the other, more intimate, areas. He recognised the group: Maggie's lot from the Smithson Estate. He knew it'd be trouble, but he was fired up. "Which of you red-hot lovelies wants to meet the boun—"

CAMERA!

Sid bent over double and clutched his back. Couldn't be too careful in these days of modern technology. The bloke with the camera put it down. He looked proper boiling before he stormed out for some reason! Hang on... wasn't that the lad who played snooker for Merlin's Snooker Hall? Sid shrugged his mighty shoulders. "Fook it."

Sid limped away from the hen night and back to his post.

GUNNAR STORMED OUT OF THE CLAGGY MAT AND INTO THE VAN. As soon as the door shut, Sheila floored the accelerator, and instantly, she was on to him. "Did you get him? Have we got the bastard?" she asked excitedly.

"No. He ran through unexpectedly, and as soon as he saw the camcorder, he feigned back injury. There's no way of getting him tonight."

Sheila hit the brakes hard, and they ground to a halt. "What did you get, then?" she asked. She snatched the camcorder out of his hands and scanned the footage. "You fucking pervert!"

"What?" said Gunnar, slightly perturbed.

"You were in there perving on those rotten women from The Miner's Arms! You weren't trying to catch Tillsley at all!" She got out of the car, slammed the door and started walking down the road.

"Where are you going?" he shouted out of the window.

"Home."

"It's several miles away."

"Fuck off."

Gunnar flipped a coin. Heads: he'd get out of the van and talk her back round. Tails: he'd run her over.

Heads.

"Damn."

He tossed again; still heads.

Reluctantly, he got out of the van. "Sheila, wait!" he called. "As soon as those women saw the camera, they started revealing themselves. They thought I worked for the nightclub and was taking footage for the website. That's when Tillsley bounded over to have a look. He saw the camera and grabbed his back."

"Fuck off."

"What's the matter with you?" Gunnar got out of the van and followed her down the road. She didn't slow her pace.

"I'm angry."

"I can see that."

"I'm angry with you for not getting the job done, for them Middlesbrough slags spending their benefit income in that sordid nightclub, angry with Tillsley for perving on them like a lecherous beast, angry we've spent all night here wasting our fucking time."

She stomped over a bridge that ran over a canal.

Gunnar couldn't see an end to the stomping. He put his hand on her shoulder.

"NO ONE GRABS ME!" she yelled. She spun around and threw her arms up to relieve her shoulder of his hand. Caught by surprise, he fell backwards, tumbling over the railings and over the side of the bridge, landing face first on the canal barge moored below. He hadn't experienced pain like this for a while.

SHEILA LOOKED OVER THE BRIDGE and her rage was replaced with worry. She hadn't meant to push him over the edge. He was her only ally in the fight against the tyranny of the non-working class. She didn't want to see him dead...well, not yet. He lay motionless, his coat raised up like a tent.

"Oh no!"

He'd landed, genitals first, on the barge's chimney. It wasn't a small chimney either. Her misfortune in inflicting crippling injuries to male genitalia was incredible.

"I've killed him!"

"NNNNNGGHHH..." GUNNAR MOANED AND STIRRED. Excruciating pain ran through his lower regions. He dared not think of the damage. His genitals had only just recovered from their last injury.

That *woman*.

He couldn't wait for this whole section of his life to end, so he could torture her for weeks and weeks.

The door of the barge opened and an elderly gentleman, carrying a torch and a frying pan, looked gingerly over the top of his boat. He wore stripy pyjamas and slippers, certainly not equipped to deal with the situation that presented itself. Seeing Gunnar prone, he climbed onto the roof and sleepily made his way over to investigate.

"Are you all right, young man?" he asked, not noticing that the chimney had impaled him.

Gunnar grabbed the old man's leg and threw it as hard as he could. The old man fell hard with the audible breaking of bones. Gunnar pulled him over by his hair and desperately bit into the man's neck. He needed blood for the strength to push himself off the chimney. He needed it for regeneration.

The old man was dead within seconds. He wouldn't have felt anything; he was unconscious from his fall. When Gunnar's thirst was satisfied, he pushed himself up hard from the roof of the barge and escaped his captor with an agonising scream.

"Edward!" yelled the concerned voice of the new widow from inside the barge.

Gunnar leapt from the roof to the deck and rushed inside to drink more blood, vital to his recovery.

When everything was taken care of, including setting fire to the boat and leaving the gas cooker on, Gunnar walked casually outside and up across the roof. His jump onto the bridge was superhuman. Now she'd understand.

He faced her. "If I were you, I'd forget all you've witnessed." He leaned close enough for her to smell the blood on his breath. "And I suggest you never put me in that situation again."

"I thought you were mad..." she managed, looking him up and down, seeing him in a new light.

"The only thing that matters is the hunt for Tillsley. Come. We must leave before the authorities arrive."

They left for the van as the fire took the barge. The remains of the elderly couple and the truth behind their tragic end would be cremated along with all evidence of the vampire's involvement.

28

FOR WHAT SEEMED A LIFETIME, Brian Garforth stared into the eyes of the Devil himself, straight into the eyes of Death, and the only thing that could take away his ten o'clock hard-on. Brian confronted an animal that had ruined thousands before and would no doubt take thousands more.

"Not a fatty!" he cried.

He was hoping for a stunner, not this. But Brian "Any Port in a Storm" Garforth, being the liberal sort of fella that he was, decided to make the best of it.

"All right then, lass, best we get this over with as I haven't got all night, like." He dropped his red woollen trousers and then ripped down his pants to reveal the marriage-wrecker.

She didn't follow immediately. "Come on, pet. You canna be shy if you're up here in the first place, like." He pointed to the bonnet where he wished to perform the act of love.

The girl got out of the brand new Mercedes. "Hi, I'm Sadie."

Brian gave a shrug and shuffled around to the front of the car. "Howay lass."

"What's your name?" she asked.

Brian sighed and shook his head. "Listen, pet, this lark ain't about all that talking bollocks. If I wanted to talk, then I'd have phoned a porn line. This lark is about ruttin', n'owt else, so if you hurry up, we can get on with it." He pointed at the bonnet.

Sadie looked down at the ground. "I was hoping that I'd meet some new people. I thought this was more than sex."

"Well, ya thought wrong, didn't ya, ya daft cow. Now, to business, or do you want me to get in me motor and fook off?"

"No! No...OK, I'll...I'll do it," she said sadly and walked around to where Brian was already doing something obscene.

"Now, pet, if you could grab on to the badge of ya nice motor, then we can begi—" Brian was startled by an almighty crash that occurred in the woods. "What was that?"

Sadie looked scared. "I...I don't know."

A blood-curdling scream filled the air, and both Brian and Sadie grabbed their ears to protect them from the din. A tree crashed into the clearing, and into it walked something from a nightmare. Brian and Sadie both froze at the sight of it. It walked slowly towards them, and the ground shook with each footstep. It stood twelve foot high, its shoulders as wide as a man was tall. Heaving muscle wrapped around every square inch of its frame. Not a hair was visible on its entire body, but veins bulged across every muscle, tendon and bone. Tattered clothes covered its skin.

The face of the monster contorted as it unleashed another deafening scream. Its massive shoulders heaved with each breath, and sweat evaporated from its hulking body. Saliva and spittle flew from its mouth and dripped down teeth the size and shape of a shark's. Its eyes were blood red, and the pupils as black as coal. It looked humanoid, but it certainly wasn't human.

It crossed the clearing until it reached the two doggers. It bent down until its face was a foot away from Brian's.

Sadie was the first one to regain her senses. She turned and fled, running mindlessly away from the beast. The beast peeled back its lips to fully reveal its immense teeth. Its repugnant breath washed over Brian, and his life flashed before his eyes. There was only one option.

Brian put the nut on it, turned, and legged it.

For he was a man of the North, was he not?

The monster roared with anger and held its arms aloft as Brian waddled away like a penguin, still with his kecks around his ankles. He reached down and pulled them up with speed and agility, a move perfected from years of jumping out of ladies' bedroom windows and sliding down drainpipes when husbands came home.

The monster smashed its giant fists into the ground before charging at its first-ever attacker. It was unbelievably powerful, but Brian was, indeed, spectacularly quick over thirty yards. He pumped his arms and legs as hard as he could, running for the safety of his Capri 2.8i. Brian didn't look back but could tell how far the monster was behind him from the sound of its footsteps. Over the first twenty yards of pursuit, Brian put more distance between them, but Brian was at least fifty yards from the Capri, and he only had ten yards of explosive power left.

Brian hit what marathon runners know as "the wall." The only difference was that marathon runners hit the wall after twenty miles; Brian hit the wall after twenty-seven and a half yards. He managed two and a half more yards before he began to slow, and he could sense the monster gaining ground.

Brian ran through the pain barrier. Luckily for him, his Olympian start and Sadie's lack of athletic prowess meant he'd caught up to her before the monster had caught up with him.

Brian Garforth wasn't a gentleman, and in all fairness to the man, he never pretended to be, but Brian Garforth was not a coward either, even though his next action would appear cowardly to an outsider. He saw it as an act of self-preservation, not of him, but of his tackle. His next act would be for the greater good of womankind.

As Brian drew level with the fleeing Sadie, he gently, but effectively, kicked the back of her left foot, which in turn, kicked the back of her right foot. Her legs tangled beneath her, and thus, began the long and slow process of falling. Although Sadie was not running quickly, she was travelling with a lot of momentum, and it took a while before she eventually hit the deck, face first.

The monster, intent on ripping Brian to pieces, didn't notice the prone body of Sadie until it tripped over her, and suddenly, it, too, was heading for a nasty landing.

Brian jumped into the hot seat of his 2.8i Capri and hoped to God it'd start. Against all karma and everything in the world that was decent and holy, it started first time. With a mighty flooring of the accelerator, Brian roared out of Middlesbrough Memorial Park with no chance of being caught, for he was in the fastest and the most beautiful thing to come out of the eighties. Brian put the radio on and cruised along to the enchanting tunes of Toto.

His conscience was clean.

Brian Garforth was a cunt of immeasurable proportions.

29

IT WAS MIDNIGHT. The telephone rang twice and Michael answered it. He was in his London office, a massive room deep beneath the grounds of his manor. Many manuscripts and tapestries hung on the walls. One wall was completely dedicated to weapons from the ages, from basic flint hunting knives to beautifully polished samurai swords. Every kind of weapon adorned the wall, except firearms.

"Yes?"

Sobbing greeted him. He closed his eyes. All his worst fears realised.

"Talk to me," he said.

"I couldn't help it. I had to try."

That voice. He'd known it all along. There was only one person who had the power to hide the Firmamentum.

"Ricard, what have you done?"

"I thought I could handle him. I thought after my experience with Sparle that I could—I thought—I'm sorry, Michael, you were right."

"Where is he?" Michael demanded.

"We lost him in the North Yorkshire Moors. He was doing so well, but we just couldn't tame him."

"You will be dealt with accordingly, along with your accomplices. But first, we will clean up this mess you've created. You will help end what you started, Ricard. We'll be there in two hours." He slammed down the phone and initiated the mission he'd already prepared for.

HIS TEAM WAS READY WITHIN THE HOUR. When rumours of the Firmamentum had arisen, he'd assembled the vampires. It could've been the finest group to grace the earth in living memory. However, with the death of Gabriel and the exile of Gunnar, the effectiveness of the squad had diminished. All twenty were nothing compared to the might of Gabriel and Gunnar combined.

Two hundred and eighty-four years ago, Michael forged the Agreement. He'd foreseen the end of vampire domination. With the technological advancements humans were making, it was time to lie low, no matter how much it pained him. The establishment of the Coalition and the Hominum Order ensured he'd hold his seat of power, even if kings and queens no longer bowed before him. Everything moves in cycles. Soon, he'd rule again. Once tonight was over, he could think of the future.

Briefing the team only took minutes. Most of them were old enough to remember Sparle and the destruction he caused. The team of twenty were equipped with full Kevlar body armour, sub-machine guns, and grenade launchers. Humans certainly had a knack for developing ways to destroy one another. All the team needed briefing on was the location. It'd be a different story this time. With this technology and raw power, the monster would have no chance.

The prophecy proclaimed the Bellator was the only one who could end the Firmamentum. Tillsley was the Bellator. A lamia needing a human...the thought made him sick. The last human born from the prophecy killed his father, and it had haunted Michael for two thousand years. He killed the original Bellator, but it was the beast he longed to face.

Two gunships flew, with all haste, to Ricard's home.

Michael briefed the troops in the air via intercom. "We meet with Ricard in forty minutes. You've trained for this. Death will come swiftly to the beast. We'll surround it and hit it with everything we have. Then, I will behead the freak. Personally."

"Initiating landing, sir," buzzed the pilot.

They touched down, and the troops filed out of the back of the helicopter. They were not finely ordered like a regiment; they weren't trained for discipline—they didn't need to be.

Their task, in principle, was a simple one: search and destroy at any cost. Their natural killing instinct was their greatest ally. How easily could the beast be taken down, though? Would their killing instinct and their cutting-edge weaponry be enough? Many lives would end tonight, but it was of no consequence to Michael.

Ricard was waiting for the group outside his cottage. He ushered Michael and the more senior members of the team inside. The small house could barely contain the massive lamia and their equipment. Once they were all in, Ricard disclosed all that he'd held secret for so long.

"I'm sorry, Michael. I'm sorry for what I have done." At least he'd managed to regain control of his emotions.

"Spare me. You'll be punished in good time. For now, all that's important is that we find and destroy it." A flicker of grief crossed Ricard's face and was gone in an instant, but Michael wasn't going to let it go. "I will end your life without trial if you do not give me all the information. And I won't hesitate to feed your corpse to that beast before ending its miserable life."

"I do not doubt it for a second. Remember though, I didn't have to contact you about Sparle—"

"Sparle? How sentimental of you to name him after your pet from two thousand years ago." Michael shook his head in disgust. "Did you honestly think you could tame it? Was I right? Would your ego not allow you to let go of past failures?"

"My ego? No, I couldn't condemn an innocent being to death before it was given a chance."

"Your missionary voyage was doomed from the start. Why did you call me? What has happened?"

"There were five of us to begin with, but I'm the only one left alive. All of us helped to keep Sparle at bay. We placed electrodes under his skin when he was an infant. If he became too boisterous, we'd electrocute him until we could bind him and take him back home. He needed to run free. It would've been cruel to deprive him of what he was put on the earth to do.

"Everything was fine. All his kills were sanctioned for the others and I. However, as he grew, so did his bloodlust, not to mention his incredible strength and speed. On more than one occasion, he evaded us, which is why some of the cleanups for your teams have been considerably troublesome.

"We always managed to recapture him for he'd spend a great deal of time feeding and playing with his prey. He's had no external influence of violence; sadism must be ingrained in his soul. We stopped taking him out into the open, but the effect was degenerative. I should've ended his life, but I couldn't. My weakness, as you well know, is my compassion." Ricard's voice faltered once more.

"What happened?" pressed Michael.

"This evening, the electricity we passed through his body didn't affect him at all. It didn't even slow his pace. He killed the others...and I knew he was past my control."

"I take it there is a tracking device?" asked Michael.

"Of course."

Michael pointed to the door and the troops immediately began to fall out. "We must find him before he reaches a population. If he does, the Agreement is finished."

THE HELICOPTERS PASSED LOW OVER THE NORTH YORKSHIRE HILLS. Ricard's tracking device showed Sparle travelling at a rapid pace across the moors. "We're lucky he turned west," said Michael. "He's heading out into the wilderness. Why hasn't he stopped to feed?"

Ricard stared at the laptop screen in front of him. "He's been held captive all his life. He's running free. I'm the beast, Michael. I'm the beast for imprisoning him."

Michael's knuckles cracked, but he held his anger at bay. The sentimental old fool was starting to annoy him. He would've killed him, but he could prove a useful distraction if he'd built up any sort of relationship with the animal. Michael reached for the intercom. "ETA, pilot?"

"Five minutes, sir."

"Troops!" called Michael through the intercom that connected both gunships. "We can pinpoint his location to three hundred metres. He won't be hard to find. Let's end this quickly."

The gunships set down twenty feet from the moorland heather, and the two squads of vampires dropped down, hitting the ground running. The two squads spread out, covering the moor at pace. The gunships hovered overhead, scanning the land with infrared heat detectors.

Their surroundings were far more tranquil than the business they attended. A gentle breeze blew the sweet-smelling heather across the moonlit hills. The gunships would have impeccable vision on this cloudless night. If this thing was anything like the original Sparle, there would be no chase; it'd be yearning for a fight.

Michael ran through the night, the vampires keeping pace behind. He was the only one that didn't carry a firearm. He detested them. Michael carried two butterfly swords, although in his massive hands, they were more like daggers. He'd need these deadly weapons against Sparle. He accepted it, no matter how much it hurt his ego.

In the distance was a large farmhouse. The lights had been left on. He took the radio from his jacket. "Make a perimeter two hundred metres away from the house. Remain invisible." He changed the frequency of the radio to that of the gunship. "Pilot?"

"Sir."

"Contact the Coalition. Have Sanderson's team follow Sparle's path from Ricard's to our present co-ordinates. Also, block all telephone lines and mobiles."

"Yes, sir."

"What heat signatures are coming from the farmhouse?"

"From this height, it's difficult to be accurate. There seems to be several people in the house, heat radiating from all. Whether they're all alive or not, I cannot tell. There is movement though."

"We're going in. Sanderson's going to have a busy evening."

Michael's instincts told him Sparle was feeding. It would've heard its noisy pursuers from a mile away. Attempting to satiate its unquenchable thirst was the only reason it hadn't charged them. A few outhouses were dotted around, but these didn't concern Michael. Sparle would've massacred any animals first, the smell of their flesh being stronger.

It was late and unlikely the whole family would be up. The lights were on because the inhabitants weren't able to turn them off. In the blink of an eye, his hypothesis was confirmed: one of the windows was streaked with red.

Sparle was here.

He grabbed the radio. "It's in the farmhouse. Hold the perimeter. Move in to one hundred metres."

The shadows moved closer. He hadn't expected to be this fortunate. He thought the beast would find them first. Catching it feeding and completely unaware was an unbelievable stroke of luck.

"Shall we move in, sir?"

"No, Viralli. We'll force it out, and then hit it with all we have. We don't know where it will escape from. All blindsided soldiers will have to reconvene with the utmost haste. I'll call in a strike." He changed the radio frequency. "Gunship Echo, hit the centre of the building."

"Aye, sir."

The farmhouse exploded and Michael drew his swords. The blaze lit the night sky, and debris showered the waiting vampires.

Sparle's roar of agony could be heard clearly over the fireball, a monstrous cry of anguish and rage.

Sparle leapt from the centre of the inferno to land on the grass twenty yards away, running at an astounding speed away from the burning building. His tattered clothes had burnt away along with most of his skin. He left a trail of smoke behind him, screaming to the heavens. All but the hardest of hearts would've cowered from that sound, but the vampires following Michael were born without hearts.

"Open fire!"

Twenty machine guns burst into action but didn't slow the monster. The two gunships followed Sparle with their mini-guns blazing, but he easily dodged the slow-manoeuvring weapons. With every step, his skin healed, his cries of pain diminished, and his burning rage replaced his burning skin. Without warning, he turned and faced his merciless attackers.

Sparle wasn't just a freak of nature, he was an abomination. Larger than the last rendition of the animal, quicker, and undoubtedly stronger, Nature had seen fit to bring forth a life form that could cope with the technology of the modern world. Mother Nature had unleashed her worst.

The corner of Michael's lip turned up.

He'd waited so long for this.

The gigantic vampire ran straight for his nearest attacker, thundering, uncaring for the bullets that tore apart his body, uncaring for anything but glorious violence and total decimation. The redness of his skin could be seen in the moonlight, stretched across heaving muscles that ached for vengeance.

Otto Klaisman was the first to fall. He'd walked the earth for fifteen hundred years and had once ruled the Bavarian lands. Sparle ripped Otto's throat out in a second and then tore his head clean off with a second swipe of his hand.

"Yes!" cried Michael, his bloodlust impossible to suppress.

Sparle lifted Klaisman's ruined body in front of him, shielding him from the unrelenting bullets.

Michael checked on his team, who had taken steps backwards as seeds of doubt entered their minds.

Sparle charged into Julius Alberto who, to his credit, did not yield an inch. For two thousand years, he was a power to behold, and in an instant, Sparle ripped him in half with a slash of his razor-sharp claws. The beast screamed with delight as he was soaked with the blood of his victim. He drank from the carcass while still hiding behind Klaisman's dismembered corpse.

"Rally to me!" ordered Michael. Fear didn't touch his heart, it never had, it never would. Four were lost before the vampires stood by Michael's side, setting lines of covering fire. Sparle, strengthened by the blood of his victims, screamed a roaring challenge before charging at the gunfire.

Carlos El Rivia, the youngest vampire of the squad, turned and ran in fear. He lost his head to Michael's flashing blade.

"Hold your ground or die!" he roared. Cowardice could never be forgiven, not even by death.

Sparle bowled into the firing squad, sending several flying back with his momentous power. Those who didn't lose their footing tried to fire at him, but it was all in vain. Many lost their lives until only nine of the squad remained.

Michael grimaced. They were weak. They were the best, but they were still weak. Only he was born with true power. The sound of metal scraping on metal filled the air, and the gunfire ceased. All, including Sparle, turned to face him. Michael's swords gleamed in front of him, dripping with blood. He'd stripped to the waist and cut himself deeply from the top of his chest to the bottom of his stomach. Almost instantly, he began to heal. His powers of regeneration were staggering.

Sparle's head was a mess of rage and murder, but even he could understand this was a challenge. And this was a worthy one.

"No matter what the situation, no one will interfere," Michael said calmly.

A grin split his face before he slammed his foot down, taking the fight to the monster. He rushed forward, butterfly swords gleaming. A second later, Sparle replied, up to full speed in a heartbeat. The clash would've been fatal to all but the two titans battling under the moonlight.

Michael plunged one of his swords deep into Sparle's chest but not far enough to reach the heart lying deep within his massive torso.

Sparle caught Michael's other hand that held a sword millimetres from his eye. With his free hand, Sparle gripped Michael's throat and squeezed hard. Blood oozed from his fingertips, causing Sparle to grin in delight.

He has no comprehension of what I am, thought Michael, not deterred that Sparle treated the sword in his chest as nothing more than a splinter.

This was a stalemate, with neither combatant willing to relinquish their hold and neither able to finish their opponent.

"Sir, shall we fire?" shouted Viralli.

Michael could say nothing due to his crushed larynx, but he didn't need to. The look he gave Viralli told his loyal soldier all he needed to know.

Sparle sunk his long fingernails into Michael's wrist, wanting to rid the threat of the knife millimetres from his eye. The pain didn't faze Michael in the slightest, but if his tendons were ripped apart, he'd lose a weapon. Even though it pained him, he couldn't defeat Sparle without it. He twisted the sword in the monster's chest, before pulling it out with a spray of blood. It gave Michael the opportunity to slip the vice-like grip holding his throat.

Michael retreated, slashing down, severing a couple of Sparle's fingers. The beast screamed with rage. The vampires yelled victoriously. Michael licked the blood off the blade, taunting the animal. Its screams turned into insane laughter as it looked upon its enemy. Now, it realised what stood before it, and it relished its own pain and the spilling of its own blood.

Sparle charged again.

Michael flourished his swords, flicking Sparle's blood from the blades. The weapons shone in the moonlight, mirrored by the gleam of the monster's fangs.

Sparle leapt with the intention of crushing Michael into the ground.

Michael swiftly dodged to one side and cut powerfully downwards into Sparle's descent.

Sparle roared with pain and frustration as he collapsed into the moorland heather.

Michael had cut deep into the giant's hamstrings, disabling him, halting the constant attack. Michael didn't allow Sparle to rest, turning back, and attacking with renewed vigour. Michael cut down and Sparle threw his hands wildly in the air to protect himself from the blade.

Michael fell back. *The lucky...* He clutched at his eye. Sparle's talon had ripped across it when he lifted his arm to protect himself. Michael would've been dead if Sparle could've moved fast enough, but his hamstring was still regenerating from the huge gash.

"Sir!" shouted Viralli, "Are you OK? Shall we—"

"If you dare think of interfering—!" Michael shouted in between spitting out the blood dripping into his mouth.

Michael assessed Sparle's injuries against his own and decided not to attack.

Sparle crawled towards Michael, uncaring for his own physical state. All he desired was death. His hamstring had almost healed, the strength returned, and he powered into another ground-shaking charge.

Sparle was on Michael before he knew it. Michael was not able to judge the distance because of his ruined eye. He only just got his swords up in time. They bowled over until Sparle came to rest on top of him, impaled, the monster's vast mass skewered by the upturned blades. Sparle screamed, but it was in delight rather than pain.

Michael's hands were trapped in the sword hilts. There was nothing he could do to stop the onslaught.

"Open fire!" screamed Viralli.

I'll have your head for that, thought Michael as the darkness came.

THE HALL OF THE LAMIAN CONSILIUM WAS FULL TO THE RAFTERS. All the chairs were pushed to one side, and humans stood within its great walls. The elders had called the emergency meeting after hearing of Michael Vitrago's demise. The Firmamentum was here. Sid Tillsley was the only answer.

Only three of the twenty had survived Sparle's onslaught, fleeing to the gunships, which had held the beast back with their powerful guns. The survivors had briefed the elders by radio, and the area had been sealed off to the best of their limited capabilities. To keep this a secret would require a miracle. The humans were called as soon as the elders knew the truth.

Before Sparle's emergence, both sides had contacted Tillsley to see what they could gain. Now, it was obvious they must work together to put an end to this.

"This is the first time that humans have entered this chamber," spoke an elder, Nawa Bwogi, an ancient vampire, fair and righteous. He'd seen Michael's rule as the best thing for the species, not that he'd liked it. The Firmamentum had caused a personal vendetta to overshadow sanity. With Michael's death, the hierarchy of the Lamian Consilium would be in a state of unrest for years. "Michael Vitrago has been killed by the beast spawned by the Firmamentum."

Bwogi waited for the gasps and outbursts from the humans to die down. The news was an immense shock to all. "The beast is raging through the North Yorkshire Moors. We're trying to pin it down with gunships. I don't need to tell you what it will mean if it reaches a major population." He sighed and rubbed his brow. "Only a beast born from the prophecy could bring down Vitrago. We have no alternative but to fulfil that prophecy. We must find Tillsley and force him to fight."

"What happens if Tillsley won't fight?" asked Caroline.

Another elder answered the question. "If Tillsley doesn't fight, then Tillsley will be killed. If Tillsley dies, then we'll have to atomise with beast."

"But—" began Caroline, but was pre-empted by Bwogi.

"What other option do we have? The coverup operation will be more difficult than anything since Lockerbie."

Caroline nodded in agreement but chewed the inside of her mouth in annoyance at his interruption. Their only hope was the great right hand of Sid Tillsley.

RICARD SAT IN THE HELICOPTER with the surviving members of Vitrago's squad. A variety of emotions raced through his head: relief that Sparle had survived; hope that he'd somehow escape; guilt at the death of Michael and the squad; disgust at himself for not being able to help Sparle.

Reinforcements had arrived, and he and the squad were now leaving the catastrophic mess. They all stared at Ricard. Each had lost friends. Each had sustained horrific injuries because of his idiocy, his naivety, his weakness, his love.

"I'm sorry." It was all he could muster.

None of them dignified him with a response.

He put his head in his hands. Never had he felt such guilt, but it was not for the death of Michael. It was for turning Sparle into the Lamian Consilium.

Did he have an option? No. Once Sparle had escaped, there was only one course of action. He did, however, have one more choice to make, and it was a decision that was, without a doubt, the most important one of his entire life.

30

SID STROLLED DOWN THE ROAD with a skip in his step and a gleam in his eye. It'd been a funny old few days. He'd never been treated to so much free booze in his life. After the *them lot* vampires had been sent packing, him and the lads had been on another free bender because of some blokes in suits who had dropped in to The Miner's. Rich had said they were with some poncy committee about vampires or something, but the important thing was: they got the beers in.

It was all a bit hazy. They'd wanted Sid to go with them, but then, he'd had a few too many. He couldn't remember if he'd hit one of them or both of them, but it had all turned nasty when Rich had told him the name of the organisation they were in was called the "Homo Order."

Sid shuddered.

Anyway, it was a good night. Brian had turned up and told everyone about the dogging he'd got up to. Apparently, he'd got into a scrap with some big fella for getting in the way of him ruttin'. He's a card, all right.

With all the free beer and odd jobs, Sid was pretty flush. It was time to treat himself to a good ol'-fashioned all-dayer in The Miner's.

Yep, everything was going great for Sid, that was, until the riot van pulled up in front of him and mounted the curb. Six big policemen, dressed in full riot gear, jumped out and approached him, hands on batons.

"Sid Tillsley, you're under arrest for benefit fraud," stated the nearest copper. "You have the right to remain silent, but any—"

"I'm not Sid Tillsley," said Sid Tillsley.

"Yeah, right! Now get in the van!" shouted the copper. He was only young, but Sid was a man who deplored rudeness.

"I ain't taking that from you, young'n!"

Sid suddenly grabbed at his buttock, pulling out a dart. "What the fook?" Two more darts replaced the one he'd removed, and the effects began to take their toll. Sid spun round to look at his attacker, a police marksman in the passenger side of an unmarked car. "You...you..."

The tranquillisers began to kick in as they were forced round the big man's narrow arteries. He staggered towards the car in what proved to be a vain attempt to stick the gun up the copper's arse. Sid only made it halfway. Sleep took him before he reached the ground.

SID AWOKE WITH A START. He was pretty sure he was in a cell. He sat up gingerly, although he had a remarkably clear head considering the drugs. Cowardly bastards, hitting him in the arse with darts. He'd been arrested a few times before and had always come quietly, so he must be in deep shit this time. If his benefit fraud was at the end of its long and financially lucrative road, then the next few years were going to be a struggle he could do without.

He settled back down on the bed. This was not the type of cell he was accustomed to. The bed was extremely comfortable, and most prison cells didn't have a bottle of water and sandwiches waiting by the bedside. Something was going on here.

In an immediate answer to his question, the door to the cell opened. Light streamed in to reveal a room that couldn't come close to being called a cell, not even by those posh lasses that lived in semi-detached houses, had coffee mornings, jostled for strawberries in Wimbledon SWfooking19, and were proper twats. An amazingly attractive shape was silhouetted in the doorframe.

The tranquillisers hadn't affected Sid's blood flow.

"Good afternoon, Sid. I'm Lucia. Please follow me, as there are many of us who wish to speak to you."

"Aye, pet, I'll follow you anywhere," he said lecherously. No lass at the benefit office looked like that. She was red hot. More suspicion from the big man, who rubbed his chin thoughtfully. Luckily for Sid, who had never been overly fond of thinking, following that magnificent behind made all suspicion drift away.

"I suppose you're wondering why you're here?" asked Lucia over her shoulder, spilling her immaculate black hair across her back as she turned.

"Eh? Err...wassat?" managed Sid, dragging his eyes away from her tight trousers.

"I said, Mr Tillsley, I should imagine that the question: 'Why am I here?' is going through your head, right now?"

"If I'm honest, pet, no," said the crooner.

Lucia smiled at Sid. He concluded that the smile wasn't forced at all, and she probably just had a bit of wind. "All your answers are waiting through here, Mr. Tillsley," she said, throwing open the doors to a massive, fancy room, full of twats in suits...and *them lot*.

"Fook."

Sid wasn't the brightest penny in the pile, but he was clever enough to realise this wasn't just about benefit fraud. Maybe they found out it was him who carried out that despicable crime in Middlesbrough Library, 1993. Even he had to admit it was the worst thing he'd ever done, and he'd known it would come back to haunt him.

Most of the people here were them vampire fellas. If any of the dirty buggers made a play for him, then he didn't care how many there were, the first one with the wandering hands would get a black eye.

Vampires were quite distinguishable to Sid now. Some of the angrier-looking ones had those pointy teeth going on. All of them were big lads though, with big, bright, sparkly eyes. He hadn't seen the lasses before. If they'd sent the lasses to see him in the first place, things would've been different. Sid was all for making love, not war.

"Sid Tillsley?" said a black African fella with a shaved head.

It was best to be polite, just in case he was in shit and needed to sweet talk his way out. "Aye, I'm Sid."

"Do you know why you're here?" asked the African.

Sid remembered back to that dark day in '93. Never in the history of the world had so many pop-up books been so terribly defiled. Still, best to plead ignorance, as usual. "No, sir."

"Sidney, you're here because we urgently require your help," This time, the speaker was a short, black, English woman. She reminded him of a female version of Trevor McDonald. "You can save humanity. You can prevent the world from descending into civil war."

"Can ya get someone else to do it?" he said with a grimace. "Me back. Me back is in terrible shape and I canna work, ya see?" He grabbed at his spine.

The congregation gave him looks of disgust and several unpleasant comments were shouted.

Sid made a note of a couple of the more offensive comments. He'd be meeting those responsible in the car park after.

"Do you know what your purpose in life is, Sid?" the question came from a young vampire with a blonde ponytail. He was a good-looking lad who must have got his fair share of action.

"Young'n," he said, "I need at least six or seven pints to start talking shite like that. This place got a bar?"

Everyone ignored him except for an ancient, old-looking fella who was sitting next to the African. "Sid, have you ever wondered why you're able to kill vampires with a single punch?"

The big man looked down at his right fist. "Not really, mon. I've always had a pretty good punch on me, like."

The old timer continued. "No, Sid, you can't kill our kind with strength alone. When you first showed yourself to us, by slaying Gabriel, we were amazed. You killed one of the greatest warriors in history, and our gut instinct was one of fear. We thought you'd developed a secret weapon that threatened our existence. However, now, we know why you're here and what you are."

Sid didn't have a clue what the poncy twat with the big words was going on about.

"There is a prophecy," the old timer continued, "well it was once a prophecy, that is now a way of life. The original prophecy predicted that—"

Sid stopped listening. There were distractions.

"Sid. Sid. SID! SIIIIDDDD!"

Sid looked round the room a few times, the echo confusing him, and then back to the old vampire bastard who looked proper angry. "Eh, what?"

The old fella's cries had stopped Sid perusing the hall for the greatest set of breasts, an investigation he was carrying out in the name of science.

"I'll continue, shall I?" said the old timer.

"Aye," said Sid, not before winking at the winner.

"The original prophecy spoke of a vampire unlike any other, born with an unearthly power and an unquenchable bloodlust. However, there would be a human with the strength and the will to defeat it, thus bringing nature into balance."

Sid didn't have a clue what the old fart was on about, and he didn't care, either. What he did know was that none of them had mentioned benefit fraud or the incident on the library story mat where he was caught short, and that in his forty-six years, man and boy, he'd never seen so many great jugs in one room.

Best to act ignorant.

It wouldn't be difficult.

Sid shrugged.

"Sidney, *you* are the human! You are the man who will save the world. You are the man who must kill the beast ravaging your homelands in the Northeast."

Oh, no...

"With reckless abandon, it rampages, never satisfied, always on the hunt."

Sid knew exactly what they meant.

"You're the only one who can stop it destroying the lives of hundreds of people..."

Fook. They had to be talking about Brian. He'd never been careful where he put it. They wanted to bring him down because he never rubbered up.

"We need you to kill the vampire monster roaming the moors."

The penny dropped at last. This was what Rich had been chewin' on about. Even so, he didn't want to get involved. "Look, lads, lasses," he nodded at Lucia's cleavage. "I don't want to get involved. I'm a simple man, a simple man with simple needs..."

"If you don't," said the female Trevor McDonald, "then we'll imprison you for benefit fraud. When you're finally released, we'll make you pay back all the money you have taken by working legitimately. We'll kill your friends and burn down your local pub. And then, when you think that things cannot get any worse, we'll torture you until you die."

Sid stood flabbergasted. "Fooking 'ell, you miserable bitch! Bet you haven't had a good shaggin' in a while."

Sid's comments drew gasps from the other humans, but it didn't deter the female Trevor McDonald.

"However, if you help us, all your previously obtained benefit money will be forgotten about, and you'll be paid a million pounds for one night's work."

Sid considered it. It sounded like a trap to him, and he wouldn't put it past them Benefit Bastards to set something up like this. Most likely, he didn't have a choice, but Sid was a man who didn't like being pushed, and Sid Tillsley would rather go down with his head held high.

The big, black African fella stroked his chin in thought. He looked quite regal, really. He seemed to come to some sort of decision. "If you help us, Sid," he said, all eyes turned towards him, "Lucia will show you her breasts."

SID WAS WIGGLING HIS ARSE in the most comfortable armchair in the world. He was enjoying a glass of two-hundred-year-old brandy and a Cuban cigar. The vampire lads were against him having a couple of brandies, but he always had a couple of drinks before a big fight.

A large cloud of sweet-smelling smoke rose steadily to the high ceiling. It was a magnificent room, fancy wallpaper and pictures and things. If he were to become a millionaire, he'd have to get used to it. He was ninety per cent certain it was a trap, but the chance of seeing them heavenly funbags after the punch-up was a chance that couldn't be given up, no matter what the consequences.

The lass was not too pleased about it, and he thought she was going to rip that African fella's nuts off. Thinking about it, none of the others looked particularly amused either. If he hadn't shouted out that they had a deal, it would've kicked off!

It was eight-thirty in the evening. They were going to be flying out in helicopters in an hour. Because of them vampire fellas not liking the sunlight, the lad he had to put the nut on wouldn't be out until after ten. Then, it was a case of giving him a hiding and earning a cool million before seeing something very special indeed.

What could go wrong?

RICARD KNOCKED ON SID TILLSLEY'S DOOR. He hadn't yet been tried for his crimes against the Agreement, but what of his crimes against the being he swore to protect? He'd been ordered to advise this man, Sid, on the best way to defeat Sparle, of his strengths and weaknesses. Sparle would be subjected to more betrayal, and Ricard would pay for his crime against the balance.

"Aye?" said a deep Northeast accent. Ricard was familiar with the accent, spending the past twenty years amongstst the likeable folk.

He opened the door to the overweight figure of Sid Tillsley inhaling a cigar. He appeared to be in his element, not perturbed by the horrors he was about to face. This was the man who'd killed Gabriel with a single punch and defeated four vampires while hungover. Could he defeat the raw power and aggression of Sparle? Ricard very much doubted it.

"Good evening, Sidney. I'm Ricard," he said, offering his hand.

It was shaken vigorously. "Please to meet you, Rick. Call me Sid. You're the one who's gonna tell me about the fella I'm doing a few rounds with later?"

The human threw a few shadow punches, as if he was in for a light sparring contest. His pulse wasn't racing, although, through the cholesterol, it was definitely struggling. He wasn't dressed for combat. He should be wearing full Kevlar battle armour and be equipped with copious blades and firearms. Instead, he wore jeans that were three sizes too small for him and a leather jacket. A fading tiger stared back at Ricard with the words "The Collection" written underneath.

Ricard smiled. "I suggest you change your attire. You'll need all the protection you can get."

"Nah, mon, this is what I always scrap in. I'll be reet."

"Sid, this isn't a normal vampire, you understand?" Ricard realised he wasn't dealing with one of the smartest members of human society.

Sid nodded. "Aye, mon. Me mate Brian had a tussle with him up in Memorial Park, few nights back. Big ol' bastard apparently, good chin. Brian said he got all his balls into a head butt and it didn't even shake the bugger. Brian did a runner and the thing was nearly as quick as him over thirty yards! Fast, hard fooker, by all accounts."

There was no fear in Sid's eyes. "Sid, how old are you?"

"Forty-six, Rick."

Ricard had never been called Rick before. He quite liked it. "When did you realise you had the gift of battle, Sid?"

"Eh?" asked Sid, screwing his face up.

Ricard dumbed down the question. "When did you first realise you could fight?"

"Oh, reet. Let me think..."

Sid scratched his head like a great bald gorilla. Maybe he was the Missing Link.

"Was always big as a kid, like, always a lot bigger than the other lads my age. When I started school, some of the older lads tried to bully us 'cos I stood out."

"What did they do to you?"

"Well, n'owt. That's when I first realised that I could fight. One of the older kids came up with a group of his mates, showing off, like. He tried playing silly buggers, so I give him a right hook and none of the others wanted any after that."

"How old was the boy you hit?"

"About fifteen, I reckon, but he had a shit jaw."

"How old were you?"

"Five."

Ricard blinked. Sid wasn't like other humans, but that wouldn't stop Sparle tearing him to shreds. Sid didn't deserve that, not under the circumstances. He was not Remo, the Bellator of two thousand years ago. Ricard shouldn't have allowed the situation to reach this point. He'd no idea how similar this Sparle would be to the one born two millennia ago. They were almost identical, although this rendition was undoubtedly stronger. Now, he was to send this human with a "gift" against Sparle.

"Sid, I don't think you can beat Sparle." His comment was not taken seriously.

"Don't be wet, lad. This right hand's never failed to knock out a client. It's just you buggers react a bit differently, which is unfortunate for yous, like. He'll go down the same way as the rest. Don't worry."

There was no way to convince Sid of anything else but a round-one victory. It was futile to tell him of Sparle's weaknesses. *Weaknesses!* Only his intelligence held him back from being a perfect killing machine, and that wouldn't help Sid. It was likely Sparle had the higher IQ. The only thing Ricard could do was to tell him of Sparle's strengths. At least then, he'd know what it was that would kill him.

"Sid, Sparle has no weakness, but let me tell you his strengths."

"Aye, you should know your opponent before going into a fight.

Clever thinking that, Rick," commended Middlesbrough's answer to Sun Tzu.

"You already know about his speed and his ability to regenerate?"

"Eh? Regen...regenter...Eh?"

"He heals quickly, almost instantly, in fact. The blow your friend landed on him would've felt like a fly landing on his face. He could be hit by a car and heal within a minute."

"Shit the bed, mon!"

Ricard hoped that he was finally getting the point across.

"Poor bastard has no hope of getting anything on the sick from benefit office."

Ricard was learning to expect the unexpected from Sid Tillsley. "That's not the only thing, Sid, his power is immense."

He was cut off by Sid's recollection. "Oh aye, I saw the bastard lobbing trees like darts, very impressive, like. Thing is, Rick, darts ain't a power game, it's about accuracy and nerve. Got a 137 getout, last year, ya know?"

Ricard unfurrowed his brow. "The only other things are his teeth and nails," continued Ricard, as if Sid hadn't spoken. "His teeth are the size of your little finger, and his nails are like tiger's claws. If they catch you, you're dead."

Sid didn't look impressed by this latest revelation. "Scratching and biting! Is he a fooking girl or summat? I don't like that, Rick, I don't like that at all. But, if it's fighting dirty, then Sid Tillsley is willing to go there. I don't like it, but I ain't having some fairy trying to pull me hair."

Ricard looked up at Sid's shiny bald head.

"Me chest hair...or worse. He'll regret it if he plays silly buggers."

Ricard sighed. It was futile.

A knock at the door preceded the beautiful Lucia.

"Mr. Tillsley, your helicopter awaits."

"Howay the lads!"

31

SID SAT IN THE HELICOPTER, as excited as a schoolboy when his mum's Littlewoods' catalogue came through the post boasting an extra large lingerie section. He'd always wanted to have a go in a helicopter, especially as he'd never flown because of his fear of air stewards. It was scary to think that thirty-nine per cent of people in the air at any one time were *them lot.*

A helicopter was different. A helicopter was man-travel. None of them orange-hued feminine fellas putting your seat belt on and...He went into a cold sweat and grabbed the armrests of his chair.

"You OK?" The voice came through his ear-guards from the vampire opposite.

"Aye, mon," he said through his own intercom. "Never been in a chopper before, that's all," he lied about the reason for his unrest.

The vampire looked away in disgust.

The big man's anxiety began to pass. *Relax, mon! Just think about the chopper, just about the chopper and not the air steward's chopper...Hang on.*

Sid was sick into a paper bag.

The helicopter soared high above London and raced towards the North. After a quick shot of whisky from a hipflask, the taste of cigar-smoke-flavoured vomit subsided, and Sid began to really enjoy the ride. There were some beautiful views of the towns and cities lit up below. It was almost a shame to give someone a pasting at the end of it.

He didn't know where they were headed for the scrap. Apparently, they had to find the fella first. What was his name? *Spam?* Good name, that.

That Rick did go on. A funny fella, but the best vampire Sid had met so far. The African fella was a good lad too; he was gagging to see that lass's jubblies! With Rick, Sid had got the impression he didn't want the fight to kick off for some reason or other. It didn't matter now. He'd no choice but to get on with it.

"Eh-up, fella, when we getting in?"

The pilot spoke through the intercom. "Half an hour, tops. It won't be long. Prepare yourself."

RICARD WALKED BRISKLY though the corridors of the Lamian Consilium. He was about to stand trial for his crimes against the Agreement. He'd be tried by the elders, and sentenced immediately. This would be the first trial without Michael being present since the setting of the Agreement, and he was curious to see how the elders would function without the Bloodlord. Who would replace the irreplaceable? Would they rule as a council rather than a dictatorship now there was no obvious figure of power?

Ricard reached the doors of the courtroom, grand double doors similar to that of the Great Hall. He pushed them open into a room surprisingly larger. Several pillars were required to hold up the ceiling, high above the stone floor of the gigantic oval hall. At the far end were twelve identical chairs set in a semi-circle surrounding a dais where the accused would be interrogated. Where *he* would be interrogated.

Eleven seats were occupied with eleven vampires dressed in blood-red robes. There was no way the Consilium, or the elders, could foresee Michael's death, but Ricard did. Michael held the Agreement above everything, except his own ego. It haunted Michael that the human who killed his father had defeated the last beast in battle. And it was ironic that Michael had accused Ricard of the same mistake with his ego. There was no way Michael could resist the chance to fight the most dangerous creature ever born. He would've broken the world to face Sparle in battle.

Ricard stood on the dais. He was older and wiser than every elder present. He knew it, and they knew it, but it'd do him no favours. There was a mix of friends and enemies in this group, but all would judge him fairly. It wouldn't be difficult. Bwogi sat in the centre, but Ricard doubted he was striving for leadership. He was a good vampire with a righteous heart. Ricard didn't like putting him through this nightmare.

To his left was Helga Khan, a Bavarian he'd known for fifteen hundred years. She was younger than he, but not by many decades. She was as striking as when he first met her. Grey now flecked the long, dark curls that fell gracefully over her slender shoulders. Her eyes irradiated with the intensity they did all those centuries ago. They had worked together many times over the years, but their mutual fondness for one another wouldn't hold any sway this day.

There were others that Ricard could not call friends. Henrik Sleant was an animal, but not in the same sense as Michael. Torture and cruelty were his speciality. Being an accomplished diplomat was no excuse for being an abomination.

Who these people were was not important. He was the one standing trial.

THE HELICOPTER'S WARNING SIGNALS SCREAMED at the pilot as he lost control of the vehicle. The helicopter regained stability, and the reason for the loss of control became apparent. A fireball rose hundreds of feet above the moors, and the thermals had sent the chopper spiralling into the atmosphere. "Looks like we have him," said the pilot.

"Never mind him!" shouted Sid. "Watch how you're flying this bastard! I nearly shat myself then!"

The pilot ignored the cries from his unhygienic passenger. "This is Prophecy. We have Tillsley with us. Update on ground status?"

"Glad to have you on board, Prophecy. This is Alpha Gunship. Apologies for the explosion back there. We suspected Sparle was in—" The transmission cut off abruptly.

The pilot of the Prophecy attempted to regain contact. "Come in, Alpha! Come in, Alpha!"

"This is Alpha. We have contact, repeat, we have contact. We'll patch you the bearings."

The vampire opposite Sid lifted the visor of his helmet. "This is it, human. You'd better be all that they claim. If you're not, you're a dead man." said Viralli. "I watched that thing kill twenty powerful vampires while taking constant machine gun fire. What can you do?"

"Death from above!" Sid loudly broke wind to the tune of "The Ride of the Valkyires."

Viralli, although disgusted, couldn't help but be impressed.

BWOGI BEGAN THE PROCEEDINGS FOR THE TRIAL. "Ricard, you're accused of jeopardising the Agreement. How do you plead?"

"Guilty," said Ricard in a far away voice.

Bwogi nodded. "It's understood you've harboured 'Sparle,' as you have named him, the vampire born from the Firmamentum. You attempted to 'tame him,' is this correct?"

"Yes."

The council members looked at each other, passing different comments with their eyes.

It was Helga who spoke first. "Ricard, what did you hope to achieve? Did you really think you could succeed where you failed two millennia ago?"

"I had no choice, Helga. I couldn't forsake my son."

It took a moment for the enormity of Ricard's confession to sink in.

"Sparle...is your son?" asked another elder. "What about the first Sparle? What other lies have you told us through the centuries?"

"The first Sparle was also my son. I have told two lies in my life, both to protect my blood. The first time I harboured Sparle, the death of thousands on my conscience was my punishment. This time, my actions could break the world."

"For someone so 'wise,' surely you would've realised this when you set the beast free?" asked Miguel Samorro. He'd always considered Ricard a weak entity because of his love of the human race. If it weren't for the severity of the situation, he would've enjoyed the predicament entirely.

"I have no excuses. My love for my son stayed my hand, and I'm willing to accept any punishment deemed fit."

"It's lucky the Bellator has been found. He's the only hope we have," said Helga.

Ricard shook his head. "Tillsley is not what you think."

GUNSHIP PROPHECY RACED OVER THE MOORS with Alpha following closely behind. The monster had taken refuge in an abandoned mine and left to hunt as soon as the sun set. Since his initial escape, Sparle drove west, killing everything in his path. Houses were evacuated wherever possible and excuses made to the locals. The vampires plotted his path by using herds of cattle and sheep. They placed them at strategic points for him to feed. However, all attempts to trap the creature were unsuccessful.

"Are you ready, human?" asked Viralli. "We're pushing him towards an old quarry where we'll be able to hold him for a short while."

The human threw a series of jabs and stretched his arms laboriously across his chest. "Aye, mon, that should do it. Don't want to peak too soon, like."

Viralli didn't comment. What was the point? He was not someone who believed in prophecies. Sparle was real, and putting this human up against him would be like setting a child on a bear. Prophecy or not, Sid Tillsley was going to die.

"WHAT DO YOU MEAN, RICARD?" demanded Helga.

Ricard played with his hands, anxiously, nerves finally getting the better of him. He'd betrayed Sparle once, and that is why his son endured the chase over the moors. Could he let him down completely?

"Ricard! Explain yourself!" shouted a younger vampire, not old enough to have seen the Firmamentum of two thousand years ago.

This was it. This was decision time. His son would die whether he faced the Bellator or not. Modern artillery was too powerful and had the ability to atomise his son if the need be. It'd be at great risk to the Agreement, but not compared to Sparle running through a city. It wouldn't be right for things to come to that. If Tillsley fought Sparle, it would be in vain.

"I'm so sorry, my son."

32

"WE CAN'T TOUCH DOWN WITHIN HALF A KILOMETRE OF THE TARGET," said the pilot. "Sparle bought down a helicopter that was flying low. We cannot risk losing another bird."

"Affirmative," replied Viralli. "From the drop-off point, we'll proceed to the quarry, on foot."

"Eh?" Tillsley, for the first time, looked shaken about the mission. "What the fook you talking about? How far is half a kilothingy, when it's at home?"

"Five hundred metres."

"Eh? Stop playing silly buggers, mon. How far in real distances, in yards?"

"Five hundred and fifty."

Tillsley put his head into his hands. The magnitude of the situation had finally hit home.

Viralli said, "It will all be over, soon, human."

Sid looked up from his hands. "You're having a fooking laugh, ain't ya? Five hundred and fifty yards! It's gonna take me a good half an hour to make that sort of ground. No one said anything about me walking anywhere."

The pilot announced their descent.

Viralli's mission was to accompany the human to the battle, and as ever, he'd follow his orders to the letter. Viralli looked the big human up and down. Gabriel's bane. Viralli had fought beside Gabriel and had seen him defeat overwhelming odds on numerous occasions. Viralli would love to have a go at Tillsley, this "champion" of humans. He was a wreck of a man, but his eyes, though small and beady, showed something else. Where the eyes of the vampires were bright, beautiful, and piercing, Tillsley's were like dark pools, which reflected no light. He was unlike anything Viralli had seen before.

The landing was a smooth one.

Viralli jumped out of the helicopter while Sid climbed awkwardly, but safely, out.

The helicopter took to the air to avoid attack. The two began the walk to the quarry, the gate of which could be seen in the distance.

"What is your strategy of attack?"

"Eh?" said Tillsley, screwing his face up.

Viralli raised his eyes to the heavens. The man was an idiot. "What I mean is: how do you intend to fight your opponent?"

"I knew what you fooking meant, smart arse, but it's a stupid question, ain't it?" snapped the human, muttering under his breath, "Fooking vampires are all *them lot* and wankers."

Viralli didn't like humans, especially Tillsley. "How is that a stupid question? You're about to fight a ferocious animal, you need to have some sort of plan!"

"Well, I don't do that running around bollocks. I'll wait until it comes to me. Then, I'll fooking smack him!"

"And then what?"

"What do you mean, 'then what?'" asked Tillsley, an annoyed look on his face.

"What are you going to do after you've 'smacked it?'" Viralli added two finger dittos when he said "smacked it." He sensed Tillsley's heart rate increase exponentially.

"I guess I'll leave him to you bunch of arseholes. You seem keen to get your hands on the lad," he said through gritted yellow teeth.

"What I mean is: what are you going to do after you've smacked it and your blow does not even shake the creature? What are you going to do when it is ripping your head off with its bare hands?"

Tillsley kissed his right fist. "Don't you worry, son."

They were almost at the quarry. Tillsley was sweating as if he'd run a marathon. Suddenly, a deafening roar filled the air. It echoed off the quarry walls, making the sound even more terrifying, if that was possible.

"Noisy git!" said Tillsley.

"It awaits you, human." Viralli was torn between wanting an end to Sparle and wanting to see him rip this ridiculous human being to shreds.

The two passed the gate and stood at the top of the quarry—it was a bloodbath. A large herd of cows had been left in the quarry to keep Sparle occupied while Sid got into position. Carcasses, ripped to pieces, were thrown the length and breadth of the vast pit. The moonlight glistened over the rocks drenched in blood. It was impossible that Sparle had fed on all the cattle; he'd killed them for the fun of it.

Sparle stood in the centre of the mayhem. His naked body gleamed in the moonlight. In each hand, he gripped the decapitated head of a cow. He held each aloft to the moon and bathed in the glory of murder. He roared again and threw the heads of the cattle out of the quarry. Viralli marvelled at his strength and savagery. Missiles couldn't stop him, so what could this fat idiot do?

"He's got no kecks on!" cried Tillsley. "I ain't fighting him if his tackle is flying all over the place!"

"Ssshh," hissed Viralli.

Sparle looked up and saw them silhouetted against the moon. He unleashed a challenging scream and bounded towards them.

"Too late."

"RICARD, NO ONE HAS THREATENED THE AGREEMENT with such dire consequences, so don't make the situation worse. It is imperative that you tell us everything you know and everything you've done," Bwogi pleaded.

Ricard's attempt at holding his emotions at bay broke down completely. "Do you think you can do anything to me that can come close to the pain I'm suffering for betraying my son?" Tears filled his eyes.

"Your crime against the lamian race and the continuation of the species is more important than your pain!" shouted Miguel Somarro, a vampire who'd killed and abused thousands of children. Yet, their deaths meant nothing compared to the war that would rage across the planet if the Agreement was shattered. Ricard's crimes were worse than this animal's, the lowest of life-forms.

"Tillsley..." Ricard gathered control of his emotions. Grieving could take place another day. It was time to do his duty. "Tillsley is not the Bellator."

The elders wilted in front of him. Ricard had placed the weight of the world on their shoulders.

"What have you done, old friend?" said Bwogi.

Ricard began his tale. "When Sparle was born, I knew immediately what he was. My partner died during childbirth, and the similarities to the birth and the baby were mirrored two thousand years ago. Her relatives were distraught at the loss, and the baby was their link to their loved one. They helped me raise him.

"As soon as Sparle was born, I knew, from personal experience, there'd be a human born to oppose him. I had to find him, but not to kill him. I knew that one day I might need him. More importantly, if I found him, then no one else would. If the Bellator was discovered, then the hunt for my son would begin.

"Finding the human was not a difficult task. History suggested he'd be born in close proximity to his vampire brother. As soon as Sparle was born, I monitored medical records for all deaths during childbirth, and there were only a few cases, making my job easy.

"I abducted the child, soon after. He was overdeveloped for a human baby, and by three years old, he was as strong as a human adult. He was incredibly intelligent and a beautiful, wonderful child. I raised him as my own—Jacob. Jacob was what we wanted to call our child, but when he emerged...I could only give him one name.

"I built a home for Jacob underground. The home, if I'm honest, is a prison. He grew until he reached six foot ten and three hundred pounds of muscle. I educated him in history, the arts, and the sciences. I told him there had been a nuclear war and fallout meant we couldn't breach the surface. I grew to love him as my own flesh and blood, but my need to tame my biological son outweighed my love for my adopted one.

"After Sparle's escape, I couldn't let Jacob out. I couldn't bear for them to fight, but I've accepted it now. They were born to fight, to kill each other."

There. It was done.

Ricard took a deep breath. "Call to the gunships on the moors and cancel Tillsley's futile attempts. I will take you to Jacob."

Bwogi pressed a part of his chair that doubled as an intercom. "Cancel Tillsley's mission. Arrange helicopters to the North Yorkshire Moors with the utmost haste."

All looked at Ricard with disgust, even the members who once considered him a friend.

Bwogi shook his head sombrely. "This is a grave day, Ricard, a grave day. Your trial will continue when we return, but first, Sparle must be destroyed. If Jacob cannot complete the task, then I'm afraid we'll have no option but to use force that will be seen across the world. This could've been averted years ago if it wasn't for your deluded sense of love."

Helga nodded agreement. "How have you fallen so far from grace? Your punishment can't come close to the magnitude of your crime."

"Helicopters are ready, sir," announced a voice from a hidden speaker.

The vampires rose and headed towards the chamber doors. Ricard followed dejectedly.

VIRALLI SHOOK HIS HEAD AS TILLSLEY ROLLED UP HIS SLEEVES. Sparle charged up the quarry walls below, scrambling, but unable to climb the sheer rock face.

"This fella is in a real rush to get a bust lip," said Tillsley.

The monster realised it couldn't reach its prey that way and bellowed in frustration, looking around for an alternative route. It had some intelligence, Viralli noted.

"TAKE YA TIME, YA DAFT BASTARD! I AIN'T GOING ANYWHERE!"

It was definitely more intelligent than Tillsley.

Viralli backed off to a safe distance from the imminent battle. Once Sparle had finished with Sid, it would soon be ready for more violence.

"Viralli. Come in," buzzed the radio.

"Viralli here."

"This is base. Tillsley is not the Bellator. Tillsley is *not* the Bellator. The gunships will keep Sparle in the quarry. Your orders are: take Tillsley back to Middlesbrough, await contact with Reece Chambers. Kill both. Clear?"

"Affirmative, sir!"

Viralli sprinted back to the gate where Sid stood shouting obscenities at the monster below. "Tillsley! Tillsley!" he yelled when he was within earshot.

"Eh?" Sid turned round. "Get out of here, mon! I need to get ready for this bastard!"

"Change of plan. We don't need you anymore. We're going to hit it with heavy artillery instead. There is another coming to fight him, the real Bellator."

On cue, a missile rattled into Sparle's path, which sent him tumbling back down the quarry. He roared, no doubt the frustration of not reaching his target being greater than the pain of the explosion.

"Come on, before we're hit in the crossfire," said Viralli.

"I ain't walking all the way back. I prefer to take me chance down here, like. Them lads of yours seem like pretty good shots, and if he gets away, then I'll put the nut on him."

Viralli couldn't believe that a human like Sid Tillsley existed. If Tillsley wasn't the one born to fight the vampire monster, what was he? It was best for all that he was finally taken out of the equation. "Come, Sid, orders are orders, and you will be paid in full."

"That's all you had to say. It's your round when we get to boozer."

33

SID STROLLED DOWN TO THE MINER'S. It was a beautiful day, and Sid was glad to put all of last night's events behind him. Luckily for him, last night, he'd managed to reach the pub while they were still serving. The short session had been an eventful one too. Them vampire bastards had played silly buggers before Sid could get his first beer down him. That twat Viroply, or whatever his name was, had ordered his vampire mates to give Sid a lift back to The Miner's, and they'd seemed a decent bunch of lads, but as soon as they'd got to the pub, they'd got rowdy.

They'd all come in for beer, which Sid could understand as it'd been a long night, and the beer in The Miner's was mint. Some of the lads were in, Arthur and Rathbone, but when Rich came out of the bogs, it all kicked off. It was the roughest punch-up Sid had been in for a while, because the vampires were tooled up to the balls, which is out of order in a pub brawl. Truth be told, if Rich weren't there, it could've all got a bit hairy.

"Sid!" shouted the familiar voice of Brian.

Sid turned to greet his drinking partner of many magical drunken years. "Eh-up, mate, you going for a pint?"

"Aye, mon, I am. Called in sick after hearing about last night. Thought I'd get the rundown while enjoying an all-dayer."

"Lovely stuff. I'm gonna be getting meself proper pissed up tonight. I've been away from me Bolton for far too long. Yesterday, I only got to have a pint and a chaser, all day, like!"

Brian shook his head. "You must be gagging for an ale. I hear you had a bit of trouble last night, like. Sorry I weren't around."

Sid dismissed his apology with the wave of his deathdealer. "Don't be silly, Brian. Though I will tell ya, it was some nasty shit that went on, and Kev even shut up shop afterwards. Normally, he only shuts if the pub is wrecked."

"Jesus, what happened?"

Sid regaled the story of Spam, the big vampire monster bastard; the vampire's bollocks about the million-pound fight; his benefit immunity, and his escort to The Miner's.

"Anyway, the vamps said they were coming in for an ale, and more importantly, that they'd be buying."

Brian nodded. "They haven't been too bad actually, Sid. There was that nutter at the woods, but I guess I didn't actually know if he was gonna kick off or not, and I did stick me nut on him first, like. Them lads we met in The Miner's weren't too bad, and they put their hands in their pockets, which you canna argue with. I preferred them to that wanker, Rich."

"Aye, you're reet, Brian, but them two were playing silly buggers, if you remember? One of 'em wasn't our sort of man, was he, Brian?" Sid raised a homophobic eyebrow. "Anyway, these four lads were alreet, but when we got to The Miner's, they turned into twats."

"What do you mean?" quizzed the scholar.

"Well, I ordered five pints of Bolton, and then Rich came out of the pissers—"

Brian interrupted with a sigh. "Aye, he hasn't stopped hanging around here. I haven't had a pint without him asking where you are every five minutes. Pain in the arse who's gonna get a kicking—"

Sid pre-empted the rant. "Actually, he proved himself to be a good lad, last night. You see, I turned to look who came out of the bogs, 'cos I was gagging for a dump, and it was Rich, and the fooker was drawing a gun out of his coat jacket!"

"A gun?" asked Brian surprised. "We haven't had a gun in The Miner's for nearly three months!"

Sid nodded. "I know. We were saying a little while back how it was going soft. So I see Rich drawing his gun, and he's quick as fook with it too. I dodged sideways with my back to the bar so I could see what both sides were doing. Out of the corner of me eye, I noticed the vampire fella nearest to me had drawn his gun too. I gave him a shoulder barge to put him off, and he went flying into his mate. Don't know me own strength sometimes, as ya know. Turns out, all the bastards were drawing pieces!

"The two I knocked over lost hold of their guns, and Rich shot one of the other fellas in the head. It was a brilliant shot, Roger Moore style, in the centre of the forehead! I managed to land one on his mate, and he turned into that dust stuff. I landed another on the one I shoulder barged, and he exploded. Meanwhile, Arthur was taking care of business with the other fella."

Brian looked peeved. "Ah, I haven't seen Arthur take care of business for ages! Has he lost any speed?"

Sid smirked. "What do you think? He was lightning! You know, I think all that martial arts crap is a load of bollocks, but seeing him in action..." Sid whistled. "I reckon he was quicker than his daddy was. He worked the guy over pretty badly, but the guy had an iron jaw and he couldna put him down. Guess it was 'cos he was one of the undead or summat. Anyway, he spun him round with a big, spinny kick, and I caught him with a right. Seriously, before he exploded, his head was facing the wrong way!"

"That's a proper good punch-up, that. I can't believe that Kev called last orders, tho'."

"He didn't. He was well fired up after seeing the scrap. He was that pumped that he called: 'Drinks on the house!' But he got real spooked 'cos the fella who got shot in the head got up."

"You're joking..." Brian was wide-eyed. "Drinks on the house?"

"I know, I know," said Sid solemnly. "Nearly the greatest day in the history of the world, but the lad getting up with a hole in his head scared the shit out of Kev. I finished him off, but it was too late by then."

"Well, let's try and put that behind us," said Brian cheerfully. "Because now, we drink until we can't stand up."

"Howay the lads!"

SID AND BRIAN ARRIVED outside the locked doors of The Miner's Arms. A small cheer erupted from the waiting group. Guns, although not a rare occurrence in The Miner's Arms, were an unwanted part of an evening's entertainment. None of the regulars carried such weapons, and it was just non-locals who weren't man enough to fight with just a pool cue.

It was two minutes to eleven and not quite the magical time. Arthur, Rathbone, and the lads were outside waiting, gagging for that first magnificent taste of well-kept ale. Reece was waiting for an overpriced mineral water.

"Good morning!" greeted Sid who was pleased to have so many drinking buddies on the fine, glorious summer's day. He took a deep breath of fresh air. "It's good to be alive, isn't it, lads?"

His question was not answered, because the doors of The Miner's were unlocked, and the lads crashed through. Sid passed the magical boundary and took out a large Cuban cigar, one of several he'd stolen from the vampire's underground headquarters. He lit it with a gargantuan puff of smoke. "Good to be alive," he coughed.

The lads rushed to their television corner and warmed up the box. Kev had picked one up at a bargain price at one of them charity shops. He'd even managed to short-change the stupid bitch behind the counter, the shop's fault for employing one of those retard types.

Sid and his motley crew took seats near the gents. The River Tees would be running high tonight.

"Landlord, four pints of your finest ale, please?" requested Reece grandly. His request was greeted with a salute from the landlord and a cheer from the vampire-fighting heroes. "And a mineral water."

"Bummer," said the fickle Garforth.

After Kev had poured all the beers, to not a millilitre over the legal requirement set by trading standards, he took them and the mineral water to the thirsty patrons. Glasses were chinked and mutual praise was shared. All four took that first draught of ale, the most satisfying feeling a man can experience.

"To Sid Tillsley!" cried Reece, "Vampire hunter!"

In a millisecond, he was drenched in ale.

"Hang about, lad," said Sid as he wiped the beer from his chin. "We've been through this before, and I told you that I ain't getting involved. Them lads last night will be the last of it. They came at us heavy and got what they deserved. The other lot will know that if they play silly buggers, then they'll get summat similar." He waved the right atom bomb.

Reece rubbed the beer out of his eyes. "OK, I won't mention it again, but you will see a repeat of last night, I guarantee it. You'll have to join me eventually to survive. From what you told me last night, you are not the prophesied one, which means you're something different entirely. The vampires and the humans will come for you after they kill the monster. However, you're right. Let's not talk about that now. Four more beers, lads?"

With the prospect of premium ale, Sid completely forgot about the disagreement. Reece made his way to the bar.

"Sid, he's fooking minted, mon! You should have a go at this vampire-fighting thingy," said Brian.

"Hell yeah!" said Arthur. "I'd love to have another go at one of them son of a bitches, man. You have got to show me how to make them explode like that, Sid. You had 'em all shook up, baby!"

"I'll show ya, Arthur. I gave one a pastin' for pushing in the queue at the kebab house last night."

"Shut it, Rathbone."

"It ain't about the money, lads," said Sid. "I'm comfortable. The odd job here and there suits me perfectly. A few quid from the government gets me through the week. It's nice having an easy life...a beer in your local, a cigarette from the corners of the globe, good friends, and the love of a good woman."

"The love of a good woman?" said both Arthur and Brian in the same surprised tone. Reece returned with the beers.

"Aye, lads. The love of a good woman." Sid smiled lovingly at the thought of her.

"Who is it then?" asked Brian hurriedly, unable to curb his curiosity.

Sid gave Brian a funny look. "Who do you think? Sheila Fishman, of course."

The three lads tried to hide their grimaces, trying to be polite, like when a bloke in a pub brought a picture of his hideous kids out from his wallet.

"But, Sid," began Brian, "I thought you only grabbed her tit once, and she hasn't spoken to you since?"

"You're right there, Brain. I did indeed grab her titty, and beautiful it was. It was a proper romantic moment as well, I can tell ya. That was the last time I spoke to her, but she's gagging for it, like. She's been following me about in some big transit van for the past few days."

Everyone knew what it meant, everyone apart from Sid. It was down to Brian, his bestest friend, to break his heart.

"Mate, sounds like she's trying to catch you working. There's no reason a lass like that is gonna be driving a transit van, is there? There's got to be video cameras and shite in the back. Why would she follow you around secretly if she likes ya?"

Sid considered it. "Because she's shy? Anyway, she told me that she was gonna lose her job with the Benefit Bastards 'cos she stapled that fella's knackersack."

"Sorry, mate, she had to be lying. She's trying to catch ya working." Brian offered a sympathetic pat on the back.

Arthur also offered a pat on the back. "Hey, man, women are always messin' with men's heads." He considered this and realised that it had never ever happened to him. "...I should imagine. Rich, get the beers in, this man needs cheering up."

Reece didn't appreciate getting ordered to buy beers, but this was not a time to upset Sid. He looked quite dejected, and Reece needed to stay close to him, convinced that he'd turn against the vampire eventually. Once involved in their world, one couldn't help but become exposed to the pain, misery, and death that they brought. He bit his tongue and went to the bar. Hunting was turning into an expensive venture.

"Fooking 'ell, how could I be such an idiot?" said Sid. "I canna believe that Sheila would try and get me done. We connected!"

"Didn't you just grab her tit?" asked Arthur.

"Exactly!"

"Listen," said the smartest man on the Smithson Estate, "I've got an idea. Sid, you need closure on this. You need to know for certain that she's still one of the Benefit Bastards."

Sid nodded as he finished his ale and puffed away at his Cuban cigar. Oxygen levels in The Miner's Arms were now dangerously low. "You're reet, mon."

"I've got an idea." Brian went through the plan with the lads. "Rich can drive us in his motor 'cos I've had one too many to take out the Capri, or rather...I will have done."

The designated driver returned. He was beginning to grudge having to buy Rathbone beer since no one else liked him. "There you go, lads. That's the last round you're getting for a while."

"That's OK," said Brian, "'cos after the next one, we've got ourselves a mission, and we're gonna need that nice big black motor of yours."

"Shit."

Sid walked down the road, trying to keep to a straight line. The "just one more round" had turned into a few rounds that had turned into a session. He was definitely on the drunker side of sober. He looked around. Nothing. There'd been a lot more walking in this plan of Brian's than he'd been hoping for. Still, if it proved his lass was on the straight and narrow, and not trying to send him to prison, then it'd all be worth it.

Brian hadn't disappointed with his plan. It was simple thanks to some of the gadgets Rich had up his sleeve. When Sid suspected that Sheila was following him, he was to simply press a button on a little gizmo and they'd track him down. He was then to walk down Bishop Close, the nearest cul-de-sac to the docks, and then Rich and the lads would block the road, giving Sid the opportunity to confront his lass. It was a win-win situation. He'd either obtain closure on the relationship or a guaranteed jump in the back of the transit.

Sid reminisced over the last few days. He'd hardly touched a drop, and the amount of exercise performed would impress Roger Black. He could've sworn that his jeans were slightly less constrictive than they were a week ago. The next few days of solid drinking would put an end to all that.

Was that a glimmer of white?

He risked a look over his shoulder. Bah! It was only Terry the Roofer's van. He wasn't up to all this secret agent stuff. Roger Moore was the only man who could really pull off a caper like this. Sid didn't have the chic to pull it off...not that he called it "chic."

Sid took another look over his shoulder with only a hint of a stagger. His heart beat quicker and his loins stirred. "Shit the bed." It was her. It was Sheila.

He played it cool, trying to be the man he admired so much. It was only a minute's walk to Bishop's Close and he was convinced he could make it, although he was starting to need a piss.

He pressed the gizmo.

"THE GIZMO'S GOING, RICH!" said Brian who'd "shotgunned" the front seat. Reece was glad that Rathbone wasn't in front at least. He and Arthur sat cramped in the back. "It's going!" he yelled

Reece sighed. "I can see that, thanks. He's a minute away. We'll rendezvous at the top of this road." Reece ignored Rathbone who was mocking his use of the word "rendezvous."

"What kind of car is this, man?" asked Arthur.

"What do you think it is?" asked Reece, hoping to finally impress these imbeciles.

"Escort?" ventured Rathbone.

Reece didn't like Peter Rathbone, the horrible, greasy, little bastard. He thought about the grease the horrible, greasy, little bastard was smearing on his upholstery, merely by sitting on it, and his hatred grew.

"I don't know what this car is, man, but it sure as hell ain't a Cadillac."

Reece grinned. "You can't recognise it because there is no other car like this in the world."

"That's bollocks," stated Rathbone. "Me brother-in-law's got one just like it...except it's got a spoiler."

Reece thought about opening a whole magazine into the fucker's heart, but luckily, Brian spotted Sid heading into Bishop Close.

"Let's roll," said Arthur in a way that only he could, Hollywood style.

They rolled.

34

SID HAD REACHED THE END OF THE CUL-DE-SAC. Sheila had taken the bait and parked up. If she was trying to be subtle, she wasn't doing a good job. Rich blocked her in and the mission was accomplished. Sid turned on his heel and walked purposefully and confidently towards the van. Women love confidence, as well as feelings and shit.

"FUCK! HE'S ON TO US!" yelled Sheila hysterically. The surveillance work and discovering the reality of vampires had taken a toll on her already-fragile nervous system.

Gunnar was finding it more and more difficult not to rip her throat out. When Tillsley was behind bars...

"Relax. If you keep jumping around like that, he'll know for certain something's up!" he snarled through the intercom.

"We're boxed in!" she screamed.

Gunnar's eardrum knitted back together. He looked through the cameras mounted on the rear of the van to see a black car parked across the road. It used the other parked vehicles to block any chance of escape. The car was unlike any he'd seen before. Gunnar smirked. Only Reece Chambers could be so pretentious.

"Calm down," he said coolly through the intercom, although he knew his words fell on deaf ears. "Confrontation was inevitable. Wait to see what Tillsley does."

But confrontation was not in Gunnar's plan. He was armed with many blades if it did happen, but gutting Tillsley wouldn't be a complete victory, although it'd still be pleasurable. "I have a plan," he said to her. "No matter what, don't panic."

SID APPROACHED THE VAN. Sheila wore a snazzy, baggy jumper, and its appeal tickled his loins. She looked gorgeous. Perhaps she had a mattress in the back of the van, anticipating the event. Yeah, that sounded about right.

He walked up to the window and gave it a seductive *rappety-tap-tap!* She ignored him—must be playing hard to get. Eventually, after shouting at the radio for some reason, she wound the window down.

"Eh-up, pet. I see you've been following me around, like?" he said with a wry smile.

She stared straight ahead. "Yes."

"Why have you been following the young Tillsley?"

"Yes." She wasn't blinking.

"Eh? You're a bit pale there, love, you alreet?" he said, concerned. Sid was not just a physical being.

"Yes."

"Anyway, what you got in the back of this van?" he asked suspiciously. She wasn't acting like she was up for some action. He looked through the window at the van's interior. It looked like a normal, white Ford Transit, except it had no pornography or McDonald's wrappers scattered inside it.

"Yes," she said.

Sid read the sign on the side of the van. "Morgan o' Co...you don't work for...What's tha...?"

Sid's heart dropped like a stone. The love of his life! How could she do this to him? The Os on the sign were not letters, they were the shiny coverings of lenses.

"Pet, I'm pretty upset now, and I think you should close your ears after you have answered this question: Who is in the back of the van?"

Sheila didn't answer Sid's question. She didn't even have the dignity to look him in the eye.

"Very well," he said calmly. He walked to the back of the van where the most indecent and offensive torrent of abuse was directed at whoever sat in the back. After thirty seconds, the abuse was accompanied by right and left hooks. Each punch came closer to smashing a hole through the metalwork. Someone was in for a nasty pastin'.

"JESUS, WOMAN!" Gunnar screamed through the intercom. "If he gets through that door, the sunlight will kill me! Distract his attention, otherwise I will perish along with your chances of catching him! You need me!"

Sheila considered it for a moment. She had grown to hate Gunnar as much as he hated her, and the idea of him being burnt to a crisp by the sunlight appealed to her immensely. But he was right.

"Sid, stop!" she yelled from the window. A second later, he stopped, but she suspected it was due to him being out of breath, not because of her plea.

"Wh-wh-who?" he managed in between wheezes, pointing at the van.

She didn't reply. She didn't know what to say or do. Gunnar would have to think of something.

"I'm gonna open them doors up, Sheila. You better tell me who's in there 'cos I'm gonna find out either way, you understand?"

Gunnar buzzed through, "I have a plan. Repeat after me."

"Sid," Sheila repeated the words Gunnar spoke into her ear. "I can't show you who's in the back because the door's locked. There's a computer in there and it is controlled back at base. I can take you there, if you want." she said monotonously.

He walked round to the passenger side and got in the van. "Reet, let's go meet the bastard."

SID GOT INTO THE VAN. He clocked that Rich was following when he glanced in the side mirror. Sheila drove past the docks into an industrial estate. She'd told Sid they were based in a big, underground warehouse where they launched all their surveillance work, but he wasn't really listening. All he was thinking of was finding the bloke responsible and sticking the nut on him, before getting pissed, very properly pissed. Could he ever trust a woman again? Why was he cursed with being a hopeless romantic?

"This is it," she announced. It was a warehouse just like any other on the estate, except to Sid, this was a place of evil. She kept the engine running and got out of the car to open the warehouse doors. It revealed a vast space containing absolutely nothing except a ramp down to a lower level. She got back in the van, drove into the warehouse, and headed for the ramp.

Sid wanted to ask her why she'd done this to him. He just couldn't put anything into words. It was going to take at least eighteen more pints to get over this romantic entanglement. If she let him grope the other tit, then he'd have the grace to forgive her, but he was just too upset to ask.

The lower level of the warehouse was pitch black. As the van's wheels touched the tarmac of the lower level, lights came on and a heavy shutter came down, blocking the entrance. The warehouse was the same size as the one above ground and empty—completely empty.

"What the fook? I thought you said—"

"I lied," said Sheila, suddenly sparking into life.

"Fooking hell, woman, you really are a miserable ol' cow!"

"You bastard!" she screamed. She threw herself at him in a frenzy of teeth, claws, and greasy hair, the crazy bitch!

Sid, pushed her back gently but firmly and got out of the van, dejected.

"Tillsley!" boomed a voice from a speaker on the van. "It was I who turned your woman against you. It was I who tried to put you in prison for benefit fraud. It is I, Gunnar Ivansey!"

A bloke leapt out of the rear doors of the van to confront Sid. "Who the fook are you?" he asked

The skinhead fella looked a bit confused. "We had a fight," he said. "About a week ago? You killed a spectator in the crowd? No? You must remember."

"Don't you play billiards for the The Pheasant Inn?"

The bloke sighed and his head dropped. "I'm a vampire trying to arrest you for benefit fraud," he muttered.

"You!" Sid's face flushed with rage. "You're a vampire wanker, ain't ya? You bunch of bastards! That's it! I've had it up to here with you fookers. You're going down!"

"No, human. It is *you* who will die this evening," said the vampire confidently.

He picked a knife from his coat and hurled it at Sid, who only just managed to get out of the way. He was regretting those extra six pints.

"You sissy bastard, needing a blade. Fight me like a man!" challenged the old-school brawler.

The vampire laughed. "I just want you dead, Tillsley. I toyed with ideas of a duel, and then I toyed with the idea of seeing you behind bars. Now, all I want is to gut you."

A second knife came at Sid's head. He couldn't get out of the way in time and could only get his left hand up. The knife skewered through the middle of his palm, spilling blood over the concrete floor.

"Bastards!" he yelled as if he'd just hit his thumb with a hammer. He didn't have a chance if he stayed out in the open, so he ran for the cover of the van. A knife stuck out of his right arsecheek as he made it to safety. "Bastards!" he repeated as he pulled the knife out.

The vampire laughed heartily. He was bloody enjoying this. "Sid, come out, so I can turn you into a living pin cushion!"

"Fook off, ya twat!" Sid had never been good at witty comebacks during scraps.

"The prophesied one, scared of a little blade. Who would've thought it?"

"I ain't him, mon. They've found some other fella."

The vampire circled the van, and Sid matched him, not wanting another knife in the arse. Sid passed Sheila in the van. She was rocking backwards and forwards. She was fooking nuts.

"So you are not the chosen one?" said the vampire. "So what are you, then? Shame we'll never find out."

"Fook off, ya twat!"

Sid had to think of a plan and fast. He was so desperate for a piss now that it was starting to hurt, and this bloke really was a wanker.

"Think, Sid, think." he whispered to himself. "What would Roger Moore do? In *Octopussy*, he dressed up as a crocodile and floated across a river with no one suspecting a thing." He scratched his head. "That ain't gonna work!"

"I can sense the panic in you, Tillsley. Your heart gives you away!"

Sid ignored him and continued to think of a plan. *You're not Roger Moore, you are Sid Tillsley. What would Sid Tillsley do?...Run up to him and put the nut on him.* "Aye, that's more like it."

Sid charged around the van at the vampire bastard. Sid took a knife in the leg, but it didn't matter as the momentum carried him through, and he got hold of the prick. He landed three consecutive head butts, each one making Sid feel a little bit better about himself. Whoever said "violence doesn't solve anything," had never given a right dickhead a pasting in a car park before.

GUNNAR'S NOSE WAS OBLITERATED, and he only just managed to stay conscious. Staring into the eyes of Sid Tillsley, he saw his fate coming. The right hand that had taken his brother would soon take him. He could see it drawing back slowly. He knew that his time was up.

"You are the biggest twat out of all 'em," said Sid angrily. "I've been saving up the old Tillsley Special for a while, and it looks like you've earned it."

"Do your worst, human." Gunnar managed the words with difficulty as blood filled the back of his throat. "I'm not afraid of death."

"No, but you may be afraid of this."

And with that, he launched it—The Tillsley Special. The right hand that was pulled back clenched even harder so that the knuckles whitened. Then, as if in slow motion, it started its arc of destruction towards Gunnar's jaw: the deathblow.

Wait! Something was wrong. The punch altered trajectory. Sid dropped in stature, as if he was falling. Had Sheila struck him on the back of the head and saved him? As Tillsley fell, Gunnar could see Sheila sat in the van. What had happened? Why did he fall?

The answer presented itself.

Tillsley's secret weapon: Its target was not the jaw.

The pain that Gunnar expected didn't come. He stumbled backwards as he was released from Sid's mighty grasp. Tillsley stood with a hand on one knee and the right hand still clenched, shaking with tension.

"I'll give it to ya," he said. "You're the toughest man I've ever fought. I've landed that punch twice before, and both times, the unlucky fella ended up in a coma."

Gunnar was confused. "What are you talking about?"

The punch had been aimed at his genitals, but he could've sworn he only felt initial contact. Gunnar felt for any dama—

Hang on...

He grabbed desperately.

"What the fuck?"

THE VAMPIRE BASTARD YANKED THE BELT OFF HIS TROUSERS and pulled the waistband out. A fine dust drifted up into the atmosphere.

"H...h...how?" he stuttered, before turning and running for the door at the end of the warehouse. Sid heard the door lock after the vampire was through it.

Sid looked at his right. It had brought him justice once more. He walked to the transit van where Sheila sat bolt upright with her eyes wide open, unblinking. The lights were on, but no one was home.

"Sheila, it's a shame that it ended like this. I hope you leave me alone from now on, pet." He was a gentleman to the last. She wouldn't bother him again, and Sid hoped her days of taking away the benefit cheque of the unfortunate, like himself, were over.

He limped over to the ramp and found a switch to raise the shutter. When he was out of the warehouse, Rich and the lads were there, waiting anxiously for him.

He needed to drown his sorrows. It was only three o'clock, which meant he'd the rest of the day to drink in The Miner's, and hopefully, get some plasters on these knife wounds.

Rich and Brian rushed out of the car to help him. They weren't expecting him to be covered in blood.

"What happened to you?" asked Brian.

"I'm reet, mon. Sheila was working with a vampire bastard. I'll tell you all about it over a beer."

"Is he still down there?" asked Rich.

"Nah, but don't worry, he won't be bothering anyone for a while. Come on, Rich, it's your round."

35

SID LOOKED INTO HIS BOLTON BITTER, his sixth pint since his encounter with Sheila. He was moping like a brokenhearted teenager. He took out a blood-stained Cuban cigar and attempted to light it, but it was too wet. Sid's mood darkened.

"So, let me get this straight," said Brian. "His old fella came clean off?"

Sid gave a depressed nod. "I reckon so." He put down his empty glass and looked at Rich with puppy-dog eyes. At least the beer was free.

"Tell me about the fight once more, and I'll buy you another beer," replied the out-of-pocket vampire hunter.

Sid rolled his eyes. Talking was shit. "When I saw all the surveillance shite in the back of the van, the red mist came down, like. And when he jumped out the back..." Sid shook his right hand, re-living the anger. The others drew back.

"He made the mistake of throwing knives at me. That's why he got The Special. It was weird, like. It normally feels like I've popped two balloons."

Everyone in earshot cringed. Folk always turned a little queasy when Sid mentioned "The Special." Three spectators had fainted last time he landed it.

"What did it feel like this time?" asked Rich.

"Well, it's hard to explain really. It's a bit like when I hit them in the jaw and they disappear. I know I've hit 'em, but I don't get much feedback through the ol' right. Anyway, when he pulled his kecks out to have a look, he went white as a sheet when a shitload of dust blew out. He legged it after that. I reckon summat exploded, like."

"No one wants to lose the use of their old fella," announced Brian, "but you shouldn't mess with a Northerner's benefits."

"Ivansey will be back," Rich warned. "He won't rest until you're dead. You killed his best friend, you've taken away his honour, and now, you've somehow removed his genitalia." The hunter smiled. "You won't be on his Christmas card list next year."

"But he didn't send me one last year," replied Sid.

"I don't know why I bother," mumbled Rich.

RICARD STOOD IN THE ELEVATOR HEADING DEEP UNDERGROUND. Bwogi, Viralli, and two other warrior vampires, armed to the teeth, in case the Bellator needed a calming influence, accompanied him. Ricard fought to control his emotions, but his hands were trembling. He put them in his pockets and grabbed the lining tight. Telling his adopted son he'd been lied to his whole life would prove as difficult as turning his biological son in to Michael. This was a day when all of his misdeeds would be punished.

The elevator came to a halt and the doors opened to a concrete corridor, twenty-foot long. At the end of the corridor stood vast, impregnable steel doors, the gateway to Jacob's home. Jacob would end the battle raging across the North Yorkshire Moors.

"What does he say when you leave him?" asked Bwogi. "How do you account for your absence?"

"He trusts me completely, and questions me not. This is the longest I've ever left him. He can't escape, but even if he could run, he wouldn't."

Ricard stared at the door, preparing himself. Bwogi placed a comforting hand on his arm. Although he'd judge him to the full extent of the lamian law, he was still Ricard's friend.

Ricard opened the door.

"SO, WHAT YOU PLANNING ON DOING WITH YOURSELF? You can't hang round here forever, can you?" Brian asked Reece in a tone which said "fook off."

"Nice of you to take an interest." Reece gave him a patronising smile and Brian simmered. "Firstly, I have to be sure the beast has been destroyed. I'd dearly love to see the human answer to the monster, the Bellator, but I can't risk it. After that, my plans depend on our large friend over there," he pointed to Sid, who was limping back from the toilets.

"You all right there, man?" asked Arthur to the big man.

"Dunno, like. I'm still bleeding a bit, even with the plasters. I'm not sure if the blood in the pan was from me leg, or if it's a new batch of piles. Just my fooking luck."

"You need to get those wounds stitched up," said Reece. "Do you want me to take you to hospital, or I can perform the task myself."

"Thinks he's fooking Quincy now," mumbled Brian under his breath.

Sid scowled and shook his head. "No way, mon. I ain't doing anything until I'm completely shitfaced! Then, all I'm gonna do is pass out and possibly spew me ring."

The three lads around the table raised their glasses. There weren't many things grander to drink to.

Brian saw an opportunity for the stirring of shit. "You were saying, Rich, that your plans depended on our Sid. What did you mean by that exactly?" Brian was Middlesbrough's answer to Jeremy Paxman.

Sid wasn't listening though. He was too busy drinking, and it was starting to go to his head.

"Glad you should ask, Brian," said Reece sarcastically. "With the emergence of the Bellator, it begs the question that was asked all them weeks ago: What is Sid?"

"I'm brokenhearted, mon!" Sid said and went to the bar for the comfort of the depressed man's favourite depressant.

"Sid is completely unique," said Reece."

"Aye," agreed all round the table.

"There's been no human or vampire in history with the power to recreate the effects of sunlight in a punch. The vampires will be back, the humans will be back, and I will protect him. He'll have to join me eventually. I won't let him down."

Sid arrived back with beers for all except Reece. Sid was never going to pay actual money for bottled water.

Reece looked a bit dejected, much to Brian's delight, but continued unabashed. "I was saying, Sid, you are different—"

He was interrupted by Sid flapping his hands and jeering. "Not now! I've told you once, and now, I've told you twice. This is a day of mourning, so leave it out!" He downed half his pint to show he meant business. "Why do all them bastards want to pick on me? There's billions committing far worse benefit fraud."

"Hey, man, don't think about it," said Arthur. "Let's just have a laugh and a joke and forget about Benefit Bastards, vampires, women, and..." His head picked up. There were two women at the bar. "Be back in a minute." He went over to take care of business.

Brian's "Swordy-sense" had been tingling, a missed opportunity. He got back to the problem at hand: Sid. "He's right, mate. Forget about it all and enjoy the evening. I'll get the beers in."

Kev was on form, offering a fast turnaround. Brian was back at the table in no time where Sid was looking expectedly at Rathbone for some words of condolence. Rathbone drank his beer, staring indignantly back. "She probably had a cock, anyway," he said, eventually.

"There you go, mate," said Brian, laying down a pint and a budget brandy before Sid's brain could compute what the horrible, greasy, little bastard had said. "Get that down ya. It'll put hairs on your chest."

"Cheers, mate." The brandy was washed down with half a pint of bitter. "I can't believe that I'm single again. I can't believe she did it to me, lads. Poor old Sid, a born romantic, shot down in a moment of madness by his beloved."

Brian decided it was reality check time. "Whoa, fella. You only grabbed her tit once, and she didn't want you to."

Sid dismissed it with a shake of his head. "There was electricity in that titty. Its mate was jealous 'cos it wanted a grabbin' too. Sheila didn't know it, but her titties did, Brian. Her titties did."

Arthur came back from his recon mission. "Sid, see those chicks over there?" He nodded at the two who he'd chatted up.

"Aye, what about 'em? They gonna try and get me done for claiming my well-earned benefit?" he said miserably.

"No man, don't be stupid. I've arranged a double date for tomorrow night!"

Sid's eyes lit up. "Which one's mine," asked the miraculously cured Tillsley.

"What?" said Arthur, face screwing up behind his shades. "No man, I'm gonna bang both of them. Was just telling you the good news."

Brian's hand slapped Sid on his back as he wailed. "Naaarrrgggh, all bitches, mon! All prick-teasing bitches! They all hate Sid, and Sid has nothing but love to give in return!" A dark glint sparkled in Sid's eye. "It was that vampire that put them thoughts in her head. It was that vampire bastard that turned my Sheila against me."

Reece said, "It's what vampires do, Sid. They manipulate people and will do anything to take your benefit from you."

'boro's finest scholar saw the intent. "He's talking crap! Bloody 'ell, Sid, Benefit Bastards have been trying to catch you for years! It has nothing to do with vampires!"

"But Sheila only came onto the scene once you'd killed one of them, Sid. They've used her against you," said Reece.

"Bastards, mon! Get me another pint, Rich!" He took out his last Cuban cigar which, like the last, was soaked in blood. Sheer force of will (and increased alcohol in the blood stream) had the cigar smouldering instantaneously.

"You'll forget it all in the morning," said Brian. "Just have a few more beers and the world will be reet again. Come on, mate, snap out of it."

"I gave them bastards a chance, Brian. I admit, I killed a few of 'em, but they were either accidental, or they were trying to cop a feel. I tells ya, they've got it coming to 'em." His face reddened in what was either anger, or a heartattack. "I'm getting to the stage where I ain't gonna take any more."

It was anger.

"What're you going to do, Sid?" asked Arthur. "I haven't seen you this upset since you came back from Michael Barrymore's pool party."

"I don't know, mate, but it's gonna be pretty fooking violent."

"Sid, mon," cautioned Brian. "What're you thinking? Even you can't fight all the buggers! If you go do something stupid now, them bastards are gonna do everything they can to stop your benefits. It will be the end of your career."

Reece was struggling to contain his excitement. "Sid need not worry about money. If he joins me, I'll be back him financially for the rest of his life."

"Look, you!" Sid pointed threateningly at Reece, although the booze had affected his depth perception and he actually pointed past Reece to a man at the bar. The man ran out of the pub, never to return. "I've told you, I'm not joining you, or any of them...*them*...I ain't into all that funny business that you get up to!"

Sid got up shakily and went to the bar to drink the lager that the scared patron left.

"Things must be bad," said Brian.

"I'm gonna go sort all this out for, me—Sid. Kev! Another round for me and me mates!" he yelled.

Kev obliged, "Sid, I haven't seen you this fired up since Will Young won *Pop Idle*."

"Shurrup!" Sid paid up and walked back to the table, spilling beer as he went.

"Cheers, man," thanked Arthur. "Maybe you should take it easy. There's an hour until closing time, and you've had at least eighteen pints since we got back."

"'Cos of her, Arthur!" he slurred, "'cos of her and them bastards is why I'm drinking like this. They drove me to drink because they took away my girlfriend and me benefits!" He downed the entire pint in a world record time for a man's nineteenth pint and then stumbled off to the toilet, swearing as he went.

"He's in a bad way," commented Arthur. "I haven't seen him this angry since he bumped into George Michael in that public toilet."

"That twat ain't helping." Brian snarled at Reece.

"You can blame me all you want, but Sid's life will never be the same. He lives in their world now. I can help him, and in return, he can help us all. You've seen how the vampire ruins lives. Sid can regain the balance. Finally, we can fight back!"

"It's your fight, your vendetta. You're using him for your own personal war!" shouted Brian.

Sid returned from the toilets, and from the state of his trousers, it was obvious the attack on the urinal was unsuccessful. "What're you lot shouting about? You arguing about me?"

"Yes, Sid," said Brian. "Rich is trying to use you."

Sid stumbled over, picked up Brian's beer and drained it.

"Everyone tries to use me. Sheila... my love...she used me. She tantalised me with her titty, and then, she used me!" He was close to tears. He slammed the empty glass down on the table. "No more! I'm gonna do summat about it. I'm gonna tell them vampire bastards what I really think and give 'em a slap while I'm at it."

"Sleep on it. Decide tomorrow. Tomorrow's another day," said Arthur in a vain attempt to calm the big man's aggression.

"No!" he shouted and stood up in a way that suggested action was afoot. He grabbed the last remaining pint on the table to make it number twenty-one. "I'm off, lads, off to avenge my honour and to avenge my benefit cheque!" He ended his mighty speech and made his way, with difficulty, to the door.

"Where are you going?" asked Brian.

"You ain't going to stop me. I'm going to the moors. If they want Sid, they're gonna get him!" A belch of monstrous proportions ruined his movie-star line. With the lingering smell of ale and smoky bacon crisps, the bald angel of vengeance left in search of justice.

Everyone rolled out of the pub to see Sid Tillsley staggering down the road.

"Where are you goin', mon?" called out Brian.

"To my justice wagon!" he called back without slowing his mighty, staggering stride.

"Not his Montego?" said Arthur with rightful worry in his voice.

"We canna let him get behind the wheel of that death-trap!" said Brian. "That car has caused more accidents in the 'boro than lasses missing the pill! It ain't a vehicle to take charge of after twenty pints of ale!"

"Where's he parked?" asked Rich.

Brian scratched his head. "Outside his house, I guess."

"Where does he live? We can jump in my car and head him off."

The three Smithson locals scratched their heads, and then shrugged their shoulders. "Dunno," they said in unison.

"What do you mean, you don't know? How long have you known each other?"

"Years. But what's that got to do with 'owt?" said Brian.

"Yeah!" agreed Arthur. "We don't do afternoon tea. We meet down the boozer!"

"Idiots, the lot of you! I'll get my car and meet you here."

Brian scanned the horizon for the striding figure of Sid. He didn't find the striding figure, but the urinating figure was clear for all to see. "Take your time."

BWOGI, RICARD, JACOB, AND THE GUARDS ascended to the surface in the elevator. Jacob couldn't be classed as human. He was as fair and beautiful as Sparle was terrible and vile. His beauty surpassed most vampires, and he was Herculean in stature. It was rather ironic that they suspected Tillsley of being Sparle's negative. Jacob was dressed in a tracksuit because it was the only type of clothing that would fit him. Blonde hair trailed gracefully across his face and bright green eyes seemed to fluoresce, just like a vampire's. Bwogi wondered what strength and speed Jacob possessed. Did he have the regenerative abilities of the vampire? Would he have the killer instinct he'd need to survive the night? One thing was certain, he wouldn't be beautiful after the battle.

Ricard had visibly aged over the last twenty-four hours. Bwogi fidgeted uncomfortably as Ricard confronted his adopted son, ready to tell him of the lies he'd spun for the twenty years of his imprisoned life.

"Hello, son."

Bwogi was impressed with Ricard's control. The ancient had been on a roller coaster ride for two decades, and it was all coming to a head. "This is Bwogi, he is from the surface. I have some explaining to do."

"Hello, sir." Jacob's voice was surprisingly light and musical for such a huge man. There was not a part of him that was not fair.

"Jacob, I have not been truthful with you over the years. There was no nuclear war, there is no fallout, and the earth is untainted."

Jacob didn't react to the revelation. He was regimental in his manner: a natural soldier.

Ricard continued the speech that he had rehearsed ever since he made the decision to imprison the child that would grow into the man. "You were brought up as a warrior, because I told you that we would have to fight for survival when we breached the surface. I'm sorry to tell you, that part of the tale is true.

"You are different to other men, and you are the only man alive who has a true purpose. Your purpose is to fight, my son. You were born onto this world to fight a monster, and tonight, you fulfil your destiny. Come."

Jacob wasn't perturbed in the slightest. He simply nodded and followed. So many questions begged for answers, yet Jacob was surprisingly quiet. His manner seemed that of an excited schoolboy.

His curiosity of the outside world outweighed the tension of the imposing fight.

The helicopter was waiting outside Ricard's house. Jacob was enthralled by the sights that surrounded him after only seeing them in books and in film. He closed his eyes and took a deep breath of the fresh air that had been denied him.

"We must go, Jacob," called Ricard.

Jacob followed without hesitation.

36

REECE ARRIVED AT BREAK-NECK SPEED. His impressive driving skills were wasted, because Sid was still dispensing his thirteenth to sixteenth pint in the doorway of a terrace house. The lads got in the car.

"GET OUT OF MY DOORWAY, TILLSLEY, YOU DIRTY BASTARD!" yelled Doreen Fish as she threw a plant pot, with deadly accuracy, onto the head of the offending gentleman.

Sid staggered backwards and fell onto a parked Fiesta where he unwittingly covered it in the same offensive liquid.

"GET OFF MY FIESTA, TILLSLEY, YOU DIRTY BASTARD!" yelled Edith Smithers as she threw a frying pan, with deadly accuracy, onto the head of the offending gentleman.

Sid clutched at his throbbing head as nature took its course and halted the flow.

"Vampire bastards," he mumbled, channelling his rage. He headed for his Montego Estate.

The concerned friends followed slowly behind him down the narrow roads of the Smithson Estate. Cars were parked both sides of the road and Reece's car held up several angry motorists. This was of no concern. The important thing was stopping Sid Tillsley's death drive. Eventually, Sid stopped and marvelled at the car that would carry him towards his goal of vengeance.

"There it is!" shouted Brian.

The men jumped out of the car, much to the annoyance of the cars waiting behind them. A wave from Arthur Peasley swooned the lady drivers into a state of calmness. Brian, pointing towards Sid and then sticking his finger up, scared the male drivers into an equal state of calm.

"Sid!" yelled Brian, covering the thirty yards between them in Olympic time. "For God's sake, knock this on the head till morning!" He jumped in front of the driver's side of the Montego to stop Sid's entrance.

Sid, however, was going for the boot, as he required fuel for his long journey. "Don't try to stop me, Brian. Love has turned my hand. I'm at war!" He pulled out a rubber pipe and petrol can. Looking around for the biggest car, he picked out a Jaguar, a rare beast on the Smithson

Estate. He didn't feel bad stealing the Jaguar's petrol since the owner was obviously not local.

"Sid, he's right," said Reece, agreeing with Brian for once. "You cannot fight this war tonight. Begin your quest tomorrow!"

"No!" yelled Sid as he used a screwdriver to gain access to the petrol tank. He threaded the hose into the pipe and sucked with all his might until free fuel was his.

"Did you drink some of that, man?" asked Arthur.

"How dare you!" said an outraged Sid. His petrol-flavoured burp gave him away. Once he was satisfied that he'd enough petrol for the trip ahead, he rose awkwardly and made for the Montego in order to refuel the beast.

Brian took position in front of the driver's door.

"Please, Brian, you more than any bugger should know that I need to do this."

Brian shook his head. "You can't drive in this state. It ain't gonna happen, mate."

"You drive pissed all the time!"

"But not thirty odd miles and not to fight vampires! You're gonna have to trust me on this one."

"Bah!" The wily old fox dodged Brian by getting in the Montego on the passenger side and climbing across. However, his attempt to climb across the car to the driver's side was not as graceful as his masterful dodge to gain entry. The gear-stick caused all sorts of bother with his piles. He screamed out at the interference with his behind. "Vampire bastards!" he yelled.

He started the Montego, and a huge billow of smoke disguised his escape, which would've been seamless if he hadn't driven into three parked cars. He left a trail of wing mirrors on the road. Even the most inept of trackers could follow his escape.

Sid was away, and he'd have his vengeance, although he wasn't sure how he was going to achieve it. It most likely involved finding as many of the bastards he could and then handing out slaps until he got bored or tired.

He put the radio on. "Wind of Change" by the Scorpions rocked the Smithson Estate.

"Howay the lads!"

THE HELICOPTER RACED OVER THE MOORS to the quarry where Sparle, for the moment, called home. It was perfect for him as there were abandoned mines littering the surrounding area and he could travel underground at pace, avoiding the helicopters. The supply of cattle being transported to the quarry through the day ensured that he'd not want to run...yet.

Jacob was not given a helmet with a walkie talkie. The vampires didn't want him to hear the conversation about the approaching battle. Bwogi stared at him, unable to believe that Jacob was actually human.

"Why doesn't he question anything you say? How can he accept that his own father has lied to him over the years? Is he less intelligent than normal humans?"

Ricard shook his head. "He has an IQ of over two hundred. He's beyond a genius—he is perfect. As for his manner, he was brought up with love. He is kind, fair, and gentle, but he is a fighter, pre-programmed to battle my biological son."

"How can he be ready for what he is about to face? He'll be ripped apart and all of this will be in vain. We'll still need to use heavy bombing," despaired Bwogi.

Ricard still found it hard to believe the gentle giant could turn into a killing machine. "I first built a gym for him. He was lifting human world records before he'd reached puberty. My wife's brother was responsible for the evolution of many of the modern martial arts; there was nothing he could teach Jacob. He knew it already. His body mechanics are flawless in everything he does. He can use any weapon to its deadliest potential. As I said, he was pre-programmed, like Sparle's lust for sadism."

"That's all well and good, but he's had no opportunity to fight. Sparle has, and he's taken every chance. That will give him the advantage."

Again, Ricard shook his head. "Jacob has experienced combat. He has fought and killed three vampires...another crime I'm to account for."

Bwogi looked to the heavens. "There will be much more to discuss once this night is over."

Ricard nodded. "Jacob simultaneously took down Peter Stalzburg, Carlos Ganchuri, and Abdul Shahn. All carried bladed weapons. He was unarmed."

"Three old and powerful lamia. How come this wasn't picked up in the Coalition's reports?" quizzed Bwogi.

"It happened recently. When Sparle became difficult to control, I had to test Jacob. If he passed the test, then I could continue taking Sparle to the surface. If he didn't, then Sparle would never see the moonlight again. I asked them to my house in friendship, and I told them of the human I had captured. I asked them if they would like to try and kill him for sport. Of course, they accepted. They knew that something was afoot, but their love of combat outweighed everything else. Jacob disarmed one of them and decapitated all in seconds."

"They will be missed," said Bwogi forlornly. "Tillsley kills with a single blow, a punch that mimics the effect of sunlight or decapitation. Can Jacob do this?"

"No, but if you ever saw Michael Vitrago punch in anger, you would have realised the extent of his power. Jacob's punch is twice as devastating as anything Vitrago could have mustered. Tillsley needs to be captured. We need to unravel his secrets. He's a danger to us."

"ETA: twenty minutes," buzzed the pilot.

"I have already ordered his death," Bwogi said. "A group was sent yesterday to kill him and Reece Chambers. The next time the two are together, they will be assassinated. Anomalies like Tillsley are best nipped in the bud along with the legends that flourish from them."

"HIGGGGHWAY TO HELL! Sid's on a HIGGGGHWAY TO HELL!" Sid sung out loud to the rock classic by AC/DC, powering the Montego Estate through the night. He was making good time considering he'd fallen asleep four times and ended up in three hedges and a cow, poor bastard. The lads in Rich's stupid car were behind, but there was no way they could catch him in the Montego.

Sid was nearing his destination, and it was a race against time. Could he arrive before pints seventeen to nineteen won their battle for freedom? He wanted to show the vampire bastards that he meant business, and having a trail of piss running down his leg wouldn't help matters. Up ahead in the distance, Sid could see a roadblock. A copper was parked across the middle of both lanes and his lights were flashing.

"Fook!"

If Sid turned back now, he'd look suspicious. If he drove up to the copper, he'd be arrested for being smashed in charge of a motor vehicle.

Turning back was the best option, but Sid had a point to prove, and tonight, the point would be proven. Sid pushed on. He turned up the radio.

"WHOOOOO-*hic!*-OOOOOOAAAAA, LIVING DAYLIGHTS!"

THE HELICOPTER TOUCHED DOWN, and the guards jumped out to check that it was safe for the elders to leave. At the guard's signal, they alighted along with Jacob. They were dropped at the same point that

Sid had faced the beast. Ricard faced his adopted son, the man that he'd send to kill his own blood.

"Jacob, tonight you will fulfil your destiny. You are to face a monster. You are to face a living vampire. He's as powerful and fast as you, but he can regenerate. Only decapitation will kill him. You may not survive the encounter, my son." Tears welled in Ricard's eyes. "Do you wish to take a weapon?"

"Is he armed?" asked Jacob without a tremble in his voice. He didn't know fear; it was something he'd only read about.

"His teeth and nails are like daggers," added Bwogi. "He won't fight with honour, for he's savage and wild. You won't face a noble enemy. It is a monster whose rage is uncontrollable."

"Then I will take my mace." Jacob took off his top to reveal bulging muscles and a shoulder holster that held the mace he spoke of. It was three feet long with a narrow, rectangular, metal head on the end. It was a simple weapon, yet undeniably brutal. He removed the holster and gave it to Ricard.

Jacob looked up at the full moonlight in awe. "Its beauty was not done justice." He spun the huge mace around his hands like it was a baton and stopped it dead with perfect control. Closing his eyes, he breathed in the warm evening air. "I can sense him." He turned to look at Ricard. "Father, leave us."

THERE WAS NO GOING BACK NOW. Firstly, because Sid didn't have enough petrol, and secondly, because five miles back there was a smart-arsed copper lying in the road with a broken jaw.

It was the vampire bastards' fault.

The quarry was just ahead now. He'd relieved himself by the roadside after the incident with the law and was now ready for a scrap. The lads were following behind, so if things got a bit hairy, they could help out. He'd sobered up enough to ensure he wouldn't fall asleep again and the radio was pumping. Tonight, he would avenge his lover.

He burst dramatically through the gates of the quarry to see the helicopters circling above. "BASTARDS!" he yelled, seeing the vampires in the air and out of the range of his mighty fists.

The radio momentarily calmed him. He took out a lighter, held it out of the window, and swayed in his sea. "PURPLE RAIN! PURLPLE RAIN!"

JACOB WALKED TOWARDS THE QUARRY, HIS HEART BEATING SLOWLY. He didn't know how, but he knew it beat in harmony with his opponent whom he could sense beneath him. He looked up, once again, at the moonlight. Never again would he venture underground. He'd too much to see and too much to do. Whatever he was about to face wouldn't take that away from him. He wouldn't allow anything to take his future from him, not even his father.

However, his lust for the world was not as strong as his want to meet what was travelling at a remarkable pace beneath his feet in the tunnels of the quarry below. He felt his want reciprocated by what his father had called a "monster." He was connected to this animal, and he could feel the bond that joined them. The closer their proximity, the more intense was his need to face it, to fight it, and to kill it.

He reached the edge of the quarry. It was carnage. Bones, blood, and gore were scattered everywhere along with bits and pieces of cattle and sheep. There were also human remains scattered amongst them. The sight of the slaughter didn't turn his stomach; it made him keener to see what had caused such destruction.

Jacob's destiny walked out of the mineshaft and into the moonlight. It held the bloody thighbone of a cow like a club. Jacob and the monster stared at each other, trying to sense the strengths and weaknesses of their enemy. Both knew they were linked. Both knew why they were here. The monster held the bone aloft and unleashed a roar, a challenge.

Jacob held his mace aloft and yelled a deep, powerful bellow that matched his enemy's in magnitude. Both ceased their cries simultaneously, and then...

Pain, the likes of which he'd never experienced, overcame Jacob like a tidal wave.

37

THE GUNSHIP TRANSPORTING VIRALLI, BWOGI, AND RICARD circled the quarry. The vampires all despaired when a maroon Montego Estate smashed into the side of the Bellator. They helplessly looked on as the car carried him towards the edge of the quarry. Jacob could do nothing. His feet were trapped under the car and momentum held him fast.

"That's Tillsley!" shouted Viralli.

"Tillsley?" screamed Bwogi. "I thought he was dead?"

"He should be dead, sir." Viralli picked up his binoculars. "Oh my God... He's asleep!"

Bwogi barked orders through to the pilot. "They're heading for the edge of the quarry! Intercept at all costs!"

"Affirmative," called the pilot as he rushed across the moors in an attempt to catch the speeding car.

BRIAN'S HEAD FOUND HIS HANDS. "He's fooking hit someone. He'll be in trouble with the Rozzers for sure."

Reece floored it. "Look at him! He's still moving! Only a superhuman could survive such an impact. That can only be the Bellator. Mankind's last hope."

"Ah, shite, and Sid's ran the bastard over," said Brian.

SID WOKE UP. There was a bloke on the bonnet staring at him. The bloke didn't look happy.

Things gradually fell into place.

"Ah fook, not again," he muttered. He slammed on the brakes, but it caused the car to skid on the quarry gravel, making him lose what little control of the vehicle he had in the first place.

"HE'S GOING TO GO OVER THE EDGE OF THE QUARRY!" yelled Ricard.

"Pilot, we don't have much time!" Bwogi shouted.

"There's nothing we can do," said Viralli. "It's a three-hundred-foot drop the other side. Our hope is gone. We must call in the air strike."

Ricard leaned forward as he looked on. "There is still hope! He's the chosen one!"

"THEY'RE DONE FOR," said Reece solemnly.

The car skidded ever closer to the edge of the cliff.

"SSSSSSSIIIIIIIDDDD...YAAA...BASSSTTTAARRRRDDDD!" screamed Brian, in Hollywood slow-motion style.

The car slid across the gravel. Everyone held their breath in terrified anticipation.

SID MANAGED TO PULL THE CAR AROUND. Now, it slid sideways, passenger side first, towards the edge of the precipice. The bloke on the bonnet was trying to free his leg. It must've been proper mangled.

Sid was drunk enough so that two quarry edges grew at an alarming rate. Chances were it was going to be a long drop. If he was a more agile man, he'd jump to safety, but getting his belly past a steering wheel was a job for professional athletes. The bloke on the bonnet was getting more agitated. It'd take a few pints to sort this little mess out, or failing that, a big right hand and a runner.

The only thing left to do was to hope; hope that the Montego Estate could muster the will to stop in time, hope to avoid certain death, hope that he could drink for just one more night, and maybe give some of them vampire bastards a slap as well.

Sid nearly forgot about them.

With the might of the gods and a load of luck, the Montego slowed; it slowed just enough.

"IT'S STOPPED! IT'S STOPPED!" yelled Bwogi.

Viralli pumped his fist. "Pilot, get down there. We need to get a winch on that car, ASAP!"

Ricard looked to the heavens. The gods looked favourably on Jacob this day.

"YEEEHHHAAAW!" was the ecstatic cry of Arthur Peasley as the car came to a halt, precariously balancing over the precipice.

"They still may need our help. Hold on!" Reece slammed on the brakes, knowing his would be somewhat more efficient than those of the Montego.

The Montego's passenger side wheels hung over the sheer drop, the fall of which would no doubt end in the death of the driver and the unsuspecting passenger. The driver's side wheels sat firmly on the quarry gravel, anchored down by the weight of the hard-drinking, dangerous-driving Sid.

Jacob was wedged between the edge of the quarry and the car. His leg was trapped and he couldn't free himself.

Sid got out of the car. He was bursting for a piss.

"NOOOOOO!" screamed everyone watching in unison, human and vampire alike.

The car rocked dangerously. Its state of balance was a matter of milligrams. Jacob couldn't call out; he was in too much pain. The entire weight of the car rocked rhythmically on his leg.

"AAAAAAARRRRRRRGGGHHHH!" It wasn't a scream of anguish, but the scream of relief as Sid's last few pints went home to Mother Earth.

Reece's car stopped, and the gunship touched down in close vicinity to Sid, who was zipping himself back to full dignity. All had their eyes on the car and Jacob, who rocked from safety to death and back again. The vampires and the humans got out of their respective vehicles.

Sid stumbled backwards into the car.

The vampires and humans gasped as one, as the car took an even bigger bank around its fulcrum, the Bellator's leg.

Somehow, the car didn't fall.

In the corner of Sid's eye appeared two monstrous breasts that were paraded on the front cover of his regular literary read, *Tits*. The periodical sat on his dashboard, calling to him. Sid was well aware the man under the car was in danger, but *Tits* was just under three quid, and there were some sluts from Billingham in it this week.

"NOOOOOO!" the onlookers screamed in unison as the idiotic drunk reached through the window to pick up his favourite read from the dashboard of his drinking chariot. He emerged triumphant with the one-hundred-and-fifteen-page *Boobanza of Bazookas*, clutched in his fist.

Whether one hundred and fifteen pages of normal breasts wouldn't have weighed the same as one hundred and fifteen pages of boobanza bazookas is debatable...and irrelevant. What was relevant was that the magazine weighed enough to topple the car over the edge of the quarry taking with it the last hope of mankind.

"Shit."

Seconds later, a huge explosion erupted as the first-ever Montego and the unique human fell to their untimely demise, crashing into the rocks, hundreds of feet below.

"YOU *TWAT!*" Brian shouted over the whirring of helicopter rotors. It was the most apt conclusion, considering the circumstances.

Ricard and Bwogi both stood with their heads down and spirits broken. Arthur and Rathbone both looked everywhere except at Sid and the vampires, they, at least, were a little embarrassed about the situation. Reece and Viralli's thoughts were similar; they needed to get out of the area quickly. Their fears were confirmed as Sparle's roar filled the air.

"We have to go!" yelled Viralli and Reece simultaneously.

"We must call in a full air strike immediately," said Bwogi.

"Oi!" bellowed Sid. "Now, I didn't come all this way for n'owt! I've come to tell you a thing or two, and the first thing I'm gonna tell ya is that I ain't fooking happy."

Reece pulled at Sid's shirt. "Sid, we must leave before the beast arrives."

"No, Rich! These bastards ain't going anywhere until I have it out with 'em. I didn't waste all me petrol, knock out a copper, and knock that fella down that hill for n'owt!" He turned to the vampires who were heading towards the helicopter and the safety of the skies.

"Oi!"

The vampires couldn't hear Sid over the helicopter rotors, not that they would've stopped anyway. He'd be dealt with later, and they needed to get off the ground. They needed to get away and have this place turned into an even bigger crater than it already was.

Two giant hands came down on the shoulders of Bwogi and Ricard.

"I said '*Oi,*' ya bastards!"

The elder vampires had no choice but to listen.

"Now, I've had enough with all your silly buggers! You used the woman I loved to try and get me done for fooking benefit fraud, and I can tell you, it ain't gonna happen again! Sid's here to hand out a few slaps, and I might as well start with yous twos!" He let go of them, ready to hand out a jab with each fist. They were spared the brutal strikes when Viralli bowled Sid over before he could unload.

"Fooking cheap shot!" said Sid, as he struggled to get back up.

Viralli stood, ready to face Sid.

The rotor blades gradually began to slow. Both parties turned. The cockpit was opaque with blood and gore.

Sparle appeared from behind the helicopter, chewing on the head of the pilot. His demeanour had changed. He no longer rushed for the kill. The loss of Jacob had affected him, and the balance had been disturbed. This was as close as Sparle's intelligence would take him to mourning.

Viralli and Bwogi backed away slowly from the beast.

Ricard held his ground, waiting for his son to approach. Only he could sense the difference in Sparle's character.

"That's the bastard! That's the one I put the nut on!" shouted Brian. "Have him, Sid!"

"Shut up!" barked Ricard. He needed to calm his son, but before he could try, Sparle charged past his father and straight for Sid, the man who had taken away his challenge, his fight, his true purpose.

Sparle closed in at lightning speed.

Sid wound up the right.

Sparle launched himself at the Middlesbrough local and straight into a big right cross.

The unstoppable force hit the immovable object.

A thunderclap rumbled over the hills and valleys of the North Yorkshire Moors. The windows in Reece's car shattered. Birds took flight in fear of the din.

It was one helluva punch.

Sid shook his right hand.

"Ouch!" he said.

The men from Middlesbrough drew mighty gasps.

Sid's punch hadn't even sent the monster dizzy.

Sparle stood, unaffected by the biggest haymaker in all of the 'boro. He looked at the humans and the vampires surrounding him and didn't know what to kill first. He decided to kill—

Sparle blew up in a shower of dust.

"That fella was one tough cookie, man," commented Arthur as the dust fell to earth.

"Reet!" Sid chaffed his hands together. "Now you're all gonna get one of the same! I've had enough of it! Sid Tillsley is going into vampire hunting, and you twats are first on me list!"

Bwogi stood shellshocked while Ricard fell to the ground, distraught.

Viralli, a soldier, trained to battle through the most diverse of circumstances, grabbed each of the elders by their collars and unceremoniously dragged them to the helicopter.

Sid's first official vampire hunt was under way, but unfortunately, his pace meant that Viralli had started the helicopter and winged his way to safety by the time Sid took ten paces.

Reece, although ecstatic that he had a new weapon in the hunt for the vampire, realised that actually catching them was going to be a real problem.

Sid shook his fist at the helicopter as it made its way across the moonlit sky before turning to his friends.

"Come on, lads," he said, "we can still make last orders."

38

LUCIA AWOKE WITH A START. She could sense daylight hundreds of feet above her underground chambers. She writhed on the bed, clutching her stomach. The pain started a week ago, and it was getting worse. She ran to the bathroom and was violently sick. Eventually, the pain subsided.

She washed her face and looked into the mirror. She knew what was wrong with her, but she didn't know how it had come to pass. She was pregnant. Impregnated by a human, a *mortal*.

Arthur Peasley.

With the emergence of Sid Tillsley, the world had been rocked to its core. A human can't impregnate a vampire. It's impossible. But...but...there was no other explanation. How would the world react when it found out what was inside her?

GUNNAR IVANSEY LOOKED DOWN at the place where his penis used to sit. All that remained were his lonely testicles. His penis hadn't started growing back, and he didn't think it was going to. Tillsley was going to pay. He'd taken his best friend, he'd taken his dignity, and now he'd taken away his pecker.

The last couple of months had been really, really shit.

THE HELICOPTER LANDED AT RICARD'S HOME in the North Yorkshire Moors. Bwogi had contacted the Coalition after the enormity of the situation had sunk in. The cleanup team had been on the scene within the hour, wiping out any trace of the bizarre confrontation.

The night had left so many questions unanswered. Sparle's death brought relief to the Lamian Consilium and the Hominum Order. However, the method of his demise sent shock waves across the world. A human killed the most powerful vampire born of the Firmamentum with a punch from his right hand.

Viralli, Richmond, and Ricard sat in Ricard's living room. Ricard kept silent. It was time to mourn the loss of his sons and accept the guilt for the decisions he'd made. Bwogi and Viralli, however, were captivated by the miracle.

"He exploded...exploded!" said Viralli. "We hit that thing with air-to-ground missiles and it didn't stop running. Tillsley must have a secret weapon, and Chambers is behind it."

Bwogi shook his head. "Chambers wouldn't give up something like that. His self-love won't allow it. We'll reconvene with the Consilium. The vampire faces a new enemy."

Viralli nodded. "You're right. With the death of Michael and the discovery of Tillsley, a new age is upon us."

"There are difficult times ahead. Back to London. We've much to do." Bwogi addressed Ricard and placed one hand on his leg. "We'll be in touch, old friend. I'll give you time to grieve." Bwogi got up to leave and Viralli followed.

SID SAT AT THE BAR OF THE MINER'S ARMS WITH A PINT IN HIS HAND. It was the day after he'd given that big vampire bastard a slap for playing silly buggers, and this was his first official day as a vampire hunter. He was fully dressed in his vampire-hunting regalia: blue jeans, horrifically tight in all the wrong places, a white T-shirt emblazoned with a mighty tiger face and "The Collection" written underneath it, and his cool leather jacket.

He was taking the next few days off to get drunk. Rich didn't know this yet, but he'd be here in a few minutes, and he'd get the good news then.

Kevin was excitedly sticking up a poster for the forthcoming Ladies' Night.

Arthur was telling some local red-hot lasses about Sid's new line of work and possibly setting them up for some action later.

Brian was supping ales with Sid.

Rathbone was there.

"New career, hey?" said Brian.

"Aye, forty-six years old, and here I am, a working man," he said. "Who'd have thought it?"

"Not me," said Brian.

"I'm taking the next few days off as I want to get into this thing gently. I don't want to risk me hand either as it still knacks a bit after hitting that lad the other night—had a good jaw on him, like."

Arthur left the women he was speaking to and rejoined his drinking buddies. "Hey man, we're on with them chicks tonight. I told them you are a vampire hunter!"

"Did you get me one?" asked Rathbone.

"Sorry, baby, they weren't interested," said Arthur.

"Lesbians."

"Did you get one for me?" asked Sid, bouncing on the stool, testing its structure.

"Sure did, baby!"

Sid looked over at the two lovelies, who uncharacteristically waved and—smiled! Things were looking up. Sid Tillsley raised his glass.

"Howay the lads!"

A FISTFUL OF RUBBERS

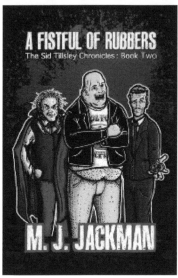

Book Two of The Sid Tillsley Chronicles (2nd Edition)

Sid Tillsley, forty-six, is an alcoholic from Middlesbrough. He's sexist, homophobic, overweight, extremely lazy, and a dogger. However, there are now *two* things setting him apart from the rest of his fellow Northerners.
Sid Tillsley can kill vampires with a single punch.

AND, he's no longer claiming benefits.

In the eyes of everyone apart from the taxman, Sid Tillsley is officially a vampire hunter. The old hunter, Reece Chambers, is using Sid to strike fear into the heart of the vampire nation, and Sid is doing so with gusto—for he gets a packet of fags for every vampire he knocks out.

But all is not rosy in Sid's world...

The Coalition, a council of vampires and humans whose purpose is to hide the existence of the creatures of the night, have shut down his local pub in a horrific act of cruelty, separating Sid and his mates from their beloved Bolton Bitter. Sid doesn't realise that he has a fight coming, one that will test him to his very limits. There's something else lurking in the shadows, or rather, the closet. A Northern man will punch anything in the face, but what terrifies him, what saturates him with carnal fear, is a direct attack on his sexuality...and the Campire draws near.

ACRACKNOPHOBIA

Book Three of The Sid Tillsley Chronicles (2nd Edition)
The end is near...

When Sid Tillsley, the most prolific and lethal vampire hunter the world has ever known, cancels his subscription to *Tits* magazine, Middlesbrough locals know that something isn't right in the world. And that's an understatement...

The vampire nation is ready to launch an assault on society. The Coalition, a council of vampires and humans whose purpose is to hide the existence of the creatures of the night, are almost powerless to stop them. Their one hope is a molecule: Haemo, a drug that suppresses the vampire's need to feed. If Haemo doesn't work and the vampires take to the streets, life will never be the same again, and a new, barbaric, violent age will devour mankind.

Unfortunately, Sid cannot be called upon, for Sid has landed himself a legitimate job, is paying taxes, has stopped smoking and drinking, and hasn't had a kebab in over a month!

But why? How? What could possibly change a Northern man so set in his ways? Vampires could never be so cruel.

Such devilry, such wickedness can only be the work of...womenfolk!

About the Author

"M J Jackman is one of the most talented, exciting, and hilarious writers to explode onto the fiction scene in the twenty-first century," was what Jackman hoped to read in the papers after the release of The Sid Tillsley Chronicles. He hoped his mastery of the written word and his elegant wit would bring celebrity status, which, in turn, would bring fast women, hard drugs and liquor, and then slower, more understanding women.

To date, he has successfully installed a decking area into his garden.

You can follow Jackman's antics on Twitter (@Mark_Jackman) and Sid's antic's on Facebook (search Sid Tillsley Chronicles)

Oh, and he's gone back to university to be a "mature student." And, no, he hasn't gone back to learn how to write (arsewipe!).

He gets an NUS discount.

Even his own characters would hate him.

Printed in Great Britain
by Amazon